EAGLE
THE LIFE AND TIMES OF
R. ALAN EAGLESON

DEIDRA CLAYTON

LESTER
&ORPEN
DENNYS
PUBLISHERS

For my parents and my sister Margaret

Canadian Cataloguing in Publication Data

Clayton, Deidra, 1948-
Eagle : the life and times of R. Alan Eagleson

Includes index.
ISBN 0-919630-97-9

1. Eagleson, R. Alan, 1933-   2. Hockey - Canada - Biography.   3. Lawyers - Canada - Biography.
I. Title.

GV848.5.E23C62   796.96′2′0924   C81-094754-4

Production by Paula Chabanais Productions
Design and jacket by Catherine Wilson for Sunkisst Graphics

Printed and bound in Canada for
Lester & Orpen Dennys Ltd.
78 Sullivan Street
Toronto, Ontario
M5T 1C1

CONTENTS

•AUTHOR'S NOTE•

That Alan Eagleson is and will remain a folk hero in the annals of hockey there is no doubt. He might even be inducted into the Hockey Hall of Fame. However, this is not a book about hockey. Hockey and hockey players enter the picture only inasmuch as they are factors in Eagleson's climb from rural Ontario to his present status as a millionaire and international media personality.

Eagleson has become a tremendously successful entrepreneur, but his power and control cannot be measured by typical business standards. A business magnate is powerful by virtue of ownership — through shares — and cannot be touched unless the company fails. Above all else, Eagleson's power and security come from his being a labour leader and public figure. As union boss of the National Hockey League Players' Association, he had to be manipulative, and he had to depend on his acute sense of people. A businessman controls through acquisition; Eagleson controls in a ''cool'' sense — through force of will. His power base exists by consent, and therefore is always vulnerable* because it is non-liquid; it has no cash surrender value.

The idea for this book was the result of an extensive research article I wrote about Eagleson's financial empire when I was a staff writer for

---

* Eagleson always kept a ''permanent'' letter of resignation on file at the union headquarters he ran out of his law office.

the *Financial Times of Canada*. Several magazine articles and newspaper stories presented him as the unknighted hero of hockey in general and international hockey specifically; although these provided informative reading for hockey buffs, they failed to show any other dimension. Many questions that had intrigued me were left unanswered and the *Financial Times* article only served to intensify my curiosity.

I was compelled to know what really made this man tick. I had to know why he received more exposure in the daily newspapers than any other Canadian except the Prime Minister. When I brought the idea for this book to Eagleson, he agreed to the project and permitted me to interview him on several occasions.

However, after I had signed a contract to publish the book, I received notice that court action might be taken if I failed to comply with Eagleson's request to see quotes attributed to him and if I didn't state in the preface that the book had been produced "without his cooperation or without his being interviewed". However, I decided to stay with my initial decision to present an objective account of an influential public figure and so refused to show Eagleson or anyone else quoted in the book the manuscript.

This work represents three years of talking to more than a hundred people, from hotel clerks to international hockey officials. I had to penetrate the legal, political, and financial machinations of one of this country's most influential networks — the hockey world — to discover how a boy from a poor immigrant family could become a prominent multi-millionaire by the age of forty-five. I learned why Eagleson felt compelled to leave the prestige and comfort of a successful law practice and a promising political career to accept the challenges offered by professional sport. I learned why he needed to win over impossible odds, and why he wanted his performance applauded.

I talked to dozens of people who had observed him in Canada, the U.S., Sweden, Germany, China, and Russia. According to some, he is a heartless rebel, defiant of convention, driven by a desire for self-glorification. To others he's a selfless, charitable, brilliant man, unique among his peers, whose devotion is unrelenting. He fosters love-hate relationships with those who deal with him. Everyone has stories to tell and opinions to give, many of them contradictory. I had difficulty at first believing that their public statements and private feelings could be about the same man.

In order to obtain supporting letters and documents, I was given unlimited access to the entire 1969–1981 collection of Hockey Canada files. No one has ever pulled together or examined the political and financial wheeling and dealing of this publicly funded corporation until now. I attempted to gauge its success or failure as well as to document Eagleson's growth as the key decision maker behind the first summit series in 1972 to Canada Cup '81.

Almost everyone I interviewed willingly and unabashedly gave me his opinions on the record. I am indebted to many people for their encouragement: to Len Coates of the *Toronto Star* for his initial suggestion to do the *Financial Times* article and to Paul Nowak, my editor at the *Financial Times*; to Bruce Powe and his family for their support; to Cherie Rogers for her advice in the early stages; to Pamela Harrison in Montreal; to Colette Letourneau and Ross Anderson in Ottawa and to Pauline Anderson in Toronto; to the Toronto Academy of Karate for keeping body and soul together. My sincere thanks go to Kate Hamilton for preliminary editing and typing and to Pauline Haward for her help in typing the manuscript. Very special thanks are due to Ian Adams, who saw a rough draft of the manuscript, gave me encouragement to see it through, and introduced me to my publishers, Malcolm Lester and Louise Dennys. Research work on the book was assisted by a grant from the Centre for Investigative Journalism.

Finally, this project was made possible only through the generous time given by R. Alan Eagleson, Q.C., his sister, Margaret Hooey, and his parents. I thank the many hockey players, officials, owners, agents, sports writers, politicians, and others who gave me their time, including Bobby Orr, Marcel Dionne, Steve Shutt, Ken Dryden, and especially Doug Fisher and Chris Lang. The omissions and errors are solely my own.

D.L.C.

A DAY IN THE LIFE

In the picture language of the ancient Egyptians, the letter A is represented by the figure of the Eagle, distinguished by its daring flight, its speed, and its close association with thunder and fire. It depicts the warmth of life, the Origin, the day.

6:30 A.M.: Ringgggggggggggg ... Ringggggggggggggg!

Robert Alan Eagleson, Q.C., curses to himself. Like a surgeon used to being summoned for a midnight operation, he gropes on the night table for his luminous watch. (It saves him the need for lights and the glasses he wears because of nearsightedness.) He picks up the telephone.

That telephone is like a patent medicine. He uses it an average of four hours a day to connect the lives, ambitions, and talents of hundreds of people who seek profit and pleasure from sport. The phone acts as the vital pump at the empire's fountainhead, shooting out verbal steam to fuel the progress of the empire's success.

Early morning calls are a routine established in 1966, when he cemented his fortunes to those of the most talented hockey find in decades. He negotiated with the Boston Bruins for Bobby Orr's first major league contract, and at the same time won control over the National Hockey League by forming the NHL Players' Association. These two important events marked his ascendancy as the brightest sports lawyer and merchandiser of the Canada–U.S. megadollar hockey industry.

Today's call was from one of his one hundred professional hockey clients, who, along with press and politicians, are free to call him any time, day or night.

1

The black receiver goes back on its cradle. His mind is already bent on solving the day's first problem.

He pads downstairs, crosses the bare hardwood floors of the huge Rosedale Tudor-style mansion, and heads for the front door. A May wind noses in as he grabs the *Globe and Mail* which has been folded twice and squeezed behind the front-door handle.

He returns upstairs checking the headlines, then climbs back into bed to finish reading the paper. His wife, Nancy, is still asleep. Her day doesn't start until an hour later when it's time to get their two children off to school. Eagleson has a game of tennis scheduled for 8:00 A.M. with Dr. Simon McGrail, and a breakfast meeting at 9:00 A.M. at the Westin Hotel Toronto.

While no morning is typical, when he is home the day will start with this pattern. On only one or two days a week does he go straight to his office. For the most part, he is away at European hockey summits or is head-table speaker at benefit luncheons. He also accepts speaking engagements on the average of once a month, each in a different province. During the past three months he has slept in his own bed only six times.

7:30 A.M.: He stops pulling at his tie knot and, like a hound hot on the trail, tilts his head to listen. Don Hooey, his brother-in-law and chauffeur, has turned the ignition of Eagleson's Cadillac Seville. It starts on the first try. The telephone ringing, the car idling are part of the early-morning vernacular.

Next to "availability", an impeccable, well-tailored appearance is Eagleson's hallmark. His expansive wardrobe consists of fifteen winter suits, six summer-weight ones, an assortment of ties, no hats, and five pairs of variation-on-a-theme Florsheim loafers. The suits are all custom-made by his empire's tailor laureate, Marty's* on Scollard Street in Toronto's posh Yorkville. Image is all-important to him, and dress is one of the ways Eagleson measures class. The only deviation from his strict standards occurred in 1974, when the Russians were playing the World Hockey Association team in Moscow. He was not involved in any official capacity, but was simply there as an observer. He dumbfounded everyone by showing up at one of the games wearing a jean jacket and an open-neck sport shirt.

8:00 A.M.: THWAAACK! Dressed in sparkling whites, Eagleson is

---

* Bobby Orr was a majority shareholder for 50 percent and Eagleson held approximately 25 percent.

smashing a serve in the direction of Dr. McGrail, an otolaryngologist at the Wellesley Hospital. The club is only a mile or so away from Eagleson's home, so often in the early summer evenings he and Nancy will bicycle over to play a game of doubles.

This morning he's booked for singles, although doubles is the game he excels at. Opponents describe his game at the net as "tenacious" and "unorthodox".

Tennis, not hockey, is Eagleson's passion. He plays tennis three times a week. Discipline is something he cherishes, some say to the point of obsession. This comes partly from identifying with the hard-muscled athletes he represents as a lawyer, but also from his knowledge that discipline is a way of monitoring his ability to perform. There is one other reason. Many of Eagleson's close friends say he feels physically threatened by others — a possible carryover from school days when he was frequently picked on by bullies. While there is some question as to whether he ever played in a hockey game (lacrosse was his sport), he once added a clause to one of Bobby Orr's Boston contracts to the effect that he wanted to play one line of defence with Orr before his contract expired.

Everything about his tennis game is controlled — everything except his language. It's very colourful, and he rants on nonstop. The game begins. His backhand swing starts from above the left shoulder, the right foot positioned ahead of the left and parallel to the baseline. The follow-through is climaxed just as the ball skims over the net. Instantly positioned at the centre of the court, two hands on the metal frame, a slight turn of the racquet into the backhand position again, and he's off. With the speed and agility of a fourteen-year-old, he's back at centre court.

They play two sets in thirty minutes. Each wins a set.

9:00 A.M.: Once again he's beside Don in the car, inching along slowly in the rush-hour traffic. Eagleson feels neither elated nor depressed about the game, but goes over the mistakes that cost him points.

Don swings the car up the circular ramp in front of the Hotel Toronto and Eagleson jumps out. He knows the first names of most of the doormen. Characteristically he notes the changeover into their summer "Beefeater" costumes. He strides through the hotel lobby.

Eagleson conducts hundreds of breakfast meetings, press conferences, and private parties here throughout the year.

The hotel is convenient, only a stone's throw from his office.

Chandeliers, wing-back chairs, well-tailored waitresses and, of course, a paging system for telephone calls suit his taste perfectly. It's a local bolt-hole for many of Toronto's lawyers, just steps away from the courts, old and new city halls, and Osgoode Hall.

10:00 A.M.: He's dashing through the lobby of another hotel. The Four Seasons Sheraton embraces the twenty-five-storey Thomson Building at Bay and Queen streets.

As soon as he's seated behind the dropleaf harvest table (circa 1860) he uses for a desk, one of his two phones rings. He pushes a button on the red-licorice-coloured desk phone and identifies himself. At the same time, Patti (who recently replaced his former personal secretary of ten years) places a cup of coffee in front of him along with the mail. She glances around the office to see if everything is in its place.

Each of the ten offices in that tenth-floor suite is carpeted in beige shag, except for the reception area which has a hand-woven tapestry rug. There are also two of these in his office. His is the corner office, naturally. In it, he shows off the valuable collection of paintings by "best-recognized Canadian artists," he says, and the antique Canadiana pieces which are his wife's passion. The hard-edged stripes of a Jack Bush hang over the soft leather sofa. A Riopelle straddles the two windows that look down between the two half-shells of City Hall. Above the Nova Scotia hutch is a Lemieux.

"It's a keepsake from the time I spent with Jean-Paul Lemieux down at Paul Desmarais' house." Eagleson reminds you constantly that not only does he represent the *crème de la crème* of the National Hockey League and serve as counsel for twenty-five gilt-edged corporations, but he is also a heavyweight in the Progressive Conservative Party.

As soon as he hangs up, Patti pokes her head around the corner to tell him the 5:00 P.M. tennis game the next evening has to be cancelled. It's with Ross Johnson, Chairman of the Board and Chief Executive Officer of Standard Brands, Inc., New York, a giant food conglomerate. A close associate says Johnson is the one man Eagleson pays more attention to than anyone else.

Suddenly he's in a flap. "Why?" he demands. Without waiting for an answer he pulls the receiver to his ear. The relaxed, foot-swinging composure abruptly vanishes and someone at the other end of the line is getting hell. "How come we can't have the court?" Just as quickly, the anger fades. "Oh, well, as long as there's something else going on and you're not giving it to someone else, 6:30's okay." Whether it is a tennis game or a multi-million-dollar hockey contract, Eagleson never allows anyone else to get the upper hand.

By now everyone in earshot knows the boss is in — his voice carries down the hallway like a rumbling bowling ball. Eagleson is the cynosure in the office every moment he is there.

His comptroller, Marvin Goldblatt, seems ripe for a peptic ulcer. And he has one, which he talks about whenever anyone will listen. He's nervous, a chain smoker, and a classic worry-wart. He has the office next to Eagleson's "to be within earshot".

"Jeeesus Christ!" Eagleson barks and Goldblatt jumps like a Wemmick to Mr. Jaggers. He can tell that Eagleson's irritated. His mouth is tight across his teeth. Also, he's taken off the gold-rimmed glasses and is pinching at the bridge of his nose. On his desk is a document which Patti brought in with the morning mail. On the surface, it doesn't look any different from the 150 contracts — all double-spaced on legal-size bond — that he goes through in the course of a year, contracts that determine whether a player's bottom line will show $50,000 or $500,000 next season.

"This is one hell of a poor excuse for a contract," he says, sweeping over the document with the back of his hand. It's a document that came from the National Hockey League Players' Association, of which he is the founder and executive director. The NHLPA's joint committee on player representatives is asking agents to use a standardized contract for negotiation.

"It won't force me to use an agreement with a client, because I have none. I'm a lawyer, not an agent," he insists.

This is only one of the conflicts that arise from his being an independent representative for the players as well as their union boss. But he reiterates the one philosophy he has when dealing with hockey players, impressing on Goldblatt his distaste for the dummy agreement by again emphatically sweeping over the document.

"If a player doesn't like the way I do work, I say, fine, don't pay the bill. We don't have any bills unpaid, do we?"

"No."

Case closed. Goldblatt knows he wasn't being asked for an opinion, anyway. Eagleson mulls the problem over quietly for a few minutes, then simply states his decision: "No dice." He doesn't have the patience to discuss every detail; he only comes into the ring for the final round of decision making. But most of those who work with him say his decisions usually have a side door that is left slightly ajar: this permits him to change his mind. And he frequently does.

Promptly at 10:45 A.M. Patti marches in, leading two Washington attorneys, Wendy White and Larry Latto from Shea Gardner, outside counsel for the NHLPA. Then a Toronto writer is introduced and takes a chair.

As if on cue, another Eagleson employee, Sam Simpson, a young, affable fellow, wanders in. He quietly takes a seat. His is the all-encompassing title of Director of Operations. Simpson is the full-time assistant looking after the NHLPA's day-to-day business, although Eagleson, as chief executive director, is still its lord and master. There are rumblings of "growing unrest" among some of the players who do not feel Eagleson is giving them enough of himself.

"The grievance procedures of the NHL will be the best of any sport," he promises to everyone and no one in particular. (There is no discussion here about his statement, but there is talk about pitching the 400-strong players' association into full union colours, sporting sweaters stamped with AFL-CIO on the front.)

If it is true that Eagleson has been giving less priority to the players' association, it is not evident this afternoon. For the next four hours Eagleson, Simpson, and the two American labour specialists will be redrafting a new collective-bargaining agreement for the players. For looking after their combined and separate needs, Eagleson gets a fee that may go as high as $200,000 in one year, but on a yearly average is closer to $70,000. They begin with the problem of spelling out the terms of reference of the agreement.

"Eagleson and not NHL President John Ziegler has the sole right to invoke arbitration," begins Latto, who has been called in to assist Eagleson in revising the 1976 NHL-NHLPA collective-bargaining agreement. "Let's insert a 'closed shop' clause as a condition of employment," suggests Eagleson. "That'll eliminate the necessity of getting players to sign up every year." Latto points out that in some U.S. states the term "closed shop" is prohibited.

"So we get around it by saying 'union shop'," interjects Eagleson.

"We virtually get 100 percent support now," Latto adds.

"Who didn't sign up this year?" asks Eagleson.

"André Savard wouldn't join."

"Savard!" The air escapes from Eagleson's pursed-up lips. "It was us who got him up to the majors!"

The telephone rings and Latto takes the opportunity to get up and stretch as Eagleson talks to top Canadian Olympic swimmer Graham Smith.

Like sandbags, dozens and dozens of red, blue, and manilla files stacked on the agent's desk barricade the man behind it. A Quebec hutch and bookcase complete the L-shape of his working area. On the wall behind Eagleson's desk hangs a weathervane topped with an eagle, its wings spread, about to take flight. (He recently removed a huge wall hanging from behind his desk because a Toronto writer referred to its design as "the world's largest jockstrap".) A pine-panelled blanket box (Quebec circa 1840) serves as his coffee table. For a first-time visitor, he will dig inside this chest and hand over a couple of trinkets. One of the treasures inside the box is a brushed-copper paperweight half the size of a normal hockey puck, which has been engraved with the double-stick logo of the Canada Cup '76 hockey series. Another is a silver charm with the same logo, which he presents in a brown jeweller's gift box.

On a small dropleaf table from Prince Edward Island, dated 1860, is a Honey Rothschild clay sculpture of two hockey players frozen at the moment their bodies touch, their eyes wide with excitement.

Eagleson's collection, however, does not compare in value or direct snob appeal with the extensive personal collection of Krieghoffs housed upstairs. In the out-of-bounds penthouse office on the twenty-fifth floor is Canada's illustrious newspaper tycoon, Kenneth Thomson. Eagleson likes to drop his name whenever possible and will occasionally seek his advice.

"Come up to Toronto, we'll talk, and I'm sure I can do something about generating some revenue for you," Eagleson promises Smith as Latto wanders around his office.

Talk resumes. Latto reads from the revised agreement and Eagleson quickly shoots out deletions, revisions, and affirmations: "'May' should be 'shall'. It makes a helluva difference so put 'shall', it's binding then." Then he goes off on a tangent: "Orr's contract of 1971 involved a very lengthy series of negotiations, a dozen drafts, and a dozen documents ... [starting in January 1970 and concluding on February 14, 1971] Charles Mulcahy [Jr., Chairman of the Owners' Committee] did not write one letter, not one piece of correspondence was in the file from Charley during that time, only phone calls. ... Now it says we must have a unanimous vote by the twenty-one reps. Problem is NHL should be a party to the agreement, not just twenty-one clubs; therefore, we won't accept binding arbitration.

" ... I think we should put the squeeze on to have ourselves involved ... players are like cattle at a barter, but there are certain players' rights that should be considered. No trade ... do you think a guy can play as well in Toronto as in L.A.?

"Question unanimous vote of the owners ... once had Vancouver's owners kicked out.... Fifty owners, lawyers and accountants. Harry Sinden kicked out, yet his trainer could stay ... we are doing him a favour. Ziegler shouldn't be going to meetings, only the executive director."

Then Latto picks up the thread: "If Alan appoints an arbitrator the [Buffalo] Sabres will come in on the 1977 amendment to the agreement." "Unless twenty-one reps signed the agreement it is not valid," says Eagleson. "And only two signed, therefore it's not valid." Eagleson refuses to invoke arbitration. Then he starts to dictate a letter to Latto — with a little prelude.

"Sabres will have to come up with $20,000 to $25,000. ... You get back to me whether or not we're going to stop arbitration, having told me in advance all the other shortfalls of your position. Tell them Eagleson told you to talk to Ziegler and make a settlement of $50,000; let them go to arbitration, but if he says $25,000 I'll talk."

Latto turns to the writer in the room and says, "Did you understand any of that?"

Another problem to be considered that afternoon is the 1972 WHA player contracts: what did their contracts provide for now that the two leagues had merged?

But before they can tackle this enormously consequential and expensive question, the door opens and Darryl Sittler enters. The familiar line of his square jaw makes his generous smile crooked. Eagleson immediately glances at his watch. "It can't be noon already!" Sittler is here this time for a press conference at 12:15 P.M. to launch a radio promo for a new "scratch and win" hockey lottery for Toronto's Big Brothers. Eagleson is the organization's director.

Eagleson makes many of these "marriages of convenience" — he will connect one of his corporate concerns with an athlete to promote a cause. Sittler keeps in shape by playing hockey, but promoting products will make the difference between his retiring comfortably or retiring with style. At a time in his career when playing for a Stanley Cup contender should be given top priority, Sittler and Eagleson think there is far too much at stake in terms of "outside" involvements in

Toronto to permit him to consider a team change.

In the matter of endorsements, Sittler is locked into five-year contracts with such companies as Neilson's, Weetabix, Bauer skates, Sico paint, and the Bank of Nova Scotia.

Like his clients', Eagleson's own name has become a household word. His face peers out among the whisky and travel advertisements in magazines as he tells readers that when it comes to making international hockey deals the airline of his choice, naturally, is Air Canada. Or he's promoting a television station, doing a commercial, faking a call to Harold Ballard.

"Give me five more minutes to work on this goddamn agreement, okay?" he asks Sittler.

12:15 P.M.: Although the press conference is just a stone's throw away at the Hotel Toronto, Eagleson, complaining about a bad back, accepts a drive over in Sittler's Jeep. The two Washington attorneys, Eagleson, Sittler, and the writer make their way to the tenth floor.

Two hotel rooms are opened up and twenty or more sports scribes are sipping the usual chilled white wine and nibbling bits of sardines on crackers.

The Big Brothers are hopeful of attracting the born-again bingo types — the New Lottarians — to finance more big brother–little brother associations. "Each match costs approximately $750 annually. This year Big Brothers expects to add 5,500 needy 7-to-13-year-olds to its already swollen waiting list of 7,500," reports a press release.

Everyone is then ushered into a room ablaze with TV lamps. A CBC cameraman holds up a light meter in front of Sittler's face. A woman representing Big Brothers is enthusiastically passing out metallic scratch'n'win lottery tickets.

When Eagleson enters he is immediately handed a ticket. "I'm so lucky, I won't show you how to do this for fear I might win and cause another controversy," he tells the camera. "We'll let Sittler do it to prove the tickets are legitimate." He hands a writer his ticket.

"Is Ballard allowing this commercial?" quips a Toronto Star reporter, picking up on Eagleson's lead.

Then the Big Brother barker mounts the podium and gives a few words in appreciation of Sittler's generosity.

"See, Darryl, you've got to play in Toronto ... the people love you," says Eagleson in a not-so-quiet stage whisper.

Then he spots the writer rubbing a dime over the lottery ticket. "Did you get anything?"

"I won $10.00."

"See, I'm a lucky son of a bitch," he laughs.

"Quiet, please," yells the barker.

Then a large screen crackles and jumps until the familiar faces of Eagleson and Sittler come into focus on it. They sing a cute jingle based on the player-agent theme, and everyone resumes his place back at the hors d'oeuvre table.

Eagleson picks up a paper cup of beer and takes a bite of a cheese sandwich before he is whisked away for an interview. In thirty minutes the whole thing is over. Eagleson collects his group and audibly complains again about his back pain. As if on cue, a bottle of aspirin is produced, and the name of a chiropractor is hastily scribbled on a piece of paper by a scribe.

On the short ride back to the office, Latto and the writer fight for possession of a parking ticket Sittler received that morning.

"In Montreal the cops don't ticket the players' cars," Sittler grumbles. It's true. But Toronto's finest are cut from a different cloth. Sittler autographs the ticket for the writer, then thinks twice and retrieves it, saying if he doesn't pay it, the leasing company will be out money.

Eagleson and the others head up for another round with the NHLPA agreement, leaving Sittler and the writer in the Jeep.

"I was flying back from Barbados on American Airlines a few weeks ago," Sittler tells the writer, "when a stewardess hands me a baseball lottery ticket. I scratch it and I won. The ticket says I could be upgraded to first class. What was I supposed to do, I was already sitting in first class!"

A moment passes; then the writer inquires: "Why was the Canada Cup cancelled? What about Mike Milbury and the group of seven? Do you want the players to become part of the AFL-CIO?" But these questions are just stage setting for the big one: "Your agent told me this morning you would be happy to sign a new contract with the Leafs for $350,000 for five years with the right to let them trade you. Is this possible?"

"Eagleson's never said that to me and I've never said that to him ... that I'd be happy with $350,000. I signed a contract with the intention of playing another four years here. I have a lot of involvement in things outside of hockey, a nice home and a place up north that I go to. . . . Listen . . . I went through a lot of crap and hassles last year. I wasn't getting enough ice time and things like that. I survived it all. . . . I think from here on it will be a piece of cake . . . if I just go out on the ice and play the way I'm capable of playing. . . . ''

"What kind of megabucks are you looking for?"

"I would never say to the Leafs: here's a number of dollars and 'no trade' is waived because they could trade me whenever they wanted to."

Was Eagleson up to his old tricks again, sending out trial balloons through a writer just to see what kind of response he would get? This way he could gauge his next move. An earlier call to an editor at *Maclean's* magazine revealed that Toronto Maple Leaf coach George "Punch" Imlach had trouble pinning down the number: "Imlach called Bill Watters (recently departed from the Eagle's nest) and got a figure of $500,000. Then he called Eagleson who said $1 million — maybe Sittler would say $2 million!"

With a range from $350,000 to $2 million, does Eagleson just want to keep Leaf management dancing on a pin? This latest puzzle has its advantages, especially for Eagleson. It takes attention away from the departure of Bobby Orr and Bill Watters from his fold. And the press has been nosing around trying to verify a few stories leaked to them about Orr, his money, and Eagleson.

Even those high up in the Eagleson organization were "waiting to see how long Eagleson can keep the balls in the air".

Sittler has been looking out the window of the Jeep at a couple of people talking in front of City Hall. He recognizes them as friends from St. Jacobs, Ontario, where his parents currently live, and he runs over to chat. The break is welcome. The writer thinks of a new angle to get Sittler back on track. He's been promoting Eagleson for the past few minutes with the standard party line: "He's a very fair person. He has too many hats, but I think he's capable of wearing them all. I know Al's been at the job for ten years now and I don't see anybody with a mind like he has. Not many can do all the things he can do and do them efficiently", and so on.

(A few weeks later Sittler shut out his "capable and efficient" agent from his negotiations when he reinstated himself with the Leafs. Some said his Jeep had been seen on quite a few occasions parked on Redpath Street in front of a building where an Eagleson competitor, agent Gerry Patterson, has his office.)

The writer rejects the impulse to pocket the parking ticket still lying on the seat. Sittler returns and, without prompting, sums up.

"Listen, my parents live in St. Jacobs, my wife's parents live outside Kitchener. If something happens and we decide we want to go to Buffalo it would depend a lot on how much they would pay, conditions of the contract. ... " The talk was all dollars, conditions of payment, and endorsements. Today's pro can talk as much about what is happening to the price of gold as any stockbroker.

Of a dozen or so of Eagleson's clients the writer had interviewed, only Steve Shutt, a left-winger for the Montreal Canadiens, wanted no part of the après-hockey corporate career. He wanted to retire on a farm and "raise chickens".

The writer presses the off button on the recorder and thanks Sittler for his time. She tries to reconstruct the series of events surrounding the Sittler-Leaf contract and apparent Sittler-Eagleson fallout while waiting for the elevator.

Eagleson has told the Leafs he would charge $500,000 before he would permit Darryl to be released to another team. So far the Minnesota North Stars, Buffalo Sabres, and Chicago Black Hawks have expressed interest, but none has offered to buy out the "no-trade" clause.

Yet you can't file an NHL contract with a "no-trade" clause. You file an agreement and, as was the case with Bobby Orr, you have a separate letter agreeing to "no trade" between the club and the player. Such an agreement had been signed on Sittler's behalf, stating: "It is understood that Sittler will not be traded during the term of his contract." Even hard-hearted Harold Ballard had deferred to Eagleson and never contradicted the myth of the "no-trade" contract. The ultimate test would be if the letter could stand up in court.

3:00 P.M.: Once again the office is empty and Eagleson is alone for a moment. Behind the enormous desk he looks as fresh as he did at 9:00 A.M. His tie is knotted over the top button of the white shirt neatly between the two points of his crisp shirt collar. He is tapping a paper clip on his desk, sounding like a geiger counter searching out some radioactive material — his hands are never still. He cradles a phone on his shoulder and speaks to Bill Torrey, general manager of the New York Islanders. It has taken three months to wind up a contract for a former Toronto Marlboro junior hockey player, and he is going over the last details. But the final price can't be agreed upon. Eagleson gets his way by having the dollars written into the contract on a bonus basis.

" 'Tough' is the one word I have for him," says Torrey. "He's as tough as anyone I've dealt with, maybe more so because he not only knows how to talk hockey, but he can lay some pretty heavy courtroom histrionics on you."

Anyone who has ever been on the opposing side of Eagleson concurs with Torrey's description. He doesn't hesitate to use small points to improve his leverage when there is disagreement over big dollars. When an impasse is reached over what a player is worth, Eagleson can quickly pull out a new strategy that ends in a bonus for his client. He's your best friend when the negotiations begin, the passive listener with the poker face, but he enjoys confrontation. He will appear openly arrogant and display impatience with the proceedings in order to keep the other side on edge. At any second he may adjourn a meeting in a fit of feigned rage. A former employee says he always mixes a few boyish antics with any orders he gives, but he gets his point across.

One day a political associate met Eagleson at his office for lunch. They stood in the hall waiting for the elevator. Just as it arrived, packed with business types, Eagleson ran back, opened his office door, and hollered: "Just because the boss is gone you don't have to stop working."

4:00 P.M.: Goldblatt enters his office and absentmindedly lights up a cigarette, something Eagleson despises. He quickly cuts into him.

"Hey, I thought you were going to stop smoking."

"It was either keep my fifty extra pounds off or quit smoking," Goldblatt replies.

"Bullshit," Eagleson charges, "self-discipline, that's what it takes." But Goldblatt is saved from further reprimand when Patti buzzes him on the intercom with a potential recruit.

Goldblatt, a certified general accountant, started with Eagleson at the law firm of Blaney, Pasternak, Smela, Eagleson and Watson, and after ten years in the business manages the financial affairs of approximately sixty athletes of his own.

The buzzer is going again and this time Patti stays on the line. Intrusions by the public are common. People who Eagleson says "are a little above begging level, but not far" see his name on the directory downstairs and feel free to walk in.

This one is a little fiftyish-looking woman, who enters and says she needs a lawyer to talk to.

"I don't think I know you," comments Eagleson.

"No, but I know you. My son owes me $20,000 and he won't pay me back." He listens to the whole story.

"Okay. Here's my card. Go home and show your son this. If you have any trouble call me. Maybe the card will convince him," explains Eagleson.

The buzzer goes again. A surprise visitor. Eagleson bounds out of his office to the reception area. A plumpish man in a poorly fitted brown suit grins bashfully. His aluminum-looking hair has been greased back and, by the look of the overfilled ashtray, he has been chain-smoking. He offers Eagleson his hand. The meeting takes three minutes and the man leaves. He represents the Czech national hockey team, but Eagleson doesn't have any more time to talk today.

"When these guys come to Toronto they head straight for my office," he says to the reception room. "I'm more popular than the CN Tower."

Eagleson picks up his calls from the receptionist, who has just returned after being away from work for sixteen months following a severe car accident. She is grateful that he kept her job open for her. One of the calls is from a "concerned parent", a father whose underage son has been pestered by an agent.

Eagleson calls such agents "jackals". "They're not lawyers." His favourite pastime is lambasting his competition. He points a bony finger: "There are two of them who go and chase kids who are fourteen on spec. They say look, if I get every good fourteen-year-old I'm bound to hit the jackpot ... best example was young Gretzky ... I get frustrated when I see a young kid like Gretzky tied up with an agent ... he didn't need one until he turned pro."

The early bird was Gus Badali. Ironically, Badali was a candy bar auditor for Famous Players Theatres when he first met Gretzky. Badali is an agreeable sort who mixes well with youngsters. Being a fast learner, Badali managed to sign Gretzky to a four-year contract with Edmonton at $875,000 with a $250,000 signing bonus to a high roller named Nelson Skalbania. Skalbania, a Vancouver real estate dealer, had a WHA franchise at the time in Indianapolis. Badali takes 5 percent of Wayne's hockey income, whereas Eagleson would probably take twice that.

Eagleson has a different way of doing business. "When I first get a call from a kid's father that some guy has been pestering his kid to sign a contract before he's out of juniors, I suggest he show up with his son at my office. I tell him to forget I'm his lawyer until after the season is over." Eagleson starts his staff working on the new recruit immediately, checking out the client's friends, teachers, and teammates. If Eagleson can handle the kid's disposition and likes his attitude, he takes him on, but doesn't announce it. By the time he's finished the juniors they get together with the kid's parents, the team owner and general manager and they talk turkey. Until 1980 Bill Watters, his vice-president of Sports Management Ltd., handled all of the preliminary negotiations. Eagleson came in for the big finale, the actual signing-up ceremony: champagne, pictures, and the big bonus cheque.

He compares his business to that of a used car salesman's. "I have to know my product and the market. I think of only two things when I come up with the final dollar figure: what the team's requirements are and how good the player is." Luck never enters the picture, he claims.

But today there are fewer juniors taking up his time. He concentrates more on the money makers — the superstars who are his clients. He has only one rule when dealing with superstars. "They have to trust me 100 percent. Once that trust goes, or someone questions my judgment, I hand back the paper and say, do it yourself, no bill."

4:40 P.M.: While he's finishing his conversation with the "concerned parent", Chris Lang, Hockey Canada's treasurer since 1969, enters the office. He nods to Eagleson, then sits down on the leather couch across the room. He's a smaller version of Eagleson. His mannerisms and speech are curt and sharp, very imitative of Eagleson's. He doesn't mind shooting the bull if it's for a reasonable cause. Most people say he's " a good guy".

Eagleson hangs up the telephone and crosses over to the window. Is it coincidence that the view is of the city hall and the old courthouse? These buildings represent two ambitions he sacrificed — being a trial lawyer and a politician — in order to run the country's national pastime.

"Is it that time already?" he asks, snapping out of his reverie. He calls Patti for some coffee and pulls a chair over to the couch so he can look at some of the papers in the manilla folder that now lies open on the blanket box.

Eagleson doesn't get paid for his Hockey Canada work. In fact

Chris Lang says that "Eagleson has left virtually millions under the table with Hockey Canada".*

Lang and Eagleson discuss points to raise at a meeting that evening with the Canadian Amateur Hockey Association past president Don Johnson. The CAHA withdrew from HC in 1979 but there is still a matter of a $1 million trust agreement between the CAHA and HC to settle.

5:15 P.M.: Eagleson and Lang leave. The stately Rosedale mansion looms up to the right. Don manoeuvres the Cadillac past the family's General Motors station wagon, and parks in front of a green Datsun belonging, Eagleson finds out, to a reporter from a daily newspaper. He curses to himself.

He leads Lang and the reporter past wide expanses of highly polished hardwood flooring. They enter a family room with a dove-grey carpet, and dark wood shelves full of Nancy's art books. His wife's taste is further reflected in the mix of folk art and early Canadian furnishings which gives the room its immediate warmth.

The fire crackles in the natural stone fireplace; Nancy is whistling a tune from *New York, New York*; and Heidi, a small terrier who matches the carpet, jumps around Eagleson's feet. His children, Jill and Allen, he's informed, are doing homework.

Eagleson picks up two ice-cold Tuborg beers on his way back from showing the reporter where the front door is, and seats himself on the couch. He takes a swig of his beer; Heidi nestles in a comfortable nook between the outside of Eagleson's thigh and the arm of the sofa.

Eagleson and Lang continue their conversation. Eventually Eagleson goes upstairs and changes into a grey suit for their meeting tonight.

---

* A management consulting firm from Edmonton, M & M Systems Research Ltd., looked into the feasibility of Hockey Canada and came up with a study called "The Organizational Development of Hockey Canada". One of their conclusions was that in "... formal and informal discussions with persons directly and indirectly associated with HC ... one increasingly hears suspicions such as the following expressed. ..." The study listed ten situations where a person or organization had motives other than the good of hockey in joining Hockey Canada's board. Names were withheld from the report, but the blanks could easily be filled in by anyone close to HC. Past chairman of Hockey Canada Doug Fisher says the statement that might explain the motivation behind Eagleson's involvement was: "[Eagleson] is using HC to make personal contacts which will have social and commercial value." Thus, Eagleson's efforts may not have been completely altruistic. He retains his seat on HC's board representing the National Hockey League Players' Association, and is also its chief negotiator for all North American international hockey matters (see also p. 84).

11:00 P.M.: In his bedroom at last, tired and a little impatient, he sighs loudly, as if the length of the day has only now fully reached him. Today, the press have seen him on three occasions, once in his office, again at the Big Brothers' press conference, and privately in his own home.

As he begins to undress the phone rings.

·2·

POTATOES AND POINTING

*... the foot soldiers always fight the fight
and Eagle's a foot soldier ... if this was a
class in England he would have come from
the yeomen as opposed to the officer's
class, the guys who carry the pikes as
opposed to the guys who ride the horses.*
Morley Kells, Ontario MPP

Robert Alan Eagleson was practising law at the age of five. Lying flat on his stomach, a recycled black taffeta cape concealing running shoes, shorts, and a T-shirt, the young Chief Justice went about his daily business of trying his friends and enemies for their injustices in his collapsible cardboard courtroom. To carry out his role as agent of the law, young Alan had erected a tiny law court out of cigar boxes, egg crates, and fruit cases. The supply of accused, the jury, court clerks, and a horde of spectators was frequently replenished by clipping pictures of models from the Simpson-Sears catalogue. Men, women, and children in colourful modes of seasonal dress and undress were assigned names and titles and carried out special duties. He ran a quick, efficient, and at times merciless institution. A steady flow of accused approached the witness stand, a suspended strawberry box which jumped up and down on a chain of elastic bands. The closed lid of the cigar box signalled that the jury members were deliberating their verdict. Punishment was doled out in one-week or life sentences, and the guilty were consigned to a discarded birdcage hidden behind the cellar steps.

A textile worker from St. Catharines, Ontario, and his nine-months-pregnant wife sat next to their radio on a cold April evening, waiting anxiously for the outcome of a Toronto-Boston ice hockey game. It was one of the longest overtime games in the history of the Stanley Cup playoffs and didn't end until 2:00 A.M. The Leafs won the game, which excited Agnes Eagleson so much, she claims, that it brought on her labour and the birth of another hockey legend.

The Eagle was born on April 24, 1933, in a tiny bungalow in St. Catharines, Ontario. His father, a repairman at Grout's Mill, christened him Robert Alan Eagleson. (Alan's father spells his name "Allen". His full name is James Allen Eagleson.) His mother called the baby simply "wee Alan".

The name "Allen" is a typical British surname, and had been the father's paternal great-grandmother's maiden name. The name has been passed on to the first male in each generation. However, The Eagle was given the true Celtic spelling, "Alan", which means "harmony".

James Allen Eagleson, a miller's son, left school at age twelve, as was the custom in Ballymena, Ireland. He apprenticed for eight years as a loom fixer at the Phoenix Mill, keeping the giant weaving machines in good running order. Ballymena had been in the linen and carpet trade ever since the Adair family started making cloth in 1732.

Agnes Jane McNabney met Allen Eagleson, Sr., "at the mill", where she worked until they were married. She was the daughter of a Ballymena blacksmith and one of twelve children. The McNabneys are referred to as "the Ballymena Scots", and are the reason for the Irish accent in that market town being so different from the Belfast accent just twenty-nine miles away.

Shortly after the couple were married, when they were expecting their first child, two of Agnes' brothers, Sammy and Bobby McNabney, were sipping a draught of the wee Bush and talking about a place called Canada. The McNabneys booked passage for the New World in 1929. Agnes, Allen, and their new child would follow the next year.

The world depression and the crisis following the collapse of the stock market that year fostered intense anger and resentment among the already disgruntled loom workers in Northern Ireland's linen industry. In 1925 unemployment teetered at 47.7 percent; by 1930 there would be a general strike by 200,000 loom workers in the United Kingdom.

The young couple had many talks about the opportunities for advancement in Canada. In spite of the British Parliament's "step-by-step" economic improvement policy for Ulster's linen and shipbuilding industries, and a noticeable drop in unemployment, the Eaglesons eventually decided to leave the peaceful Antrim glens to find their fortune in Toronto's commercial centre.

Wearing a cloth cap and a silk scarf knotted and crossed over in front, the young pioneer, with his young daughter and pregnant wife, set off on the twenty-nine-mile carriage trip southwest to Belfast. Allen had liquid assets of £10 which he carried in his sock.

A small tender carried them to the Canadian Pacific "M" ship docked five miles out of Belfast Lough. Cramped quarters and seasickness for the next seven days didn't dampen their expectations of the land of plenty. The arrival in Quebec City at Wolfe's Cove was shared by more than 64,000 other Britons arriving that year in Canada's several major ports. The total immigration in 1930 was 104,806 and, with 164,993 arrivals the year earlier, the two early depression years marked the greatest influx of foreigners to Canada since the 1913 total of 400,870.

Less than half a day's train trip away was the Eaglesons' destination, Toronto. Canadian Pacific's convoy of colonist cars pulled into the newly built Union Station, emptying working-class, white, Anglo-Saxon Protestants onto the platform. Eventually these rank-and-file blue-collar workers would swell the Progressive Conservative ranks, colouring Ontario's political future true Tory blue.

The Eaglesons were met by Sammy and Bobby McNabney, who quickly steered them past throngs of dewy-eyed reunioners and out onto Front Street. The McNabneys, like most Britons, had settled in Toronto's east end, a section of the city characterized today by a mosaic of ethnic groups, predominantly Greek and Chinese. But at the time Agnes and Allen first moved into the area, there was a saying: "If you're on the trolley going east along to the Danforth, you have to show your English or Irish passport."

And if you were Irish, there was another ritual you had to go through. The first thing on the McNabney brothers' agenda was an Ulster United soccer game at the Ulster Stadium at Greenwood Avenue and Gerrard Street.

Allen Eagleson, Sr., doesn't recall the score at the end of his first Ulster United soccer game, but he does remember what he considers to be far more relevant details. Out there on the soccer field were the two McNabney boys. Sammy played outside right and Bobby, well, he's not sure about what position Bobby played. The team's manager was a man called Imlach and the twelve-year-old ball boy was his son, George "Punch" Imlach.

Watching the game was as closely as any Eagleson got involved in soccer, though many attempts were made over the years to enlist Eagleson's services. Soccer, however, was not particularly high on the newcomer's list of priorities. With no money, a daughter, and another child on the way, Allen Eagleson, Sr., immediately took whatever work he could find in Toronto. His first job was dishwasher at Bowles' lunch counter at Bay and Queen streets for minimum wage — fifty cents an hour. As it turned out, his son would set up a law practice some forty years later in exactly that location.

By the end of the year the Eaglesons were saying goodbye again to Sammy and Bobby to take a better-paying job at Grout's Mill in St. Catharines. They would move several more times between Toronto, Guelph, and St. Catharines, each time to a higher-paying job. By the time she was twenty-five Agnes had four children: Fran, Margaret, Alan, and Carol; Allen Eagleson, Sr., was earning $6 a week.

Hard-pressed for time and money, Allen Eagleson, Sr., found it impossible to upgrade his formal education to compete for a more lucrative white-collar job, and his taxable income never went above $7,000 in his life. It wasn't until he retired and moved with Agnes to their winter home in Florida that he earned a high school diploma after taking courses in history and geography. On graduation night, the school principal took down the Cocoa Beach flag and presented it to him. It still flies at their summer residence near Owen Sound, Ontario.

Allen Eagleson, Sr., was a hard worker who usually took whatever overtime or shift work came up to ease the financial burden at home. He was a good mixer and at one time was a shop steward. "He was a union steward but not to protect the workers," one previous employer said. "He did it to make sure the workers worked! ... He got quite upset if some bloke from Britain sat around smoking instead of working." It was the heavy dose of the Protestant work ethic in his blood that made him that way, his co-workers said.

Raising and educating their four children was always left up to Agnes. And "Aggie", as her friends called her, never forgot why she left her family and homeland to come to Canada. "It was to better ourselves in the new country. ... We wanted to give our children the opportunities we never had in Ireland."

Aggie was a spunky and confident person who prided herself on being a frugal home economist. If necessity is the mother of invention, certainly Aggie, raising a large family almost singlehandedly through the Depression and the Second World War on factory wages, had all the incentive she needed.

During the next decade and a half, Aggie invented a number of economic practices that Marx, Keynes, or Galbraith would have had difficulty in faulting. And even when the financial burden had been eased, Aggie could not forget her strict working-class ethics.

One of her principles, which she admitted had its roots back in Ireland, was "potatoes and pointing". The purpose of Aggie's potatoes and pointing was to bring home the theory of the Irish Protestant work ethic. Potatoes and pointing is a typically Irish dinner served when the family has been seated around the table. In the middle are set two large plates. One dish contains potatoes, the other a solitary piece of meat. Every member of the family takes as many potatoes as they want, but only the breadwinners (usually the men) are given the meat. The rest may point at the meat — they may have all the pointing they want — but only those who work get the meat.

An empty stomach has always been a great motivator. The children grew older with one strong instinct: to get at the meat. Potatoes and pointing and the Protestant work ethic were Alan Eagleson's introduction to economics.

The Eaglesons were not a family who gathered around the radio to listen to programs. The news and Saturday night hockey games were the extent of their listening. Any music that entered the Eaglesons' home did so sporadically, usually through school choirs or church hymns. It was not unusual for Alan to go around the house singing at the top of his squeaky voice: "I went to the garden alone, when the dew was still on the rose."

Outside of school their literary education was a hit-or-miss affair. Books arrived occasionally from aunts and uncles as Christmas gifts; otherwise the children, left to develop their own tastes, tapped the public libraries. Alan, of course, read the "books for boys" — such as The Hardy Boys — but he preferred animal books of any kind. Lassie Come Home was a favourite by seventh grade. "Alan and I would take turns reading it in front of the class," his sister Margaret remembers.

They always had a houseful of "company", and Alan saw a great deal of his uncles, who, besides a few neighbours and teachers, were his childhood heroes.

With no other exposure to "good books" or other sources of philosophical tempering during his so-called formative years, Alan developed a keen awareness of religion. Sunday was "family day" and most of it was taken up by going to church — that is, to any one of the range of religious facilities that were heated and only cost the price of a donation. The children would attend Century United Church on Ninth Street in the morning, where they had Bible lessons and sang hymns. In the afternoon they would go to one of the Bible schools to memorize psalms and sing more hymns.

Young Alan was quite impressed by the Sunday routine and for a while went around the house announcing, "When I grow up I'm going to be a minister. Only I won't make sermons, I'll just take the collection and leave."

Later in their teens, the children taught at Westside Sunday School in New Toronto (which later became part of Etobicoke), and Alan was involved with the young adult social life there until he was about twenty-one years old.

"Dad always did church work, but Mom would only do a bit of quilting occasionally," Margaret recalls. "It would be an embarrassment to call my parents religious." Margaret is the second of the four Eagleson children.

"Religion" entered the Eagleson household through moral guidelines which taught the difference between right and wrong, good and evil. It was called Christianity but it had little to do with God, except that everyone was expected to believe in Him and everybody did. "Do unto others as you would have them do unto you" was embroidered on a sampler and kept on the wall above the refrigerator. The children had to observe fundamental principles: be generous; behave in public; share what you have; don't swear; be courteous to older people; don't talk back to your parents. Being a good Christian also meant no ice skating or riding bikes on Sundays. "But we broke the rules," says Margaret.

Without grandparents or other relatives to aid them, the Eaglesons had to finish their "growing up" with their children, relying on church socials, family picnics, and neighbourhood baby christenings for recreation. When the children were tucked away in bed, their parents would gather around neighbours' wood-burning stoves to chat about common experiences and sort out problems. At night they would play euchre at the kitchen table — except on Sundays.

It was important not to become "puffed up" about yourself. Aggie wouldn't allow any kind of individual glorification or self-indulgence. If her children walked around with long faces or spent too much time alone they were called "disrespectful" and scolded for being idle. Then she would tell them to go out and play. She thought her children abnormal if they weren't always "busy".

Alan's three sisters, Fran, Margaret, and Carol, looked after most of the household chores of cleaning, cooking, and sewing, which were called "girls' jobs", so Alan had a lot of time to keep "busy" and to play outside.

Most of the children's recreation, however, took the form of family outings. The summer months away from school were long and hot; the kitchen door slammed continually as the kids zipped in and out for glasses of lemonade or home-made Popsicles. When Dad wasn't working he would take the family for a picnic and swimming at the Credit River.

The Eagleson children knew how to swim by the time they entered first grade. Allen Eagleson would wade out waist-deep carrying them on his shoulders and toss them in. "We used to come out dirty — it was so polluted," says Margaret.

Afterwards, the women would spread the picnic lunch on the large wooden tables and the kids would sit shivering in wet bathing suits trying to keep the sand out of their sandwiches. When the sun set and it was time to go home the children held towels around each other, for modesty's sake, and changed out of their wet swim suits into their street clothes.

In the winter, every night after work, the neighbourhood fathers would take turns flooding the backyards to make ice rinks. They taught the kids how to skate by pushing them around the ice with kitchen chairs.

Because swimming and skating were public, free, and could be enjoyed by the whole family, they became a big part of their life. The seven years the Eaglesons lived in Port Dalhousie near St. Catharines are remembered as "the best years" by Agnes Eagleson.

But these years were particularly difficult ones for young Alan. "He was just like a little bird, with legs like tooth-picks hanging down from his bathing costume," his mother recalls. Ice skates were quite expensive; often Alan had to wear a pair of his sister's white hand-me-downs. Boys' skates are black, so although Alan learned to skate he didn't play shinny very much with the neighbourhood boys.

"Because of my slight build I was continuously picked on by the bullies," he has said, "something I had to live with all through my school years." Whenever he complained at home about the "bullies" his mother told him to just ignore them.

To Agnes Eagleson the best way to deal with a problem is to laugh about it, so she used to tease him about being skinny. Even at five wee Alan was alert to the Protestant work ethic — he wanted to waste no time getting at the meat — so at that young age he set about deciding the best road to take to get there.

"When I grow up I'm going to be a boxer and call myself 'The Eagle'," said the sandy-haired boy, beginning a routine that was repeated every night throughout the relentless winter months.

"You couldn't be a boxer, you're just a skinny runt," his mother responded each night between bath and bed. "The Eagle!" she laughed "You might look like a bird, but you'll never be big enough to be a boxer ... besides, I don't like fighting."

She was strict about their bedtime. "Every night Allen went off to work at twenty minutes to six, so I had the children five nights a week on my own. They were always in bed by seven o'clock."

But one night, when the children were slow in going to bed, Alan was stretched out on his stomach with his nose buried in the evening newspaper.

"No one ever taught him how to read, but he could read when he was five," says Margaret. That night he was trying to pronounce the words in the big black headlines.

"What's a Robin-ette, Mom?" he called out.

"He's a famous criminal lawyer," she said, after taking the newspaper out of his hands and studying an account of a famous murder trial in which John Josiah Robinette, a Toronto lawyer, was involved.

"What's a lawyer, then?" he persisted.

"Someone who tries to keep you out of jail when you haven't done anything wrong."

That evidently sank in deeply. "A couple of nights later when I was dusting off some of the family heirlooms I had brought over from Ireland and was dividing them up among my three girls, wee Alan shed tears when he heard that because he was a boy he wouldn't be getting anything from the collection," his mother says. " 'That's not fair,' he wailed. Then he surprised us all by announcing, 'That's it, I'm going to be a lawyer when I grow up, just like Robinette!' ... and it stuck ever since."

But what Alan didn't have in size, he made up for with speed and a keen mind. He was an overachiever even at five, and when it came time for him to go to public school, he was put ahead one grade. Within a few years he quickly outpaced those in his grade and he accelerated another year, completing grades three and four together. This put him up with his sister Margaret, who was two years older.

A certain amount of competition resulted, but both Eaglesons usually finished the year standing in either first or second place in the class. This continued until the family moved to New Toronto. Allen Eagleson, Sr., had switched jobs again, this time leaving the textile business to take a job at the Campbell Soup Company. But it meant pulling the children out of school in mid-year.

When they were enrolled in 20th Street Public School in the west end of Toronto, a teacher who had been at the school for some time argued that Alan was too young to enter seventh grade and should be sent back to his own age group. It was the first time Agnes Eagleson ever thought to question the authority of teachers or the school system, but she decided to take the matter up with the school principal.

"Grade seven is where he should be and here are his report cards to prove he can do it," she said. "If the boy can stand first or second every week on his tests why put him back? If you see he can't do it then put him back but at least give him a try." Finally the teacher had to back down.

It took a certain kind of teacher to appreciate Eagleson's curious and tireless mind. One of his high school teachers who didn't mind his "mischievous" behaviour was Miss Marguerite "Pearl" Weir. "If the rest of his class took thirty minutes to do an assignment, it only took Alan five. Then he would clown. He would even stand on his desk . . . he had to get attention some way and he certainly couldn't get it on the football field or with girls . . . he simply couldn't compete."

Margaret used to be embarrassed by her brother's clowning, but at the same time she respected what she called his "specialness". "If I was at the top of the class it was because of hard work, whereas Alan was there quite naturally. It used to frustrate me that he was so bright. Here I would be studying for a test that we had the next day, and there was Alan tripping off down the road with his lacrosse stick. He would be whacking the ball against the school wall while I was studying and he would end up getting five marks more than I did."

His physique remained a problem. He didn't make the local hockey team, and in grade eleven when he was fourteen he weighed less than eighty pounds. Concerned nurses at the school would call up Agnes

Eagleson: there must be a biological disorder; shouldn't she take him to the doctor? But it wasn't Aggie's way to fuss about appearance and she explained it away: "He never gives himself time to put anything on his bones." Both of his parents were short, too.

He suffered most because of his size in the boys' change room before and after gym class. In the academic classes he could compensate by getting better grades than anyone else, and teachers tended to put up with his clowning and talking out of turn. But the boys in gym would pick on him because he was younger and smaller. They called him names like "the brown" and "egghead". He used to beg his mother to give him a note to excuse him from gym class, but of course she would have none of it. "It's what's inside you that counts, what's in your heart and head that matters," she would tell him.

It wasn't until the beginning of his graduating year that she realized the extent of her son's plight. Alan was in the Parent's Night exercises. At sixteen, he was less than five feet tall and weighed only ninety pounds. He was in the display group on the gym floor, standing behind the first row leader, who was six feet tall.

Eagleson overachieved throughout high school. He cared about getting good grades to the point that he would disturb the household at night by reciting Latin verbs in his sleep. He became quite skilful at public debating and civics, which included setting up a mock parliament with other high schools. At his grade thirteen graduation from Mimico High School in 1950 he was written up in the school yearbook, *The Peptimist*: "Teachers wonder what Alan will think of next, but sometimes he can be serious. At Christmas he spoke at the Boys' Parliament at Whitby, and he intends to make law his career."

His interest in politics and law were firmly established, but the one activity to which he appeared most dedicated was managing the younger kids' athletic activities.

"Alan was never an easy mixer and never learned to share in the group activities of other boys," neighbours say, "but he was always involved in what was going on." Sometimes it was nothing more than taking a dozen or so kids down to the schoolyard and teaching them to play handball against the wall. He would let them get hit by the ball too, just to teach them not to be afraid of it." Margaret says Eagleson didn't date or have a girlfriend during high school.

Throughout his high-school years he spent each summer teaching swimming at the neighbourhood pools. The routine was only interrupted when the Canadian National Exhibition was on. From the day the

Princess Gates opened, Alan was working either as a garbage collector around the grounds or running a greasy hamburger stand. The pay was excellent and it provided him with spending money during school. But it was always swimming and the people who ran the special competitions that held a fascination for him.

He started managing the financial side of sports quite early. In public school he marshalled children onto a special bus each week to take swimming lessons at the Humberside Collegiate pool. "He collected their ten-cent fares each week," says Margaret. "And if one kid couldn't make good the fare he smoothed it over with the bus driver and promised the kid would pay double next time. He never kept a tally as far as anyone knew, only remembered in his head who owed and he made it his personal business to always square it with the driver."

"He was a regular little monopolizer," his mother says. "If a kid showed up without his money a second time, Alan took it upon himself not to let him get on the bus."

The Humberside swimming coach was another early influence. Gus Ryder would pick Alan to look after some of the children afflicted with cerebral palsy who took therapy at the pool. "Sometimes there would be as many as six to look after and if Gus had to go he'd leave Alan in charge," Margaret recalls. "He'd return and simply say to Alan, 'Everything okay?' Young Alan would reply, 'Everything's all right.' "

One of his students remembers him as a "hard driver" and a "disciplinarian". "He would paddle off in a boat in the chilly and polluted Credit River coaxing her on as she swam," Alan's father recalls. " 'If you go one more mile I'll buy you an ice cream,' he'd say." The twelve-year-old girl was the famed marathon swimmer Marilyn Ann Bell who became the first person to swim Lake Ontario from Youngstown, New York, to Toronto.

Although Eagleson himself never developed as a particularly good athlete in any one sport, he was known to be a good organizer and very dependable around many sports establishments. He joined typical boys' organizations such as Cubs and Scouts, but his main "hangout" through his mid-teens was the boys' club run by a New Toronto policeman. "Jack Price definitely filled an important role for Alan," says Margaret.

"Industrious, a steady worker" are the words his early friends frequently use to explain Alan's drive. His abundant energy allowed him to cover a great deal of territory, which made him always appear to be in the right place at the right time. And he always considered himself to be luckier than most.

"One time there was a car raffle to raise money to build the Lakeshore swimming pool. The whole family canvassed homes in the neighbourhood to sell tickets. It was Alan who won the fifty-dollar prize for selling the most tickets, as well as fifty dollars for holding the winning ticket," Allen Eagleson, Sr., says proudly.

By the end of the high-school years, managing the ambitions of others had become a small but significant part of his lifestyle. He still dreamed of becoming a lawyer in spite of the family's tight money situation. Agnes Eagleson had taken full-time jobs at Eaton's order desk or washing dishes at Woolworth's lunch counter during the children's high-school years to help out with the finances. Fran, the eldest daughter, had taken a secretarial course and was out working. But Margaret, who graduated the same year as Eagleson, wanted to become a teacher. Since hers was a one-year course, Eagleson elected to postpone entering university for a year, and, instead, took a job at the British-American Oil Refinery at Clarkson, Ontario, turning over most of his $70 a week earnings to his parents to help support the family.

THE IVY LEAGUE

*"A man's reach should always exceed
his grasp or what's a heaven for?"*
That's always been my philosophy.
R. Alan Eagleson

Browning's poetic passage has invoked ambition in generations of
aspiring Horatio Algers, but having digested his mother's particular
recipe for household economics, Alan Eagleson now had the intestinal
fortitude necessary to fulfill the last part of Browning's directive:
"The triumph was — to reach and stay there."

The sixteen-year-old Mimico High School graduate started work as
a lab technician at the British-American Oil Refinery (now Gulf Oil)
located about fifteen miles from his home. It was his first and only
full-time blue-collar job. By Christmas he had saved enough money
from his weekly pay envelope to buy his mother a seven cubic foot,
$350 top-of-the-line McClary refrigerator. The Eaglesons were the
first family on the block to own one.

Of course he contributed towards Margaret's tuition. Yet his ultimate goal was still quite self-centred. "Whenever I read in the society
pages of the newspapers about the wealthy sons going to Ridley
College or Upper Canada College I pledged to myself: 'I'll get a crack
at you guys one day,'" says Eagleson.

But "getting there" and "staying there" were different problems.
Eagleson wasn't born into the type of Toronto WASP establishment
(even though he is a white Anglo-Saxon Protestant) where fathers
passed on their army or college ties to their first heir. His father didn't
have those kinds of connections. The other way to compete was with

money. If you didn't have any, you had to make it. Eagleson figured the best way he could do it was to become a lawyer. That meant he would have to work to pay his way through six years of university, mostly cleaning oil furnaces part-time with his father. Over the next several years he formed a routine around early risings and a thirty-mile trip from the family home to the University of Toronto. By the end of university, Eagleson's parents had moved to Fergus, Ontario, and he continued to live in the family home with his married sister Margaret.

A few months before he entered university Eagleson realized he'd been blessed with a bit of Irish luck. "Wee Alan" had added another ten inches to his nearly five feet and weighed over 170 pounds.

He had arrived. But could he endure the full burden of three years to get an undergraduate degree, and another five to finish law school and articling? He had not yet completed his second year when his resolution to become the country's greatest criminal lawyer was put to the test. One cold February night while Agnes Eagleson was soaking her swollen feet, having just arrived home from her job at Woolworth's, the doorbell rang.

"Good God, it's Alan's old math teacher," she remarked to her daughters in the kitchen. With the solemnity appropriate to a visit by Daniel Webster's devil, she inquired: "*What* has he done now?"

The math teacher from New Toronto High School (Mimico High had by now merged with New Toronto) had been sent by the Prudential Insurance Company of America in Newark, New Jersey, to recruit students who had shown good math skills and who would be interested in apprenticing as actuaries. She had air tickets with her and some figures indicating that of all the professions, actuaries were the most highly paid.

Eagleson arrived home shortly after his former teacher left. When Eagleson heard his mother say she wanted her only son to apprentice for four years to become an actuary, he was furious. He dashed his books against the refrigerator and started shouting, "If I can't be a lawyer I'm not going to finish school, period. ... I haven't spent all this time at university to become a goddamn insurance adjuster," his sister recalls. It was the first time he ever swore in front of his mother, and it was the last time she ever attempted to interfere with his plans.

Still, it wasn't easy clinging to his ambition in light of such arguments as "you could be working for a living." Pearl Weir was present during one of the family discourses about Eagleson's lengthy education. She had been the children's history and English teacher and often came for supper. She calls their home "a very proper, sedate little bungalow with its one little entrance and no architectural ideas", and the family "plain, homey, and wholesome".

Miss Weir's father was from Ballymena, and she said there was a "kindred spirit" between them. Whenever anyone asked her how old she was, she would say, "A woman who tells her age will tell anything." And if she ever came across a book "that contained sex stuff" she would take her scissors out of her purse and cut it into pieces then and there. She watched out for the Eaglesons and would worry when Allen Eagleson, Sr., was out of work, which was "many, many times. Aggie filled in at these times by working at the Hornell Blouse Factory. It was a good outfit and they told her, 'There's always a place for you if you need it.'"

But that night Miss Weir was particularly upset to hear that Allen Eagleson, Sr., was getting raked over the coals by the men at work. "He had a humble job then at the oil refinery cleaning furnaces and the men in the lunchroom were hoping young Alan would fail university. They said it was a waste of time and money. 'What do you think, Dad?' Alan asked. His father said, 'I want you to finish school, Alan.'"

Eagleson didn't have an actual date until he was twenty-one, and then he almost married the first girl he went out with. Her name was Arlene McKee and she came from Bala, Ontario. He dated her for quite a while and she spent a lot of time with the Eagleson family. "He would have married her had she not pressed for it right away; he said he couldn't afford it and wanted to wait until he finished law school," says Margaret. But that was another five years down the road.

People have said Eagleson got his money sense from his mother — and his gift of the blarney from his father. Allen Eagleson, Sr., figured that his son's "economic" reasons for not marrying Arlene were quite different. "What happened there was he told me he made a ten-dollar bet with this fellow he would never marry her."

That ten dollars certainly would buy enough gas to keep Eagleson in "wheels" instead of hitchhiking to school on cold winter mornings. And just as he bragged to his father about winning the bet, he would boast about a red mail truck he "picked up for a song", which he drove to university.

Nancy Fisk was the daughter of Melvin G. Fisk, who ran his own sawmill in Collingwood, Ontario. Eagleson first saw her at a varsity football game: she was sitting a few rows over from him, wearing a jaunty Royal Military College Persian lamb hat. Eagleson decided to check her out during a time-break. He climbed over a few rows of people and pinched her hat. She raced to retrieve it, outdistanced him, and not only got her hat back but won the man who had swiped it. "I had just bought the hat; it was a lucky find and I didn't want to lose it," she recalls.

Everyone remarked how Eagleson had found his match in Nancy. They married in 1960 when Alan turned twenty-six and was practising law in a firm which he and a few of his "drinking buddies" from law school set up. Actually, the term "drinking buddies" is a misnomer: he didn't drink, he just preferred the company of a convivial crowd over the more sober "bookish" students. He never missed a chance to take part in — or instigate — frivolous escapades, and was often thought to be "totally soused" although he only drank Coke. "He was afraid of drinking, probably realized people who did drink only made fools of themselves, and he was so frantically competitive he wouldn't trust it," says one close friend. "There was a strong pro- hibitional environment at home and he probably promised his mother he wouldn't. ... Mrs. Eagleson ruled the roost with a heavy hand."

Professor Robert Mackay, a thirty-year-old University of Toronto law school lecturer, was one of the "in crowd" who also indulged in Irish high spirits. This unassuming man went on to become dean of the law faculty at the University of Western Ontario, counsel for the law firm of Blaney, Pasternak and for Hockey Canada, and remained a life-long Eagleson friend.

Mackay lived close to Eagleson in Etobicoke and would alternate driving the thirty miles twice a day to the University of Toronto campus.

He says the link between Eagleson and the other good buddies was that "we all lived on the poverty line". On the other side of the tracks were "the gold-medalist Jewish students from Forest Hill who were only interested in education ... they'd invite us to weddings and we'd take doggie bags."

Mackay's description of Eagleson ranges from "intensely loyal" to "fanatically loyal". "He was always faithful to the University of Toronto which at the time was the new upstart law school in competi- tion with Osgoode Hall, and he was deeply committed to his desire to keep up the athletic contacts he made." During his first undergraduate year he was manager of the university's varsity football team. The tightrope he traversed between "working his way through", playing and managing sports, and still keeping up with his studies, permitted him somehow to remain loyal to his good buddies "whether they were right or wrong," says Mackay. "And a close relationship with Al meant sometimes you were likely to get thrown in jail if you got too close."

While he never appeared to challenge the rules laid down by the strong matriarchy at home, there were many close calls with the law because of Eagleson's volatile temper. Once, when Mackay over-parked at a coin meter, he came out to find Eagleson "giving the policeman walking the beat a hard time ... he never shut up. There was the cop opening the trunk with a case of beer in there and yet Al kept yapping."

If he couldn't tolerate an invasion by the law, he was even less able to tolerate losing. Even a simple thing like another car overtaking his red shandrydan was cause for a do-or-die challenge. "In Al's mind *that* was breaking the law ... not parking too long at a meter!" says Mackay. Mackay was driving when Eagleson pulled one of these pranks somewhere on the 401 Highway. "Fifteen miles later when the cars came to a stoplight after turning off the highway I realized he'd been eyeballing one car all the way. ... He'd say, 'Just a minute,' jump out of my car and start banging on the guy's window ... then just plough him one and hop back in the car and say 'Let's go, Bob!' ... boy, did I ever go!"

Eagleson always knew he would get through those five years of law school and articling. He never made the dean's honours list and he certainly didn't get close to the top 10 percent. "His marks were very mediocre," says Mackay, but "it was generally felt among the faculty that we'd hear more about Al than any of the scholars who stood first."

The late fifties was an exciting time to be part of the University of Toronto law school. The faculty was filled with some of the giants in the legal field: The Right Honourable Bora Laskin, now Chief Justice of the Supreme Court of Canada; Wolfgang Friedman, considered to be a top mind in international law; and perhaps one of the greatest lights of legal education and a remarkable leader, the late Cecil "Caesar" Wright. These were the foot soldiers who formed a tre-mendously strong camaraderie among the faculty of an institution desperately trying to stay afloat as an independent law school. About two years prior to Eagleson's enrolment the University's board of governors was ready to call it quits, figuring the school couldn't support itself financially. The Law Society of Upper Canada had not recognized the new law school as an accredited body and so it could only grant the Bachelor of Laws (LL.B.) degree; its students had to do a further year at Osgoode Hall Law School in addition to the usual one year of articling in order to be called to the Ontario bar. This gave Osgoode a monopoly on granting the privilege to practise. Shortly after Eagleson graduated, the Law Society granted the University of Toronto parity, thus opening the doors for several similar law schools in other provinces.

Eagleson received his LL.B. in 1957, and in that same year won the University College bronze medal and arts trophy for athletics. He was never considered to be very athletic, however, and because of a weak back, actually played very little sports.

But Mackay says it was solely because of Eagleson that the law faculty won the Reed Trophy two years running for scoring the most points in intramural swimming, hockey, and lacrosse against huge faculties like the 1,000-strong engineering school. Describing his contribution, Mackay says, "He was a fanatically fierce competitor who obviously must have had a lot of help." There are a number of personal testimonials to at least one brilliantly executed solo perform-ance at a University College lacrosse game that gives substance to Mackay's comment about the "fanatical" aspect of his character.

Eagleson ignored his weak back problem once too often and in 1957, at twenty-three, he sustained an injury that would prevent him from ever again picking up a lacrosse stick. Lacrosse wasn't played at the varsity level at the University of Toronto then, just intramurally.

During the second-last playoff game of the season that year, the law-school team's two main forwards were barely ambulatory. One had a separated shoulder, the other fractured ribs. Mackay attended the match and says "Alan was the only one who could play forward or defence, and was the only one left who could pick up the ball and carry it. Near the end of the game, with Eagleson scoring all the goals, it was up to him to win the game. The score was 15-13. It meant Al had to go through the whole team, and in those days players didn't wear any padding. Eagleson received one hell of a pummelling and before the game ended, he picked up the ball and walked over to the opposite team's bench. 'Take it and the next game is yours too,' Al said. 'Take the pennant, I won't take another hammering like that again, ever!' We helped him into the dressing room . . . we had to peel off the sweater, it was entirely covered with blood."

The back injury he sustained from that game forced him to wear a body cast temporarily and has caused him relentless suffering ever since.

The other major distraction apart from intramural sports was a series of part-time jobs he took on to see him through university. In the winter he worked weekends helping his father — now a maintenance engineer at Goodyear — clean oil furnaces, and during the summer he worked outdoors as a recreational director at some of the camps around Ontario's lake district. For one summer he was in charge of the athletics at MacTier (a small town to which a decade later he returned for a historic and lucrative rendezvous).

Next to money and contacts, the "perks" that went along with a job were important. "Eagleson probably wanted to manage the university varsity basketball team because we had to spend twenty-six days in Florida every Christmas playing U.S. teams," says John McManus, who coached the team. Eventually this sandy-haired coach became perhaps the most influential "contact" Eagleson made at university through sports. Eagleson later inscribed a book he gave to McManus, "Thanks very much for the start you gave me in this business."

"What I liked about him was if you asked him to do something you knew he would see it through and it would be done right away . . . the coaches liked him for it. He would also clean my furnace during the Christmas holidays without charging me for it; that was a side of Al that few people saw."

For the most part Eagleson was remembered for his harsh bravado, not his charity.

One of his classmates in law school was Jack Batten, a lawyer now turned writer. Batten was team manager of the law school's basketball team in 1957, the year Eagleson played. "He was a guard but he didn't play much. He got heaved out for punching a St. Mike's player. And when he did make a contribution it was usually vicariously, through his many connections, rather than as a direct participant." The basketball players called him "aggressive, abrasive, and bold beyond belief". "We really didn't know how to handle him; he was a fast Duddy Kravitz type," Batten says. When Eagleson became manager, he was paid a stipend for his expenses and received the same amount of meal money as the players. "It was the desire to be part of the limelight . . . that's what attracted him to sports," McManus holds. "He was a natural entertainer and nothing stopped him from competing for the spotlight."

One time when the University of Toronto's varsity basketball team was trailing its archrival, Queen's University, by 30 to 3, Eagleson found the tension unbearable. He was sitting beside Coach Mc-Manus. Every time the varsity Blues got a foul shot, the trombone player on the opposite team's school band would let out a great RAAAZZZOOOOO.

"Hey, isn't that against the rules?" inquired Eagleson, pointing a long bony finger at the musician.

"Yeah, I'll go talk to the referee."

Eagleson felt better, everyone relaxed. But at the next foul shot there it was again, RAAAZZZOOOOO. Before the trombone player could wipe the spittle from his mouth, Eagleson delivered a shot right in his chops. When he returned to his place beside McManus, he leaned over, put his hand to the side of his mouth, and spoke confidentially: "He won't do it again."

Few people knew that Eagleson wore a back brace during university, but the basketball players discovered it when the team arrived in New York. Some kids were hanging around the airport and asked to carry their bags. "Hey, you guys basketball players or something?" Of course Al spoke up first. "Yeah, that's right, and I'm the toughest guy on the team. ... Just punch me here, go ahead and see." The kid, about fifteen, delivered a terrific lunge punch to Eagleson's solar plexus. The kid ran away hollering, holding his arm; he probably had broken his wrist on Eagleson's brace.

As manager, Eagleson had to travel with the team, look after the equipment, make sure it arrived with them, and make the hotel arrangements. The team played New York three times each December. The New York cabbies are licensed to take only four passengers at a time and must queue up in front of the airport. Eagleson figured out a system to save cab fare. He would get a cab at the end of the line, shove two players in, and when the cab came to the head of the line he would shove in four more players. They were never spotted. There were few limitations to his cunning and, says McManus, "It was always money that motivated most of his mischief — it was a rule that inspired him."

One of his last tours with the varsity basketball team was as McManus' guest. The team arrived in Miami on New Year's Day in time to see Syracuse pitted against Oklahoma in the Orange Bowl game. Eagleson had been unsuccessful, according to McManus, in wangling a ticket "his way", i.e., free. So although the Floridian police were around the gates, he tried something else. Feigning a conversation with the tuba player in the Syracuse marching band, Eagleson, knees high in step, marched straight past the cops and into the stands. Not satisfied with that, he decided to look for a souvenir. He headed for the player bench and smooth-talked his way into the team dressing room. But he was kicked out. Undaunted, he waited until the game ended, ran over to the 40-yard line, and helped himself. In front of thousands of spectators he yanked the sweater off a Syracuse fullback and walked away with his prize.

His schemes were only limited by opportunity, never imagination. During one trip to Florida there was a period of ten days with no games. Each of the players, including McManus and Eagleson, had a little cabin on the beach at Fort Lauderdale. Eagleson killed time by going up to the sunbathers, hand outstretched, telling them he was collecting $1 from each one for a party that night. He'd get $80 or so every day, spend part of it on beer, cheese, pretzels, and chips, and have some left over for himself. By the end of the furlough he had made a modest profit.

Once when the team was travelling by train from Rochester to Buffalo during the winter, they were suddenly snowbound with hundreds of other passengers. They had eight hours to kill. McManus says that within a few minutes Eagleson was standing on top of a table in the railway station, conducting the crowd in hymns and Christmas carols. If he took up a collection for his favourite charity afterward, nobody really cared!

Eagleson was full of benevolence, although not everyone appreciated it. The team complained to their coach when they didn't get any meal money on a trip to New York. McManus asked Eagleson about it. " 'Hey Al, where'd the guys' meal money go?'

" 'Didn't you read the paper today?' he asked me, and there in the front section of the *Toronto Star*: 'University of Toronto's basketball team donates $86 to the Star's Santa Claus Fund'!"

Eagleson was one of the first in his class to land an articling job with a law firm in 1957. "He could walk into any law office and immediately impress them with how personable he was ... personality counts more than good grades," Mackay explains. "We figured Al as a lawyer would make a bigger mark than the majority of his classmates ... his talent was he had a very great practical ability."

Weaning himself from university had its traumatic moments for Eagleson. He had started there as a seventeen-year-old and left at twenty-five. He was out on a last all-night pub crawl with his "drinking buddies'' the night they decided to pay their dean a fond farewell. Eagleson didn't make it home until 4:00 A.M. and then he decided to rouse his father out of bed. ''Do you want to get up for a minute, Dad?''

''I asked him, 'Where have you been?' '' says Allen Eagleson, Sr., reminding him that bars close at 1:00 A.M. ... I couldn't remember Alan ever getting drunk; he just couldn't handle booze, but this night he was all worked up and very emotional. He told me about wanting to work with people, and made a vow to me right then and there he would never work for money, said he originally went to law school to make money. ... 'Now when someone is in trouble it's my duty to get them out of it. ... I'll not worry about the money. The only money I want to make is to see that you and Mom are all right as long as you live and that the girls don't want for anything.' ''

GILDING THE LEAF

I'd shoot the agents if I could.
Harold Ballard

True to his code, at twenty-five, Eagleson had cracked the poor, working-class mold he inherited. He was the first of the McNabney and Eagleson clans to become a lawyer, and, indeed, the first to graduate from university.

Now that he had gained a social and economic toehold, Agnes Eagleson told all and sundry at her son's graduation: "All I want Alan to be is just an ordinary lawyer." She felt he could exit from the race. The rags-to-riches story could have been completed — but he wasn't "there" yet. He had taken a "crack at them", degree for degree, exceeding his grasp by extending his name to Robert Alan Eagleson, B.A., LL.B. And to ensure that he wouldn't totter from his lofty new position he set about sticking two more letters to his name — Q.C., Queen's Counsel.

These symbols of success were his investment in "getting there". But why did he feel compelled to get even? What did he mean by "getting a crack at the worthy sons at Upper Canada College?" Was power his ultimate goal?

Power comes from two sources: from influence or prestige, or from money, and while Eagleson had promised his father just before graduation he "wouldn't work for the money", he wasn't the one who wrote the rules. It is a modern-day maxim for the Protestant work ethic that money and prosperity are signs of a divine calling. Hadn't he already figured out that money is the power-tool of the rich? Education is a great equalizer; it had enabled him to cross-cut social boundaries, to climb out of one social class and into another.

Therein, however, lay a dilemma. His late-night outpouring to his father came quite naturally at a significant crossroads in his life — the changeover from being a law student to being a practitioner. Psychologists call it a "major life event". He was moving on to a modern-day temptation of St. Anthony: materialism, workaholism, competitiveness, and the cult of the self-made man, when money and prosperity are considered godly pursuits.

Eagleson had a natural tendency towards conservative economic doctrines, as had his forefathers. The Scottish divine Robert Woodrow once said:

> The sin of our too great fondness for trade, to the neglecting of our more valuable interests, I humbly think will be written upon our judgment.

Agnes Eagleson believed in a secularized morality: "everyone has a calling in life," which she translated for Alan as "do what you do best." The letters DWYDB have been framed in his mind's eye ever since. But he could appease his pangs of recurring Protestant guilt at the same time that he capitalized on his money-making talents.

The Protestant work ethic was the only religion Eagleson had: "The work ethic, that's what my father passed on to me . . ." says Eagleson. He piously followed it to the limit: DWYDB. Eagleson's calling was to act as the classic "go-between". Eagleson was not confined by socially defined boundaries; instead, as a skilled advocate, he could argue with great equanimity the case of either side in any dispute. Time and again, using his greatest talent — being "good" with people — he parlayed his position of team manager into lucrative schemes. He may not have been particularly interested in the sport he managed, but he was gregarious. A self-made man, he had the mentality and drive of the athlete — the game and winning were everything.

"The luck of the Irish" gave him the edge that is all-important in sports. He had gravitated naturally towards sports at a young age, as did the rest of the Scots and Irish he had been associated with throughout his life: the McNabney brothers, McManus, Mackay, and the McMurtry brothers (Roy, now Attorney General of Ontario, and Bill, who was to become Eagleson's law partner).

Another Scot, the late Marshall McLuhan, also had trouble fitting into a prescribed slot: he became a rebel in the University of Toronto's stuffy English department. McLuhan has said, "The Irish are a tribal people ... that's why Eagleson is in sport, it's a tribal custom, a game of instincts."

His particular brand of chutzpah, a type of open-faced, street-person bravado, got things done; this trait made him extremely useful later as a backroom boy in politics, but couldn't last long in the austere setting of the giant Bay Street law firms. Soon after he was called to the Ontario bar, after seven years in school and a year articling, he joined the late J.D.W. Cumberland, Q.C., and the firm became Cumberland and Eagleson. He left his family's house on Mill Road when he married Nancy, by then a physical education graduate from the University of Toronto. She is an attractive, witty, and intelligent woman who can match him in conversation as well as on the tennis court. He credits her with upgrading him "a hundred times".

"When Alan asked me to marry him I knew him well enough to realize it had to be a yes or no answer; he didn't have time for deliberation," she says. Their wedding was "a simple, middle-class affair, nothing to speak of, really," says Nancy. They have two children: Trevor Allen, born in 1961, and Jill Anne, born in 1964.

Eagleson's earlier vision — to emulate J.J. Robinette, one of his many childhood idols — still held. Robinette is one of Canada's finest courtroom lawyers. In the words of one lawyer, "Among the tall timber at the bar, John J. Robinette has stood out like a giant oak." If Robinette was an oak, then Eagleson might be called a willow. The oak is so rigid in stature that when it becomes overburdened with snow, its branches snap off; if there is a strong wind it can even become uprooted. The willow, although it has a broad reach, will simply bend with the wind or lower its branches with the weight of the snow until its burden slips off. Robinette was said to resemble a "bronze bust" in both his appearance and his rigidly steadfast and unyielding disposition. Eagleson was just the opposite. Flexibility and compromise marked his character.

His "flexibility" and his immunity to that professional disease, "hardening of the categories", permitted Eagleson to make many connections in sports, business, and politics. Flexibility was the essence of his talent of being "good" with people, but at the same time, it was his undoing. The art of networking implies a cementing of loyalties; this cementing was extremely important if Eagleson was going to be successful. But he ran into trouble: in order to increase his power base he started expanding his career into several other callings.

For a short period of time — several months — he was an "ordinary" lawyer bent on emulating Robinette's illustrious career. Robinette had repeatedly prosecuted spies and gold smugglers, and had saved a dozen or more accused murderers from the hangman, including the notorious Evelyn Dick.

Eagleson began to follow Robinette's path: he started off as a general practitioner, dabbling in police court work — traffic violations and the like — probating wills, foreclosing mortgages, and filing articles of incorporation. "I even had a real murder mystery," says Eagleson.

During this case his old lacrosse buddy, Bob Watson, who had joined a large, established law firm, approached Eagleson about starting a partnership. Eagleson agreed. They joined three other young lawyers and the firm became Blaney, Pasternak, Smela, Eagleson and Watson. Ray Smela had played goal with Watson and Eagleson at University College. Both Watson and Eagleson were from New Toronto, so they decided to hang up their shingle in Rexdale, a nearby suburb in the western part of Toronto. Watson says he was actively involved with Eagleson on the so-called murder case. "In classic Sherlock Holmes fashion, Eagleson cornered all the witnesses a good two days before the police did." Eagleson is reported to have worked so thoroughly on the case that no charges were ever laid against his client.

He continued to do a fair bit of police court work in Rexdale at the branch-plant firm of Watson and Eagleson, appearing on behalf of clients who were charged with offences ranging from careless driving to theft. Clients were interviewed after they found their way to Eagleson's office — the back kitchen in the former parsonage of a church. "I used the dining room for my office and we both used the living room as the waiting room," says Watson. "We didn't have many clients and didn't need much space."

Eventually, Eagleson gravitated towards rezoning law, "because I liked to get up and talk a lot", and because he tired of the duties of criminal court work: the homework, meeting deadlines, postponing courtroom dates, and shifting witnesses about. So he gave up on what his friend and client, Carl Brewer, later called the "legal jargonese" of courtroom work.

"I felt I had done it, I knew success as a trial lawyer," says Eagleson. Taking advantage of a fuller life, Eagleson became a joiner.

He joined clubs: the Albany, the Empire, the Lambton Golf and Country, the Toronto Lawn Tennis, and the Georgian Peaks Ski. He took on several directorships in various charities and business enterprises: Big Brothers of Metropolitan Toronto, the Sportsmen's Mutual Fund, and the boards of governors at Queensway General Hospital and Etobicoke General Hospital. There was, however, one other important card he carried: membership in the Progressive Conservative Party.

It was then, in the early sixties, that Eagleson also found time to socialize with his earliest sports buddy, Robert "Pully" Pulford. They had both been raised in New Toronto. The Eagleson and Pulford families had been close when Eagleson was fourteen. Pulford, a couple of years younger than his friend, had become a well-established Toronto Maple Leaf centre by the time Eagleson graduated from law school. Pully used to take his buddy to the once-private watering hole frequented by the Leafs, the Hot Stove Lounge.

When Eagleson realized how shabbily his friend was being treated — tied to contracts yielding relatively low pay, with reserve clauses and the right to transfer a player without notice, and with no opportunity for investing income against retirement — he took his first major step in sports management, or the "merchandising" of athletes in Canada. Retaining legal counsel for athletes was not new in the U.S.; a football player's father might hire a couple of corporate attorneys to negotiate his son's contract with the owners. But in Canada it was almost unheard of.

One of his earliest moves in the establishment of a new industry built around playing sports for fun and profit was to round up a handful of business acquaintances, such as George Graham of Ostranders Jewellers and Hern Kerney of Hern Pontiac, and incorporate the Blue and White Group Ltd., a holding company named after the colours of the Toronto Maple Leafs. In the beginning it was simply a small mortgage company. By the end of 1960 several other Maple Leafs were shareholders, including Pulford's close friend and teammate, Bobby Baun, along with Carl Brewer and Billy Harris. From then on all "new business" associated with athletes fell under the general umbrella of "real estate", a department which Eagleson first set up in the Rexdale office and continued to head at Blaney, Pasternak over the next decade or so. Any sport business was channeled into that department.

"We really had a close commitment to the other partners; we considered ourselves loyal friends as well as business associates," says Watson. ''We didn't even keep tabs on how much money any one department was making; we just supported each other's work. Our basic philosophy in running the firm was that we were young but growing, so a large amount of the dollars we were making was going back into developing our business; we didn't draw huge salaries out of necessity if the firm was going to survive. We didn't have second- or third-generation clients but had to grow with the new ones we started up with. Eagleson felt strong loyalties were important and wanted to accept only the type of associates or junior partners into the firm who'd fight for you to their dying day.''

Eagleson's ''real estate department'' may not have looked like a potential money maker. Most of his clients were involved in hockey when the six-team league was still in existence, and hockey players weren't making much money.

But through Blue and White, Eagleson was quickly thrust into relationships with most of the other Leafs; eventually meetings with other players on different teams around the league were set up, ''strictly on a social basis with no idea of what was coming,'' he says.

The routine was always the same. A player from some rural Canadian town would come to Toronto to look up Leaf coach George ''Punch'' Imlach. There were only 120 positions in the NHL; the competition was so intense, it was a buyer's market. A young hockey player then was so thrilled at turning pro he was happy to give the owners *carte blanche* with his life and his future. Most ''Anglo'' hockey players wanted to play for the Leafs then. As soon as he signed up to wear the Leaf crest, his right to play hockey became the sacrosanct property of Toronto. The way the ''farm system'' worked, a player could only further his career in the NHL — which had a monopoly on both amateur and professional players — by playing for the team he signed a ''C'' form* with, unless he was traded. The player still didn't have any say in his hockey future; it was then up to the investing team to dictate where, when, and whether he would play at all. What was the point of worrying about tax shelters or other investment ploys if a player had no say in where he lived or how he made his livelihood? ''Investment'' to a player meant owning a few Canada Savings Bonds.

---

* The C form was a contract signed by young players. For example, the Toronto Maple Leafs sponsored a junior club (Toronto Marlboros); anyone under 21 playing for the club signed a C form, which bound him to the Leafs when he turned pro.

The need for an arbitrator to shake the cobwebs away from the owners' eyes was obvious. There had not been even so much as a cost-of-living raise for players between 1945 and 1955, and there was no sign of one as long as the league continued in its six-team format. It was not surprising that one member of the Hockey Hall of Fame, Edouard "Newsy" Lalonde, got more money carrying a lacrosse stick than he ever did as an NHLer.

Lacrosse also made up the slack for Pulford, who moonlighted a lot playing for the Woodbridge Legionnaires. Morley Kells, who played in national lacrosse championships until he was twenty-four, had become assistant promotion manager for *Hockey Night in Canada* at the Gardens. He would occasionally stumble across Pulford selling tickets for attractions like the Ringling Brothers Circus during the summer months. "Why are you doing this, Bob?" Kells asked him once. "Because there isn't enough money in hockey," Pulford replied.

"Back in the early sixties there was no real negotiation of contracts. I would sit down and laugh at the forms [C forms] they were signing," Eagleson says. Players had pathetically short careers as it was and could never hope to make up this loss. But at the time they had only a Hobson's choice: "... if they didn't like what they were signing Imlach would say, 'fine, go to hell, go peddle your talents elsewhere'", Eagleson claims; "... with only 120 jobs in the league I couldn't tell Pully, 'Don't worry, they have to sign you, relax.'"

The early sixties was the wrong time for hard-line union organizing. That the players needed and wanted a union was clear to everyone. In 1957 New York attorney Milton M. Mound attempted to organize several big-time players, but failed, leaving the atmosphere rancid with ill feeling.

The timing was wrong for another reason. At the same time that Eagleson was playing godfather to the players, Harold Ballard, who had the controlling interest in the very house that begat the players' headaches — Maple Leaf Gardens — was campaigning for Eagleson in his political debut with the Progressive Conservatives. Eagleson was running for a federal seat in 1963. A year before, he had been invited to a meeting in West Toronto to listen to the man who would become his new hero — John Diefenbaker, then the leader of the federal P.C. Party. There he met Toronto lawyer John Hamilton, the federal P.C. candidate who would be competing with Liberal candidate Leonard "Red" Kelly for the federal riding of York West. Kelly was an NHL player who assisted the Leafs to four Stanley Cups. He swept over

Hamilton in most polls, except for the four Eagleson had canvassed.

In the spring of 1963 Eagleson was parachuted into that riding as the party's sacrificial lamb; he ran against Kelly but lost by 13,000 votes. Even Kelly's own teammates had knocked on doors for the 29-year-old political neophyte, and their owner was also stumping for Eagleson. Ballard was no stranger to Eagleson's ambitions, having learned a great deal about him merely from watching him play lacrosse. "On the lacrosse field Eagleson was a maniac ... if a coach told him to run through a brick wall, he'd have done it." That was loyalty, the type of dedication Ballard liked to see. Eagleson was able to pay his friend back for past favours by cutting him in on business deals a few years later.

In September 1963, Eagleson was asked to run again, this time in a provincial election in Lakeshore, a new seat which had been cut from the old York West riding. Eagleson knew it had been Tory country for years; he went in there as a native son and won. He owed much of his success to the strong backing of his family, friends, and partners. Irwin Pasternak and Bob Watson wrote political speeches and covered for him at the law firm. "We literally subsidized him for several years while he did virtually everything but practice law ... certainly as long as he was in politics," Watson explains.

Time and again people would talk about Eagleson as a "natural politician". "He had a fantastic ability to remember people's names — it was a remarkable experience to walk through a convention hall with Al; he'd remember the names of an old couple he might have met only once, two years before at a Rotary Club luncheon," says William McMurtry, who joined Blaney, Pasternak in 1969.

His family and partners supported his entry into politics, but some say it was his high profile in community sports that actually launched his political career.

Wayne Lilley, a Toronto writer who played lacrosse in New Toronto, feels that one specific incident — a devastating lacrosse accident — pushed Eagleson into the political forefront. "In 1963 helmets weren't obligatory in senior lacrosse. ... well, there was this guy Jimmy Smith, not a super player but he was pretty good. He had just finished his first year of commerce at the University of Toronto. Smith was playing for Junior Alderwood when one of those flukes happened where a guy is going so fast that a simple tap will send him flying. That's precisely what happened. Smith was rushing for the net and another player who just happened to be there barely touched him, sending Smith head first into the boards. Smith severed his spinal cord and wound up a paraplegic. He didn't have much money and wanted to finish school, so Al staged an all-star lacrosse benefit at Maple Leaf Gardens. Al was able to pick up the slack for him. Smith returned to university where he completed his commerce degree and later became comptroller of a small wheelchair company in Toronto. Smith returned the favour by working for Eagleson on his first political campaign.''

Between 1963 and 1967 Eagleson made a name for himself in the Ontario legislature by verbally eviscerating Vern Singer, the Liberal deputy leader, who had to tolerate four years of backbench heckling from Eagleson and his three cohorts, Tom Wells, Darcy McKeough, and George Peck. Singer affectionately called them the ''Chicago gang'' because of their shocking comments and rude interjections.

As the kingpin of the Chicago gang Eagleson goaded irascible politicians to the point where ''many threatened to separate Al's head from his shoulders if he ever got into politics again,'' as a *Globe and Mail* reporter says. At the provincial legislature, Eagleson was said to have ''liberal views in spite of his being a big C conservative''. He supported bills for legalized abortion, interfaith adoption, divorce reform, and legal aid.

But the world was young and Eagleson's ''liberalism'' was rooted in the possibility of infinite economic expansion. He was still looking for more opportunity than the politician or the lawyer in him already knew. That was the reason he went to Peterborough.

A two-and-a-half-hour drive northeast of Toronto takes you there. Peterborough lies at the centre of the Kawartha Lakes resort area, where the tourists can picnic, watch the boats being raised and lowered on the Trent Canal locks from May to October — and observe the Toronto Maple Leafs at training camp. The Leafs spend several weeks here in late summer preparing for the upcoming season.

But Eagleson didn't go for a picnic. He was trying to negotiate his first contract with Leaf management. His client was Carl Brewer, a twenty-six-year-old Leaf veteran who became a four-time All-Star. Brewer was anxious to make more money. At the pinnacle of his career, after spending seven years with the Leafs, he already had three of his four All-Star awards under his belt. Sensing he was worth more than the $9,000 he was currently earning, he asked Eagleson to talk to Punch Imlach.

Imlach had been the chief taskmaster of the Leafs since 1958. He was a strict disciplinarian whose main job in the army in the Second World War had been running hundreds of Canada's finest through their two-month basic training stint at Cornwall, Ontario. He was so effective as a drill sergeant that from the time he started as a corporal till he finished as lieutenant he never left Cornwall or saw active duty. Imlach says the army left him with plenty of ideas about training men — and the most important one, the necessity for discipline. "If you haven't got discipline you haven't got anything."

"Can he play hockey?" Imlach asked Brewer about Eagleson.

"No."

"If he can play hockey I'll talk to him; if he can't I'm not wasting my time talking to him."

"You don't understand, Punch," pleaded Brewer. "He's my lawyer: he's not another hockey player."

"Doesn't make any difference, if he can't play hockey I won't talk to him."

"Didn't make any difference to me then and it doesn't today," says Imlach, whose reluctance to talk to agents has never wavered, even though his son Brent became one.

Brewer was the first player who asked Imlach to negotiate a contract with a third party. Imlach held firm, refusing to deal with any agent or lawyer during his entire initial twelve-year tenure with the Leafs.

"Even during 1970-71, the first year I was in Buffalo starting up the Sabres, I never negotiated with an agent," he claims. "Eventually it came to pass like everything else — I had to, but I was dragged kicking and screaming."

Now it was time for Eagleson to stop laughing at the players' contracts. While individualism is purported to be the single most valuable trait of the Canadian hockey game, the concept carried no weight in salary negotiations.

Brewer's request to "talk to my lawyer" was the opening wedge in a rift between Imlach and Eagleson that lasted as long as Imlach stayed with the Leafs. Imlach's idea of what was best for the team was to denounce individualism in favour of teamwork.

That's where the two locked horns. While Imlach was against turning hockey players into prima donnas, Eagleson was convinced that a top player was worth his weight in gold and should be paid accordingly. But gilding the Leaf players would have to wait for the moment when circumstances would permit a total revolution. As in any revolution, those who need emancipating are not articulate enough to organize themselves; it takes time, money, and a charismatic leader to effect a change.

Brewer couldn't wait for Eagleson to apply the salve. The defence-man had developed an enmity for Imlach which would not subside. In 1965 Brewer severed all ties with the Leafs, kicking Imlach's militaristic establishment royally. He took a four-year sabbatical from his pro career and enrolled at the University of Toronto. If there had been union at the time, he might not have had to make such a monu-mental sacrifice; a third party or arbitrator could have argued his case.

In *Hockey is a Battle*, Imlach calls Brewer "a great defenceman who was an emotional high strung kind of guy ... who underwent some kind of change ... he was a kid who could be told that I'm taking advantage of him and he isn't getting enough money and he shouldn't have to do this, and he shouldn't have to do that. He can be led, and I think he just got the wrong guy for him. He needed somebody who instead of aggravating his problem would cool his problems down. But this guy Eagleson aggravated the problems all the time, made them bigger. I mean the game itself aggravated Brewer enough without having somebody standing behind him always giving him the rebel treatment."

Imlach still says Brewer would be a Leaf today if it weren't for his association with Eagleson, and he said it back in 1965 when Brewer quit the Leafs: "I'm talking now about Alan Eagleson, the lawyer. ... Eagleson is a rebel himself. He got into hockey as the players' lawyer and he started trying to work a revolution ... he was very chummy with Brewer, who was a bit of a rebel himself. So you have two rebels talking together, bracing each other up, telling each other that they're great guys and Imlach is the bloody villain, and pretty soon something is going to happen."

Today, Brewer takes full credit for his decision to remove himself from the Leaf crest. "All the ideas I've ever had have been my own ... a few lackeys have followed around behind Eagleson but my ideas have always been my own. The only reason I retired was I couldn't justify playing the game under Punch Imlach. ... That was it. At that time I didn't want to ever play again."

Eagleson's role was to fix it so that Brewer could reinstate his amateur standing. But Brewer said later the only role Eagleson played was to provide "moral support".

Some people feel Brewer is a little bitter about what happened in 1965. Eagleson did help Brewer in his fight with the NHL governors to re-establish himself as an amateur while he was attending university, at a time when it was thought impossible to go back and play amateur. But the event was seen as Eagleson's first victory over Imlach, even though the NHL's decision essentially came directly from Clarence Campbell, who had been president of the NHL since 1946.

Brewer never got his day in court, but he did get to play for Canada's national team from 1966 to 1969. Then he pulled out at the top of his career, when he could have been making a lot of money.* Some say his retirement from professional hockey was partly because of the infusion into the NHL of ''goon hockey'': he didn't like getting hit over the head by the players. And the problem of player violence still exists today.

Through Brewer, Eagleson carved himself a reputation as the Pied Piper of Peterborough. Before long he would have all the teams in the NHL marching to his tune beneath the banner of the National Hockey League Players' Association. Ironically, though one team manager (Imlach) had cut short his chances of gaining a toehold as a player rep, it was because another team owner did give him the benefit of the doubt that Eagleson could eventually paint his future in 24-karat gold.

---

* Brewer played for the International Amateur League's Muskegon Mohawks in Michigan during 1967–68 and was paid a salary similar to the average annual NHL wage of $22,000.

BOBBY WHO AND
THE SUMMER OF '66

*Well, Bobby Orr is the thing that made
Eagleson, no question about that at all.*
Punch Imlach

Law students often ask Eagleson, "How did you do it?"

"Find yourself another Bobby Orr, do a good job for him and you will get carried along on his coattails for a while ... then you expand."

Orr became hockey's number-one player almost immediately after he turned pro. It was the young rookie's reputation — first as the sensational OHA Junior A All-Star, executing dynamic defenceman-ship against rival teams such as the Russian Nationals; and then as an NHL pro, exhibiting star qualities by outperforming veteran players and breaking previous NHL records — that added lustre to Eagleson's reputation in hockey of being Orr's agent, friend, and mentor.

Eagleson, in his role as midwife to the child prodigy, guided Orr's career through the media, acted as financial negotiator with team owners, and later secured Orr's future by setting up Bobby Orr Enterprises Ltd. and various other companies including the Orr-Walton hockey camp in Orillia, Ontario.

Before the two Irishmen met, Eagleson had already proved his mettle to a lesser degree, receiving a groundswell of support for his handling of the Brewer controversy, as well as for looking after the legal matters of other top-name Leaf players such as rookie Mike Walton and superstar Frank Mahovlich.

But it appeared that his political career held more fascination for him at that point than did the prospect of becoming a Ralph Nader of hockey. The last attempt to organize the players had been made in 1958. Nor had Eagleson, since his earliest Leaf involvements, ever openly indicated a desire to lead the march, not even back in his university days when, on those rides in the red mail truck with Bob Mackay, the professor had discussed "how embarrassingly little" had been done in the field of "the athlete and the law".

"'Why don't you publish a book on the subject?'" Mackay remembers suggesting to his friend. "I knew there had been nothing done and Eagleson had been interceding in an informed way with Pully and Frank Mahovlich."

Eagleson's active attempt to equalize the disproportionate distribution of money and rights between owners and players came immediately after he met Bobby Orr. Orr had never associated himself with agents. Many of these brokers had earned the business its lowlife reputation of "flesh peddling". "I'm a lawyer, not an agent," Eagleson insisted to all and sundry. But as his law partners constantly reminded him, "he was doing everything except practising law."

It was in fact the deliberate flexibility provided by the group of young lawyers at Blaney, Pasternak who were collectively committed to each other's success that made it possible for Eagleson to stake out new ground in sports management. Had he been stuck in one of the larger law establishments, his association with athletes would almost certainly have fallen by the wayside. Good fortune prevailed in those early years. His partners, instead of arbitrarily charting his route, gave him their moral support and much-needed personal assistance.

He also found outside sources of legal nourishment along the way. Joe Sedgwick, whom Eagleson considers "one of the greatest legal minds in the country", saw him through his teeth-cutting days when he tackled Brewer's troubles with Imlach. "He didn't charge me a fee ... he told me, 'you just owe the same time to somebody else,'" says Eagleson. "I've always remembered that lesson."

This attitude, although not rewarding to the firm, looked good on his record as a politician, and to that ambition he gave willingly and tirelessly. Besides the numerous charity directorships he held, he was especially sought after as a speaker. He clocked thousands of flying hours annually, zipping across the country to address non-profit groups at least once a month. Frequently they were local sports organizations.

"I'd always throw in a little about the impact hockey has on our social and political systems ... whatever that means," he explains.

Hockey talk was a favourite crowd-pleaser, particularly in towns through which few noteworthy people passed during the iced-in winter months. There was little else to do but play winter sports, and it was hockey that most fathers talked about to their sons.

In the spring of 1966, Eagleson, then a provincial member at Queen's Park, was invited to speak at a baseball banquet in MacTier, Ontario, a town where, several years before, he had worked as a recreation director during the summer months. Like most northern Ontario towns, MacTier held fast to the tradition of weaning its boys on chasing a vulcanized rubber disc around frozen rivers.

One father in the audience responded particularly keenly to the MPP's stories about being a kid in a small town which didn't have television yet, where the kids would sit around listening to Foster Hewitt describing their favourite hockey heroes' passing and shooting.

Doug Orr approached Eagleson when the talk ended and, after exchanging their remembrances of having played baseball together a couple of years earlier, Doug briefed him about the move his son, Bobby Orr, was making to the pros. Doug's father had been a soccer star back in Northern Ireland and had encouraged Doug to excel in sports. It seems he developed into a promising hockey player in his home town of Parry Sound, Ontario, but missed his chance to make it in the pros because of the intrusion of the Second World War and the responsibilities of parenting. He had vowed that his son would have a fair chance.

That year the league's first expansion ended the Dickensian flesh-peddling era whereby young boys of thirteen and fourteen, coaxed off to hockey clubs, sold the exclusive rights to their professional futures. Many passed their young manhood between games and practices in grimy pool halls and bowling alleys, with little or no concern for life after their short-lived careers. This ''sponsorship''system survived quite efficiently: at the drop of a puck it could produce hundreds of testimonials confirming that players loved to play so much they thought getting paid for it was a remarkable bonus.

One whose veteran hockey career depended on the sponsorship system was Punch Imlach. ''People said the players were slaves, not getting paid ... hell, if I offered someone off the street a contract, he'd be in here to work like there was no tomorrow ... it wasn't exploitation, it was what the market would bear.'' Others who depended on the constant turnover of athletic record-breakers were the sports journalists who greased the machinery with their hyperbolic prose.

The year before Doug Orr hired Eagleson as his lawyer, the young Parry Sound puckster's career had been frozen in print. *Maclean's* indelibly imprinted Orr's image upon the hearts and minds of thousands of legend seekers:

> He is a swift powerful skater with instant accelerations, instinctive anticipation, a quick accurate shot, remarkable composure, and unrelenting ambition, a solemn dedication, humility, modesty, and a fondness for his parents and his brothers and sisters that often turns his eyes moist.

Enter the dragon. At fourteen, the newly-acclaimed *wunderkind* had already been offered a contract by the Boston Bruins in a covetous attempt to beat Toronto, Montreal, and Chicago to the Stanley Cup. Bobby signed a Bruins Junior C form, which tied him to their protected list under the NHL's prevailing "child labour laws". (Within a few years, expansion would allow the children to at least finish high school when the draft age was raised to twenty.) In *Hockey! The Story of the World's Fastest Sport*, it was reported that:

> His parents, Doug and Arva Orr, agreed to let him go, reluctantly, after the Bruins contrived a deal that included $2,800 for Mr. Orr. The father, not much older than Gordie Howe, is modestly rewarded as a crateloader for Canadian Industries Ltd., an explosives company. "Bobby was only 14," Doug Orr says, "but I felt he had a right to make up his own mind about Boston."

Doug Orr's determination to see his son have his fair chance prompted him to seek legal support in Bobby's upcoming dealings with the Bruins. To his mind, the young Toronto lawyer who was doing a bit of netminding for the Ontario Conservatives was it. "He was smart enough; he had everything he needed to be a good agent."

After Doug Orr and Eagleson finished talking, Bobby wandered over and introduced himself.

"Bobby who?" Eagleson asked.

"Orr, O-R-R," repeated his father as the captain of the former Bruins farm team, the Oshawa Generals, extended his hand.

"I didn't know Bobby Orr from a hole in the ground," Eagleson recalls. "I knew all the big time guys that were in the NHL, not these small guys in junior teams . . . but that meeting turned it all around.''

Before Eagleson could seal the contract, Bobby's mother intervened. ''My mother wanted to know what he was going to charge,'' Bobby explains. ''I remember Al looking away as if he was adding up figures in his head; then he turned to my mother and said, 'I'll tell you what, Mrs. Orr, if Bobby makes some money then I will make some money.' ''

''Making some money'' sounded great to young Orr, who promptly gave his new agent an assignment.

''I was eighteen and playing junior hockey for Boston earning sixty dollars a week. My lawyer [Eagleson] was trying to get me a raise but he couldn't get it for me . . . can you imagine, a guy in his position couldn't get me a ten-dollar raise!''

''Juniors got sixty dollars a week tops and that went for ten dollars spending money and paying room and board,'' says Doug Orr. Those were the underpaid dog days of the farm system. Every club in the NHL had territorial rights to thousands of thirteen- and fourteen-year-old youths within a fifty-mile radius of their city limits. The boys were assigned to one of the club's numerous subsidiaries. Because the major clubs footed the bill for the cost of developing amateur teams through sponsorships, the system was perpetuated, enhancing the dynasties and feudalistic order of player-owner relationships. And, once the youngsters were uprooted from family, friends, and schools, the NHL could get away with paying them peanuts.

Under such authoritarian rule, the NHL was omnipotent. At the professional level, it had for thirty years successfully survived threats of unions, improved pay, and better working conditions. With only 120 jobs, the owners could pick and choose from hundreds of examples of good pro talent. It wasn't until the NHL owners themselves were forced to forfeit their monopolistic control over hockey and permit the entrance of other franchises that any structural changes were made.

Eagleson had entered the picture just before expansion, a move which suddenly, by doubling the size of the league, brought virtually every potential pro player into quick demand. In 1965, Clarence Campbell announced that there were going to be important changes in the method of turning out the NHL's product. The corporation set up an expansion committee composed of the league's prime financial backers, including David Molson of the Montreal Canadiens and William Jennings of the New York Rangers. Hockey was still a third-rate sport in the U.S., far behind baseball and football, which had been successful in obtaining million-dollar television contracts. "No TV sponsor is too interested in financing on a national basis a program of big league hockey which ignores two thirds of the country as far as member cities are concerned," the *New York Times* reported in 1963.

In 1966, Campbell announced plans to expand the league from six to twelve teams, which opened up 120 new pro jobs starting in the 1967–68 season. The six new teams were all located in American cities — Pittsburgh, Oakland, Los Angeles, Philadelphia, St. Louis, and Minneapolis, and were each required to pay an entry fee of $2 million to the NHL. Expansion would give less competitive teams such as the New York Rangers, the Chicago Black Hawks, the Detroit Red Wings, and the Boston Bruins a chance to play catch-up.*

To facilitate the league's first expansion and the availability of choice players, today's universal or amateur (junior) draft program was set up, making players free agents. From 1967, any player younger than twenty belonged to no team until he was drafted. To even the balance, the newer teams coming into the league would have one or two first-round draft choices.

In addition, the club sponsorship system (which by 1967 encompassed twenty-seven professional teams — twenty-two in the U.S. and five in Canada — and in turn owned fifty Canadian junior teams) was replaced by local sponsorships organized under the Canadian Amateur Hockey Association, which shared in the cost of the New Deal.† The CAHA agreed to contribute $5,000 to every Junior A and Junior B team in North America; the NHL's contribution in the first years of the venture was $1.2 million annually, plus $3,000‡ to the CAHA every time a team picked an amateur in the yearly draft sessions.

The Bruins profited from the change to the universal draft system. Campbell insisted that as of January 1, 1966, all clubs' protected lists would be frozen, and every player on the list remained the exclusive property of the owner club. The Bruins had conveniently placed Orr on their protected list when he was fourteen and moved him to their farm team in Oshawa.

* Most of the top junior players lived inside the fifty-mile radius of Toronto or Montreal, were placed on "protected lists" and were off limits to other franchises.
† All amateur junior players are required to sign a CAHA registration card, which entitles the CAHA to sell the player to the NHL.
‡ By 1974, the price the NHL paid to the CAHA for first- and second-round draft picks was increased to $40,000.

This left Eagleson with only one way to handle the negotiations of Orr's first professional contract with the Boston club. The only leverage he had was the threat to place Orr on Canada's national team. The idea might not have worried Orr, who "just wanted to play hockey", but Eagleson and Orr's father were after bigger game.

While Bobby played out his last season of Junior A hockey, contract talks with Bruin's general manager, Hap Emms, commenced. During the summer of 1966 the offers drifted in. A $5,000 signing bonus plus $8,000 a year salary was what the Bruins considered an impressive pay hike for a kid earning only sixty dollars a week. The next offer, reportedly, was $10,500 a year, "our top offer".

Joe Namath of the New York Jets football team was making an annual salary of $100,000, and Cazzie Russell received $65,000 a year with the National Basketball Association's New York Knicker-bockers. It was a year when top-flight pro football players in the U.S. were pulling in salaries of over $100,000, while their counterparts in hockey were getting only half that amount.

As training camp in August drew closer, it was clear that Emms was not going to acknowledge Eagleson's presence in the negotiations, and that the $10,500 would stick. But Eagleson and Irwin Pasternak spent the better part of the month in Orillia at Eagleson's summer home, working on a contract for that fateful day when Emms would first have to open his door to a player's attorney. Emms, meanwhile, went so far as to announce at a press conference he would not be dealing with any lawyers.

"But Al was coaching me," says Bobby, "and I knew enough not to change my mind about what I wanted and what they were offering."

Emms' broadcast to the world about not talking to Orr's lawyer raised the public's curiosity and sympathy. "Emms turned out to be my best press agent," says Eagleson. Towards the end of August Eagleson received a phone call from Boston. "Let's talk." It was Emms.

On September 2, 1966, Eagleson was invited aboard Emms' forty-foot cruiser, the *Barbara Lynn*, docked near Orillia. The value of a lawyer's presence was demonstrated that day. Bobby signed a two-year contract, and his salary was reported at the time to be $75,000. His future had been secured by the stroke of a pen. He was the highest-paid rookie in the league. Eagleson promised that Orr would be a millionaire by the age of thirty.

The Bruins recovered their investment in three short months. According to Boston hockey writers, Bobby quickly raised box office receipts for the Bruins by $100,000 by Christmas of that year.

It was primarily the superstars who enjoyed a quick succession of salary improvements as a result of Orr's reputation. Billy Heindl, for example, wore the assistant captain's "A" on his sweater when Bobby was captain of the Oshawa Generals, and like Orr had signed a C form with the Bruins. Heindl was sent by Boston to Clinton, New York, in the Eastern League where, it is said, he made $150 a week. Eagleson is credited with helping improve the NHL players' salaries across the board. Only two years after Orr signed with the Bruins, Bobby Hull managed to increase his pay to $100,000, becoming the highest-paid hockey player in the history of the game.

The financially beneficial association between Eagleson and Orr marked the opening of a new era for hockey. Their potential profit-making abilities, coupled with the eventual NHL expansion, paved the way for a flourishing agency business in Canada. Eagleson was automatically pitted against competition at the level of Montreal agent Mark McCormack, who became the most expensive agent in the business with 25 percent fees which he charged to golfer Arnold Palmer, and Boston agent Bob Whoolf, who eventually arranged a $2.5 million contract for one of Orr's Boston teammates, the Niagara Falls youth Derek Sanderson.

Eagleson's reason for getting into the agency business was faith in the future: "I had a chance to live a vicarious life through Orr — what, as a kid, I had wanted to be." Emms' two fatal words, "let's talk," gave him the chance — and at the same time, according to Punch Imlach, "those two words are what did the league in."

After Orr's settlement hundreds of keen fathers began beating a path to Eagleson's door, asking him to negotiate equally lush deals for their sons. The time had clearly come for the Canadian lawyer-entrepreneur to take up the challenge to score a hat trick for player-owner negotiations.

"Like Topsy" is the phrase that Eagleson uses to describe his catapult in one short year from arguing land rezoning cases in Rexdale to becoming an acknowledged force in a major sector of the entertainment world. Eagleson brought hockey owners to heel, swaying the balance of power to the players.

By the time Eagleson returned from Orillia with this major victory under his belt, word of his triumph over the Bruins' management had flooded major American newspapers. In late September, shortly after Eagleson returned from Orillia, he received another historic phone call, this time from two disgruntled hockey players with the Springfield Indians.

This was his introduction to the third major event responsible for piloting Eagleson into his unique role as player advocate for the entire NHL: the threat of strike action by the Springfield Indians, a Boston farm team in the American Hockey League. Brian Kilrea and Bill White, along with three other defencemen, had been suspended from the team, and were highly agitated when they contacted Eagleson. He discovered the entire team was on the verge of striking, and were hot after coach, general manager, and owner Eddie Shore's blood. (Shore, a sixty-four-year-old Hockey Hall of Famer, won a colourful reputation as the ubiquitous Bruins' defenceman during his fifteen-year career in Boston; it was his career that Orr was slated to emulate.)

"Can you help us?" they asked Eagleson.

"What about going to the top and talking to the league president?" he suggested. The president turned out to be Shore's nephew, Jack Butterfield. "Butterfield threatened if we weren't on the ice tomorrow morning we would be blackballed and never allowed to play hockey again."

Eagleson immediately contacted a personal friend, Ernie Rowley, a contractor who was also a licensed pilot. Rowley had Eagleson and one of his law partners, Ray Smela, aboard Rowley's plane, the *Apache*, within a few hours, airborne for Pennsylvania.

"We met with all the players in our hotel suite," says Smela. "They weren't on strike yet but were pretty heated up and talking nothing but strike, strike, strike." Some reports claim there was an actual sit-down strike. "Strike was an unthinkable action at that time. They were still part of the old farm system and even the players didn't want to strike, but they were unhappy with the manner in which they were being treated."

The talks lasted a couple of days "without the players missing a game or even a single practice," says Smela. Shore refused to talk to Eagleson or Smela. Players lodged complaints about Shore forcing them to practice ridiculous drills, such as having to sweep the ice in the arena after practice while still wearing their skates and uniforms.

Smela and Eagleson watched a Springfield game, had dinner with a couple of the referees, and in a few days returned home. Eagleson had promised to investigate the possibility of putting a permanent end to

Shore's disciplinary action. The players were appeased and continued to play.

On his return home Eagleson found another client waiting for him. "I want to return to the pros," Carl Brewer said emphatically. "But I won't go back to the Leafs." As a reinstated amateur he had been playing hockey with Canada's national team, and was preparing for the world tournament in Vienna. However, as a former pro, he was considered commercially tainted under the Olympic rules, and would be excluded from the 1968 games. So he wanted to return to the pros. His hockey career seemed doomed: his rights to play pro hockey had been retained by the Leafs, and as their obligor he couldn't play for any other club. Brewer succeeded in transferring his pro rights to the Detroit Red Wings in 1969–70; then he played for the St. Louis Blues in 1970–72, and the World Hockey Association's Toronto Toros in 1973–74, and ended his pro career with the Toronto Maple Leafs in 1979–80.

The real estate section of Blaney, Pasternak, Smela, Eagleson and Watson was turning into a full-blown arbitration ward, what with the gargantuan task of officiating for Springfield, plus handling the growing list of Eagleson's personal NHL clientele. And hockey was not the only sport Eagleson was asked to "clean up".

One day over lunch with lawyer Herb Solway, a friend of Irwin Pasternak's, Eagleson was invited to meet with the Rifles, a football team started in Montreal in 1964, which had incurred several thousand dollars' worth of debts and in 1965 had moved its operations to Toronto. Eagleson, as Blaney, Pasternak's chief image fixer, was given the task of changing the Rifle's poor-boy stigma. And did he want to become the club's president?

Yes, he did, but on one condition. He wanted to have nothing to do with the salary negotiations; that would be left to the club's general manager! He scored a victory over the rival Argonauts that summer by signing Canadian Football League superstar Jackie Parker as the Rifles' coach for 1967. In his managerial capacity Eagleson had great visions of the total capitulation of the Canadian Football League.

"Now that the National League and the American League in the U.S. are joining," he said, "I think our league [the Continental League] will knock off the CFL. We don't have millionaires running our teams, we have multi-millionaires, and we're going to go after one of those rich TV contracts with a big American network. I think we'll just outlast the CFL."

His timing was good; but in a sense time was his most elusive opponent. His appetite for work was insatiable. He was driven by the constant fear there wouldn't be enough time to complete all the things he set out to do. There would always be consequences he had to suffer, from loss of time with his family and friends to his much-desired political rewards. Canada's centennial year would be pivotal in terms of both work and politics for Eagleson.

Besides the growing threat of Eagleson's presence in the *affaires d'amour* between the NHL officials and players in 1966, which rendered the corporation vulnerable to public pressure to bend, a great steel thunderbolt — the Teamsters' Union — attacked its soft underbelly when the union threatened to organize the NHL players. Not since the Great Players' Strike in 1925* had the NHL experienced such a drastic shake-up.

On the crest of the Teamsters' wave, Eagleson prepared himself for a showdown over the Springfield crisis at the League's front offices in Montreal. Several subsequent trips to Hershey had enabled Eagleson to collect enough evidence of Shore's questionable tactics to prompt him to fight for the owner's removal from the league. His threat of debating a player's employment conditions in the courts, which he had used many times before, won him another victory. "There would be no more disciplinary action or interference by Shore," said Smela. "I ended up negotiating Shore's retirement," Eagleson told the media. "Getting Shore and Butterfield out of hockey was the best thing that ever happened to it." Shore ultimately sold the Springfield club to a new expansion franchise, the Los Angeles Kings of the NHL, and retired from hockey. Were Eagleson's dealings really a contributing factor to Shore's "early retirement"?

"Yes, I would think so," concludes Smela.

---

* The 1925 strike was the only major players' strike in the history of the NHL or WHA. Red Green of the Hamilton Tigers signed a two-year contract in 1924 for a 24-game schedule, yet had already played 30 games and was asking for an extra $200. Consequently, the players struck. The Hamilton Tigers were later suspended in April 1925 and absent from the Stanley Cup playoffs. Each player was fined $200. The strike prompted the NHL to move its headquarters out of Hamilton to New York.

·6·

THE EMANCIPATOR

*I don't like unions but I'm glad it's
Eagleson at the head of the Players'
Association rather than somebody else.*
Conn Smythe

It was during the post-Christmas lull in Red Fisher's thirteenth year covering the Montreal Canadiens for the *Montreal Star* that he received his first call from The Eagle. "I called him 'The Eagle' in my column the next morning because of his unswerving gall," he said. "Eagleson called me at the *Star* and introduced himself: 'Mr. Fisher, I'm Al Eagleson, could I drop down and see you for a few minutes?' Nobody here knew him at the time so I said sure, he could come on down.

"He was fresh-looking, a man with a jockey's slender, nervous frame. He had a charming manner. I showed him down to the *Star*'s chrome and arborite cafeteria, filled two Melmac cups with coffee and said, 'What are you doing in town?'

"He said, 'I'm on my way through Montreal to Quebec City and quite frankly I am thinking of forming a players' association for hockey.' When I finished picking myself up off the floor, I asked, 'You're not talking to any of the Montreal players while you're here, are you?'

" 'Oh, no. No, no,' he replied. We chatted for a few minutes and I said, see you again soon, I hope. I went back upstairs and promptly called one of the players and asked if he had ever met Alan Eagleson. 'Oh yes, the whole team did today.' The very next day I wrote a column about my mysterious visit from 'The Eagle', said I invested a dime in the guy for a cup of coffee, then explained that while he was drinking my coffee he promptly told me a barefaced lie ... and I was doing him a favour even talking to him. [Later Eagleson said he found the whole thing very amusing. 'I enjoyed it.'] Something like that wouldn't bother him at all. He still reminds me about it and I never let him forget it," says Fisher.

Eagleson had been talking in person to people in the media about his ideas for a players' union. It no doubt helped his leverage at Clarence Campbell's office when Eagleson met with the NHL president the next day to discuss the Springfield Indians affair. On the same day that the papers ran a story that the Canadiens had been "talking" with a union organizer, Eagleson not only won his case for the Springfield team, but was touted all over the country as the next in line to fill Campbell's shoes, "unless he becomes a team owner first!"

The Eagle. The new name fit, and it stayed with him. He was more a legend than a lawyer or an agent.

The Springfield Indians crisis, as it would be called, was Eagleson's first major blow against the "powerless and repressed" status of the players. It became the springboard for Eagleson's grand design for the formation of a permanent mechanism for the resolution of players' grievances. Notwithstanding their recent success in subduing the Teamsters, the owners were sitting ducks.

Hockey's serfs (many of whom were Eagleson's personal clients) could outflank their owners provided they had proper leadership and provided they were united. They had been kept in the dark by their oppressors — but they could learn. They needed a Mao Tsetung, a careful helmsman; Eagleson had already distinguished himself by his audacity and skill — he could discipline the uninformed men. In addition, he had the example of the American professional sports associations to draw on.

"I don't recall any other lawyer working with Al on the players' association," says Smela, "there was just Al and Bob Pulford." Pulford was Eagleson's sergeant-at-arms; Bobby Orr flanked his other side, the side most likely to gain public sympathy against hockey brutishness.

Eagleson received a telephone call from Orr in Campbell's office which, ironically, was a request to meet Orr's teammates, Murray Oliver and Eddie Johnston, after the Bruins-Canadiens game December 28, 1966. The usual after-game beers and cheers promised to take on a more serious note. At the prompting of the Bruins' three key players, the entire team had assembled by the time Eagleson made his way through the snow to Johnston's hotel room. They had been impressed by Eagleson's handling of the Springfield altercation and, dissatisfied with the current player representative system, presented their desire for a permanent guild. Eagleson accepted the task and agreed to visit every city in the National, American, and Western Hockey Leagues to meet with the players.

That December night was a historic date: it marked the NHL Players' Association's inaugural meeting. The Association's first piece of business was to retain Eagleson's services for $2,500 plus expenses. (By 1971, his retainer was $20,000, for a job he always undertook to do on a part-time basis.)

Between January and May 1967 the first flush of his two-year odyssey had begun. He saw the insides of more hotel rooms and clocked more flying miles than any prime minister. He quickly presented the players with an ideology. The press were contacted privately, and kept, uncharacteristically, at arm's length; individual players remained unidentified. It would be a "Quiet Revolution", in light of the owners' successes in squashing earlier attempts to organize. Eagleson's word to the media was, "Some players approached me last fall and I have pursued the matter at their request. At this point I can only say the overwhelming majority of hockey players are in favour of such an organization and that ... the key players are solidly behind it now."

He tapped his personal clientele, which included at least one player on each of the six NHL teams, to solicit for him from the inside. But not only players were involved.

A key contact in the Leaf locker room was Bob Haggert, a personal friend of Eagleson's. Haggert had started out as a Toronto Cabbagetown kid selling newspapers on the corner of Carlton and Yonge streets near Maple Leaf Gardens. Then he sold programs at the Gardens during the games. He spent so much of his time there (one of the rink rats who attach themselves to hockey — only his was a bigger rink than most) that eventually his mother took over the job of selling programs just to keep an eye on her kid.

"Haggy" eventually got to be stick boy and then a Leaf trainer. In the mid-sixties, when Eagleson was gathering steam behind the NHLPA, Haggert was taking the brunt of Imlach's wrath. "Imlach still looked upon trainers as serfs," says one former employee. Over a period of time Haggert developed an animosity towards management, and so he was an ideal "inside man" for Eagleson's plans. When Imlach sniffed the air and found something more than the odour of sour socks and sweaters, he was smart enough to immediately link the new intruder, "unionism", with Haggert. "He [Haggert] was Eagle's inside man and of course Imlach knew that," says Morley Kells.

Kells, who later became an MPP, represented Maple Leaf Sport Productions, an offshoot of MacLaren Advertising Ltd., as well. MacLaren owns the exclusive broadcasting rights in Maple Leaf Gardens; *Hockey Night in Canada* is one of its clients. Kells edited the Gardens' program and Haggert, among his other duties, sold the advertising for it. "Haggy could travel around the league with the Leafs and Eagleson couldn't afford the time to do that, so Haggy did all the inside work for him when he was forming the union," says Kells. "Haggy played an important role for Eagle."

Other "putsch" activities at the time included circulating a flyer among the players. Eagleson pledged to overthrow the barony and asked for their signatures in return:

> I, the undersigned, hereby direct and authorize R. Alan Eagleson to act as my agent in pursuing the formation of a Players' Association for Professional Hockey. It is further understood and agreed that my name will not be used or released in any way without my written consent.

Within only a few months 110 out of a possible 120 signatures were obtained. Even players who were not his clients took an active part in raising the union flag. On his Chicago visit, Bobby Hull introduced Eagleson by saying: "Al's done more for hockey in two years than anybody else has done in twenty-five." The Golden Jet was never an Eagleson client.*

The last straw needed to break the management's back came in a chance meeting between a hockey player and a football player en route to a meeting with a players' representative in New York. The rep was collecting support from other pro leagues — baseball, football, and basketball — and suggested there should be some representation from hockey. "Could you suggest anyone?"

He did, and the next day Eagleson and Orr were in New York

---

* Bobby Hull formed an investment company with Eagleson and Bobby Orr to buy part of the Toronto Island Marina in 1972 to raise money for the first Russia-Canada games.

collecting details about acceptable benefits and compensation, and copies of other associations' constitutions. Armed with that material, writing hockey's first Players' Constitution was just a matter of cut-and-paste. (An official collective-bargaining agreement would not be dealt with until several years later.) By May, Eagleson had collected all but two NHL players' signatures in his hat box. The Boston team votes were the first in the box; then came the rest of the Big Six NHL clubs, New York, Detroit, Chicago, Montreal, and Toronto. He added to the pile 180 American Hockey League players' names (representing 100 percent of the membership) and pledges from 85 percent of the Western League teams. Membership was voluntary, to be renewed yearly at a fee of $150.

Eagleson chose the first week of May to call his own players' representatives' meeting in Montreal. The new constitution was ratified with great excitement. Eagleson was elected the union's executive director and his client friend, Bob Pulford of the Toronto Maple Leafs, was elected its first president. The Quiet Revolution had happened. The two childhood friends, Pulford and Eagleson, had staged a *coup d'état* in a matter of a few months, completely undetected by the owners.

The revolution had begun in Montreal, and it climaxed there. On June 6, the day before the scheduled NHL annual board of governors' meetings were to be held, Eagleson briefed the players' reps on their role, and then revealed his activities to the press.

"Before the hockey meetings started in June he called me again," says Fisher. "He said, 'We are going to have the association accepted by the NHL no matter what you hear. The owners are going to have to accept it and accept me as the executive director.'

"I told him, 'Al, that's fine but others have tried before and they've only run into trouble.'

"But he didn't believe me. 'You take my word for it, you be there at two o'clock on Tuesday and you'll see it happening before your very eyes.'"

Precisely at 2:00 P.M. on June 7, 1967, Fisher and other reporters were standing outside the room where the owners were to meet with the players' representatives. "The players walked in, took one look, realized Eagleson wasn't there," says Fisher, "and demanded, 'We want Al Eagleson in the room.' Stafford Smythe [who owned the Leafs then] said, 'That son of a bitch will never come into this room.'

Those were his precise words. . . . The players said, 'Fine,' got up and walked out. There we were — the players' reps [Ed Johnston, Norm Ullman, Harry Howell, Bob Nevin, Pierre Pilote, Bob Pulford, and J.C. Tremblay], some of Al's friends from the media and Eagleson — all on the outside, with the owners on the other side of the closed door. A few minutes passed. Then Stafford stuck his head out the door the way one of his prize horses looks over the gate. . . . 'Bring the bastard in here.' "

Now for the first time, the players were telling the owners what they wanted. This was a complete turnabout. The colonial rule had ended; no longer would owners rule with an iron fist, their word law, no discussion, no argument. "We want Eagleson in here" . . . and they won.

Some of the owners even appeared jubilant for the moment. Television cameras caught Charles Mulcahy, Jr., then Boston's vice-president, smiling into the lens as he gave the union the official nod: "We are pleased to recognize the first formal players' association. . . . This is the first time in the history of the NHL that a players' association has been recognized." The camera panned other familiar faces in hockey's financial elite: Bruce Norris (Detroit), David Molson (Montreal), and Bill Wirtz (Chicago), plus three new expansion team financiers, Jack McGregor (Pittsburgh), Walter Bush (Minnesota), and Barry van Gerbig (California). Still photographs were shot for posterity. In fifteen minutes it was all over. "He slid it through them," one reporter said, "like a greased pig."

Eagleson was retained as the NHLPA's legal counsel on a part-time basis. "They could never afford to pay me what my time is worth." But he did promise them a full-fledged collective-bargaining unit, styled after the pro leagues in the U.S., within two years.

The Eagle was scoring goals for hockey without ever having to wear skates. The focal point of the movement to form a players' union, he appeared to be the harbinger of a kind of sport socialism; players would collectively redeem their labour more equitably; the rents garnered by the union would serve to advance a new economic order within the North American hockey industry. He was the leader of a real attack on the collective financial power of the Smythes, Molsons, and Adamses. But his motivation and allegiance were hard to pin down: did he shoot right or left?

Although initially he appeared to have every mother's son cheering his power play — players, press, politicians, and the public — a few dissenters quickly made their feelings known. "I was sitting in the office of a lawyer who represented one key player who was reluctant to join the association for what seemed to be obscure reasons," says Eagleson. "I made it my business to find out why. Then the lawyer pounced on me ... 'I'm an agent and a lawyer, my client is well known and I could have formed the association....' I said, 'Just a minute here, why the hell didn't you? I mean shit, I did it, don't tell me what you could have done now that I've done it!' These were the same people who laughed at me when I first tackled [Brewer's] case saying I was crazy for trying it."

The horror stories surrounding the earlier series of failures hadn't deterred Eagleson. In 1947 the players had asked the owners to set up a pension fund for them. The NHL refused, and instead set up the annual NHL All-Star Game, of which two thirds of the gate receipts went into a players' pension plan. In 1957 a left winger for Detroit Red Wings, Ted Lindsay, led the formation of a union along with other players — Doug Harvey, Jim Thompson, and Tod Sloan. Lindsay's idea for the union "was not the creation of one household for all players in the NHL. ... What we were aiming for was to benefit the game of hockey, not just the players." They took the NHL before the Ontario Labour Relations Board and eventually the NHL upgraded the players' pension fund and agreed to a minimum salary of $7,000 a year, with an increase in the players' share of playoff money. But the players didn't get their union, and like a lamb to the slaughter, Lindsay was railroaded to the Chicago Black Hawks.

Oddly enough, Lindsay later attacked Eagleson, claiming he "ruined the game. ... and the players' association has encouraged familiarity among the players. They're one big happy family now. Coaches have no way of punishing players because the association will raise hell." Yet he had been one of the more vocal opponents of a system which had ill-treated him: "We were underpaid serfs, hired to play hockey and keep our mouths shut. ... They didn't think we had minds of our own. ... They treated us as if we were babies." It was Eagleson's motives Lindsay suspected: "I played the game and was for the players; Eagleson never has and isn't. He's only out for himself."

The Leaf coach and manager, Punch Imlach, wasn't against unions in principle. "I'm not against them because I'm in one ... Christ, I have been in one for forty years — first in the Anglo-Canadian Pulp and Paper Company* union, and I've been in the ACTRA union for the past twenty years, so I guess I'm not against unions," he says. "But a players' union, I can't see it. I don't see how the hell you can meet a guy the day before you're playing him and you're all buddy-buddy, then you go out and subdue him, you might say. I think that's tough. I think they are the enemies. I know who the hell the enemy is, it's the other team. Sometimes I don't think my players know who the hell the enemy is. It was always black and white with me right from the beginning."

Imlach did eventually come to see the union as a necessary evil he liked to slap every now and then to get its attention. He denies ever having tried to punish players for belonging to the association: "I don't think I ever did. There was some [punishing] done here before when Tod Sloan was transferred out of here because he tried to put in a union. . . . I object and I'd fight, but I don't think I ever did that. . . . Only thing that matters to me is when they open the door and face off the puck . . . I want to win. I don't care if you belong to a union or the Girl Guides, whether you're black or white, or what religion you are doesn't make a damn bit of difference. . . . I haven't changed a damn bit on that. . . ."

If there was ever a Canadian movie made about the men who run hockey, Punch Imlach would have to be played by someone like Robert Duvall in his role of *The Great Santini*. Imlach wears his principles on his shoulder like a sergeant's stripes. He has no uncertainty about where his loyalty lies. Who is Imlach loyal to? "The team I work for," he says immediately. "I have nothing to do with the union, I stay the hell away from it; rules and regulations I'll abide by; I know enough if a player wants to do it he'll do it, in other words everything is made for them and not for me . . . things I can't do they can — any damn thing they want. I just go along. If I want to fight, I fight, that's all there is to it. . . . But you can't fight what's written down — you have to go along with it."

Perhaps because such a high percentage of the Leafs were Eagleson's clients, Eagleson did appear to be "the enemy". Eagleson clients

---

* The Anglo-Canadian Pulp and Paper Company, based in Quebec City, sponsored the senior amateur team, the ACES, derived from "Anglo-Canadian employe." Imlach was an ACE defenceman before he turned to coaching. The ACES survived until 1972.

seemed to be frequently, and consistently, singled out for sour treatment throughout both of Imlach's tenures with the Leafs.

The most serious anti-Eagleson assault was brought into play in the Toronto Maple Leaf dressing room. It began with one of Eagleson's personal clients, Frank Mahovlich.

Mahovlich was caught in the Eagleson-Imlach struggle. Surprisingly, although he was a client of Eagleson's, he hadn't signed up for the union when his teammates did. "His Leaf teammates brought some pressure on him which threw him into limbo," Imlach says; Punch issued a warning to the whole team: "There's not one of you in here who's half the player Mahovlich is. ... If I ever catch any of my players bugging someone by soliciting for the union, that player's gone."

The Leafs won the Stanley Cup that year. During the final days of Expo '67, Mahovlich got a surprisingly big share of Canada's birthday cheer: "We gave him a raise and some bonus arrangements that were better than he'd expected, considering the year before his goal-scoring had fallen off to eighteen, the lowest he'd ever had in the League," admitted Imlach.

If Imlach made it worthwhile for the Big M not to become a card carrier, this was the exception and not the rule. The majority of players (as well as observers) were sure that only a collective power-play would effect a change. Dick Beddoes, then a sportswriter for the *Globe and Mail*, was one of the first to expound on Eagleson's work:

> Emancipation of the working staff is manifestly late in the American Hockey League where the owners resolutely ignore the 20th century. There is no pension plan, for example, in this so-called second professional echelon where some salaries are reportedly as low as $4,000 a year.

Gerald Eskenazi gave another account of poor pay conditions in *A Thinking Man's Guide to Pro Hockey*:

> No wonder a hall-of-famer such as Maurice Richard is constantly knocking today's players — most of them make more money than he did in his best years. Much of his jealousy and his harping about the quality of play probably has to do with the fact that today's hockey players want what's coming to them. There's nothing wrong with that. It's not so much that today's stars are overpaid — it's just that yesterday's stars were underpaid.

The Rocket never approached the $40,000 a year figure, and he saw action into the late 1950s, when his baseball counterparts, Ted Williams and Mickey Mantle, were earning $100,000 a year. Another Canadiens hero, Boom Boom Geoffrion, played well into the 1960s, when football and basketball also had its $100,000 men. The Boomer never earned more than $35,000 with Montreal.

Why did coaches have so little sympathy for the players' plight? Veteran coach Scotty Bowman says, "I was only making $7,500 a year during the 1965–66 season working the Junior Canadiens. I thought I was greatly underpaid — I was making $7,500 a year and some coaches in the Ontario Hockey Association were getting $11,000." But expansion paved the way for Bowman as well. "About that time, Lynn Patrick came into Montreal and offered me the assistant manager's job with St. Louis Blues, who were a year away from getting into the NHL. ... The money was great — $15,000 — double what I was making." Bowman coached the Blues during their first NHL season in 1967–68, and brought them to the Stanley Cup finals against Montreal.

It was just prior to that season, and only a few months after sanctioning the union, that the players began to use muscle against management. Many players refused to attend training camp, using the excuse that their contracts had run out or else that "they were obscurely worded". Management contested the holdouts, slapping down $500 fines, the highest tariffs in the sport's history. Eagleson set up temporary headquarters in New York during this period, using Ranger Arnie Brown's hotel room. He made and received hundreds of calls to and from players all over North America, running up a phone bill estimated at $3,000. Eskenazi gives an account of the players' "strike":

> ... the Ranger camp was the most significantly struck. ... Five players refused to play, including Brown, Rod Gilbert, and Orland Kurtenbach — three of the club's stars. As Eagleson sat at the phones he bolstered the players' confidence, telling them such things as, "We're all in this together" and "Don't sign for anything just out of fright." That day the Flyers' top draft choice, Ed Van Impe, was a holdout. So were the Penguins' top two choices, Earl Ingarfield and Al MacNeil. Tim Horton, the anchor of Toronto's defense, didn't show up. Neither did Norm Ullman, Detroit's star, nor Pat Stapleton, Ken Wharram, and Pit Martin of the Black Hawks.

The NHLPA survived its first teething pains, and players proved that organized muscle could move mountains. Gone were the days when players had to show up at training camp in university football jerseys or threaten to join Father David Bauer's Canadian National Team as a ploy to improve their salaries. Expansion helped too: there were no more prize heifers at the fair, only fringe players. If first draft choice defenceman A of the Black Hawks was getting $12,000 a year, Eagleson told defenceman B of the Rangers to hold out for $15,000.

The net effect of Eagleson's efforts was threefold. He was expanding his own knowledge of athletic management, which made his one-to-one dealings with the owners on behalf of his personal clients much stronger. Improving his clients' welfare gradually forced up the overall standard of remuneration to a more realistic level. Finally, generating this new cash flow from an expanded league bolstered the games' sagging image in the U.S. Players were now seen as highly paid superstars, ripe to endorse products. As a result, other agents and lawyers fresh from college jumped into the agency business, to the point where there appeared to be more agents than players. This was a complete switch from the situation when, only a couple of years earlier, players had been denied counsel when negotiating.

What was in it for Eagleson? There was prestige. When he dealt with the NHL brass, he was listened to. In 1963, Eagleson had made a proposal to Campbell that would have saved hockey players tax dollars during their peak earning years, a type of deferred income scheme. Eagleson got a nod, a handshake,and a door closed in his face. He told *Maclean's*, "I made my proposal at the meeting in Miami but the owners wouldn't go for it. Then Stafford Smythe says to me, 'Jeez, Eagleson, you were going to save the players $3,500. If you'd only offered to give us half that saving I would have voted for it.'"

One of the first pieces of business he tended to was getting an overall 5 percent increase in players' salaries. Expansion brought four extra teams to the NHL, starting with the 1968 season. Eagleson briefed the players' reps accordingly: "Don't settle for anything less than a 5 percent increase in salary, because if you do you are actually getting a cut: you'll be playing 5 percent more games." A player who was getting the estimated average salary of $22,000 at the time would now be entitled, he calculated, to $23,100 — or else his salary was being reduced. He also increased the per diem meal allowance to $15 from $10.

Another important piece of association business concerned the legal standing of hockey. Was it in fact a business — or a sport? Baseball had on two occasions been declared a sport, not a business, by the U.S. courts — but that was in 1950, before the game had obtained multi-million-dollar television contracts.

By 1967 hockey owners were after a further and clear-cut statement from Washington that professional sports operated outside the antitrust laws of the U.S. If the players were to win their just deserts, hockey had to be declared a business. The four leading sports players' associations met in West Palm Beach to discuss plans to hire a professional Washington lobbyist. Larry Fleischer, who holds a position similar to Eagleson's for the basketball players, and Marvin Miller, executive director of the Baseball Players' Association, voted with Eagleson. E.M. "Matty" Matthews of Washington was asked to take the job. Each association had to approve the appointment before it could become official. The NHLPA supported the resolution.

By the end of 1967, Eagleson's hockey client emporium was a flourishing business, boasting top talent such as Leaf rookie Mike Walton as well as other non-hockey athletes; and his personal investment portfolio was bulging. Financial management companies sprang up at the same time, as did feeder operations such as Haggert's endorsement agency. But Eagleson's personal life suffered, and his political profile drooped.

"The first five or six years of the NHLPA nearly put me in the meadows," he admits. "I made lots of personal errors in judgment and everything else."

While scoring points at one level for the advancement of "socialist" ideas, he was at the same time a victim. The success of the NHLPA gave him even more visibility than some of the players he represented. But handing out hockey tickets to ice cream vendors and store clerks, even if they were reds and not greys, did not generate enough current to mobilize a successful campaign at the grass-roots level. Eagleson suffered a disastrous fall from grace as one of the favourite sons of the Ontario Progressive Conservatives.

In 1967, the province decided to form larger ridings under Bill 83. Lakeshore — Eagleson's riding — was joined to the communities of Mimico, New Toronto, Long Branch, and Etobicoke. The New Democratic Party had been active in Lakeshore, a predominantly working-class area, and was vehemently opposed to the provincial government's joining Lakeshore with Etobicoke.

"The NDP moved in because Eagle had been busy and because he voted for the government's Bill 83," says Morley Kells. This caused the PCs to lose the riding and finished our chances of ever getting it back. The NDP exploited the issue, claiming the big provincial government was stealing the good old Lakeshore."

Eagleson lost Lakeshore by 3,000 votes to the NDP's Pat Lawlor in the 1968 election. In 1972 Kells, also a native son of the Lakeshore, tried to win back the seat for the Tories; he lost by 600 votes. "Eventually the NDP were running strong with 7,000 votes," he says.

The real Armageddon happened on election night. Nancy was interviewed as "the woman behind the candidate". Next morning the papers quoted her as saying: "The reason my husband lost was the Lakeshore has too many poor people."

Blue-collar workers have traditionally voted Tory in Ontario, and Eagleson had blown it at the grass-roots level. Many predicted that he would never catch up in provincial politics. His chief contribution thereafter was as a fund raiser for the party. Only three weeks after his defeat at the hands of the NDP, he was elected to the honorary role of provincial party president, a position to which he was re-elected in 1973.

His political affairs were settled, though not to his own satisfaction. Eagleson turned from the familiar landscape of his childhood to the burning issue of international hockey.

·7·

BALANCE OF POWER

*... There is an obvious distinction
between developing amateur sports and
promoting professional sports. I see a
loop-hole in the definition of the purpose of
Hockey Canada which enables you to get
into the promotion business, to play
impresario; but I do not think that if the
Canadian public were aware of what is
actually going on they would approve of it.*
Robert F. McNeil

The NHL overtly assigned expansion franchises to U.S. cities only, and then stocked them with Canadian talent. This was perceived by many Canadians as another aggressive attempt at preserving, enhancing, and increasing American supremacy over Canadian hockey. Western Canada, in particular, took a defensive nationalistic stance against the Eastern Triangle — Montreal, Toronto, and New York — for dominating the sport, and ugly recriminations came to the attention of the organizers of Pierre Trudeau's first election campaign. It appeared the federal government had created its own white elephant in Vancouver when that city, on the basis of the NHL's expansion plans announced in 1966, built a major league arena (chiefly with federal funds) and then lost its bid for membership in the NHL.

In response to the deepening national polarization, Trudeau made an election promise to investigate all aspects of sport in Canada and, more specifically, to maintain more control over hockey than was currently provided for in the National Fitness and Amateur Sport Act of 1960.

At the same time, both the National Advisory Council on Fitness and Sport and a special CAHA study committee were separately looking into "amateur sport" and the "poor showing" of Canada's nationally financed hockey team, which hadn't won a world championship since 1961. In 1967, former Ontario Liberal leader John

Joseph Wintermeyer assembled some prominent Canadian businessmen — among them CPR President Ian David Sinclair and the late
George Max Bell, a prominent newspaper publisher and oil tycoon
and a major private shareholder in CPR — and formed the Canadian
Hockey Foundation to solicit funds for the national team. It also set up
a scheme to provide Canadian universities with hockey scholarships.
During this early period, Max Bell reportedly raised between $700,000
and $1 million from the corporate sector.

In August 1968, Trudeau made good his election promise, and
together with his new Health and Welfare minister, John Munro,
created the three-member Task Force on Sport. (Federal aid to the
CAHA and the national team was dispensed through the ministry's
Fitness and Amateur Sport directorate.) The commission was headed
by another Toronto businessman, Harold Rea, and included Canadian
skier Nancy Greene and Quebec physician Paul Desruisseaux; its
objectives were to inquire and report on:

1 Prevailing concepts and definitions of both amateur and professional sport in Canada and the effect of pro sport on amateur
sport

2 The role of the federal government in relation to non-governmental
national and international organizations and agencies in promoting and developing Canadian participation in sport

3 Ways in which the government could further improve the extent
and quality of Canadian participation in sport at home and
abroad.

The official report landed on the minister's desk in December, and
was reinforced by Canada's regrettably poor showing at the Stockholm sessions in the world hockey tournament. The report suggested
that the foundation should be disbanded and proposed the formation
of an all-encompassing and wide-reaching structure called "Hockey
Canada". The minister agreed, and on February 24, 1969, articles
of incorporation were filed and the head office set up in Toronto.
The non-profit corporation was to manage and finance the national
hockey teams of Canada, and had as its mandate two important tasks:

1 To support, operate, manage and develop a national hockey team
or teams to represent Canada internationally

2 To foster and support the playing of hockey in Canada, and in

particular to develop the skill and competence of Canadian hockey players in cooperation with other organizations having similar or related objectives.

Following a hockey summit in Ottawa that same month, the second objective was expanded to include not only hockey players but also coaches.

Hockey Canada's first directorate read like a *Who's Who* of Canadian hockey devotees, or "snowbankers" as they were called. This was a title of esteem held by such veterans as NHL president Clarence Campbell: "If you're not a snowbanker, you don't rate among Canadian hockey people and fans." The mini-parliament selected top-drawer officials from the NHL, the Players' Association, government, the CAHA, universities, and the public sector. Their diverse interests ultimately created bickering, and several people were caught in the cross-fire.

"Snowbankers" selected for the board's first directors included the man responsible for the main thrust behind Canada's former national team concept, the Reverend David William Bauer. But not even his devotion to education, nor his nationalism (he was the first to chant, "Let's beat the Russians") combined with federal, CAHA, and provincial dollars could ice a competitive product out of the "amateur ranks". He ran the team from Ottawa and Winnipeg, and eventually his ideas for a "team in being" were subjugated by Hockey Canada's "Proposition 14" (so called because Hockey Canada's board had fourteen members).

"Old" hockey money voiced its opinions through Max Bell, the group's first chairman of the board, and Charles Hay (retired president of CPR and a Gulf Oil executive), its president, as well as Wintermeyer, Sinclair, and Warren Jackson Hopwood, a Winnipeg insurance executive. The NHL was represented by members of two familiar hockey families, the Smythes (by the late Stafford Smythe) and the Molsons (by John David Molson). The Canadian Intercollegiate Athletic Union, much disgruntled by the drain of young Canadians to American colleges via hockey scholarships, sent its president, Marcel Theodore Regimbal of Laurentian University. Health Minister John Munro's department, which was responsible for sport, sent Louis Ernest Lefaive, Director of Fitness and Amateur Sport, and Douglas Fisher (a former M.P., and now a newspaper columnist and adviser to Munro), who was largely responsible for writing up the task force findings. (Fisher later became chairman of Hockey Canada's executive committee.) The CAHA, which held jurisdiction over the Junior A leagues, sent Gordon Wainright Juckes and its president, Earl Philip Dawson, a Liberal MLA in Manitoba. The CAHA's power centred on its membership in the International Ice Hockey Federation (IIHF), in operation since the 1930s and run primarily by John F. "Bunny" Ahearne, a former London, England, travel agent. Until Hockey Canada was established, the IIHF recognized the CAHA as the sole representative of amateur hockey in Canada. In June, the CAHA and Hockey Canada agreed in a draft proposal to divide the country's hockey responsibilities into two areas: domestic and international, respectively. Hockey Canada wanted representation at future IIHF meetings as an "accredited spokesman" and was given responsibility for "selection, management and complete operations in international competition ... which teams are seen to be the 'national' representatives of Canada." Policy, programming, and scheduling of meetings or tournaments came under the aegis of Hockey Canada, "if possible with a voice and vote at IIHF deliberations". Furthermore, any alteration to the IIHF's constitution or by-laws "shall only be undertaken after the attaining of the approval of the Board of Hockey Canada". In turn, the CAHA had sole governing powers over "amateur hockey throughout Canada, as well as technical development and coaching, referee training and development of the international exchange of teams and games which involve hockey below junior level or senior and intermediate hockey, unless these threatened international matches involving Canadian 'national' teams".

Battle lines were drawn between Hockey Canada and the CAHA. Eventually, the complexion of Canada's national team took on a more commercial hue, necessitating the use of the federal sports minister to act as arbitrator when conflicts arose.

Rounding off the original board was Alan Eagleson, said to be "untouched" by the hockey authorities, "especially in the NHL". Eagleson had contributed information to the task force and, as a board member, represented the newly formed players' union. The federal government launched the scheme with a $200,000 grant in November of 1969. Chris Lang, a Toronto consultant who had worked on Munro's task force, was brought in as secretary-treasurer, and the Bruins' Hap Emms was appointed by the minister as managing director (general manager) of the national team.

Events that year decided Canada's future role in world hockey tournaments: Canada's very best or nothing. It was clear to every hockey purist — and to Hockey Canada's board — that the only "sure" way to win was to ice a team made up of pros. The federal task force's finding that the NHL dominated most hockey organizations in Canada appeared to be warning against using pros. Yet Hockey Canada was prepared to bite the bullet, and constructed Proposition 14:

> ... Hockey Canada, itself embracing NHL members, is to markedly improve international showing and the scope and quality of the game in Canada with NHL cooperation but without its domination. ... The Canadians face two problems: First, Hockey Canada must exploit the cooperation offered in getting good young pros by the NHL. ... If this is forthcoming, Canada will not have a sure winner but it will have a more competitive team than it has had for the last few years. The second problem is to decide whether to harden the issue of open competition at the next IIHF meeting. ... The only fair principle for Canada is open competition.

Canada's first attempt at selling the IIHF's Bunny Ahearne on Proposition 14 was made at the Lausanne conference in July 1969. Doug Fisher was appointed spokesman at Hockey Canada's first IIHF summit. His mandate was to propose the idea of fielding a team of pros and amateurs at the March 1970 World Championships in Montreal and Winnipeg. The format was designed after soccer's World Cup.

Already, Charles Hay had stated Canada's position: "Canada has 635 pro hockey players. That's about 30 teams. So what we send over is 31. Other countries send over their best — it's only our very best or nothing." But Hay's proposal for "open competition" was shot down by the IIHF voting members. Instead, another proposal for using nine pros who were not active NHLers received a tie vote. The IIHF's Chairman Ahearne swung the vote in Canada's favour.

In reporting back to Hockey Canada, Fisher relates Ahearne's apparently patronizing acceptance:

> Perhaps the best clue on what to do was given by Mr. Ahearne when he extolled (on the day after he shot down open competition) to Charlie Hay and Hockey Canada: "We [IIHF] would not be doing our duty if we did not help in some way that wonderful dream of Mr. Hay's to end the crisis in Canadian hockey. What a dream.

To accomplish this throughout the whole of Canada — which is a land mass of no small size — is no mean thing.

"We are at the cross-roads," proclaimed Mr. Ahearne. "The progress of our sport proves we did go the right way in the past. Instead of hindering that magnificent goal of Canada in any way we must be prepared to help. This experiment [nine pros for Canada] will be for one year only. We shall have a further twelve months then to decide which main road we'll continue to travel."

If Canada decides it won't get on the road at all after 1970 unless there is open competition one could not be surprised, after watching him in action, to find Mr. Ahearne out directing the IIHF traffic along that road.

By the end of 1969 the forces of Canadian nationalism had united against Ahearne. The CAHA's biggest task would be to get round Ahearne and win some regular competition for Canada's players and its snowbankers. But would the Finns and Swedes compromise their purity? Would playing against a team of Canadian pros endanger their qualification in the 1972 Sapporo Olympics? "Players participating in the Soccer World Cup, in which professionals played, were all ineligible for Olympic games," International Olympic Committee president Avery Brundage had ruled.

At stake were the reputations of approximately 700 Canadian pro players (perhaps ineligible for international competition) and the chance to repair Canada's national pride, which had been severely punctured in world hockey tournaments.

Former Soviet National coach Anatoli Tarasov told a Toronto paper: "Since 1963, the Soviet Union has whipped Canada in the world hockey championships. I think that's why the Canadians didn't show up in 1968 and the following years." Tarasov had been spreading the word rapidly about the growing Russian influence in hockey at the Canadian teams' expense. In 1969 four U.S.S.R. hockey defencemen, Victor Kuzkin, Alexander Ragulin, Vitaly Davidov, and forward Vyacheslav Starshinov, were proclaimed by the world hockey press the world's best for the seventh time in a row. The Soviet Selects had in fact surpassed the earlier accomplishments of the Canadians (who had won the Olympic Games and world championships five times in a row from 1924 to 1932, but who had suffered badly many times since). Not one veteran Canadian player had become a champion five times in a row.

While the format of Canada's future participation in international hockey was being raked over the coals, the drama unfolding at Hockey Canada headquarters in Ottawa was equally volatile.

Hap Emms had held his general manager portfolio only a few months when he was pitched into controversy over his responsibilities in shaping the national team. In a progress report written on August 7, 1969, he reported, "Ken Dryden has signed a three-year contract ... and all written requests for a try-out at the training camps have been assessed and dealt with." He indicated a certain disappointment with the board's efforts:

> I sincerely feel that all members of the committee who attended the IIHF meeting in Switzerland are to be commended for their tremendous efforts in trying to obtain for Canada a more equitable deal, but I understand the final decisions that were made have left us in a less favourable position than we were prior to the meeting. ... I have been informed from a reliable source that Mr. Munro has been given to understand that I have not been fulfilling my obligations as managing director of Hockey Canada. Obviously this information must have been given to Mr. Munro by some member of the board. While I do not concur I would appreciate it if any member of the board could factually point out to me where this has occurred. ... It was suggested to me at the first meeting that we try to hire as many of last year's personnel as possible. This we have tried to do but it appears that some members of the board are in disagreement with some of the people that I have hired. If such is the case then I believe that the board's choice of managing director was probably not the best one.

Emms resigned that same month.

The pot was on the boil now and there was no turning it off. On January 2, 1970, Ahearne held an emergency IIHF executive meeting in Geneva to discuss scheduling the world championships and, more important, to settle the question of Olympic eligibility if pros were used. Canada had to decide whether it should stage the 1970 games and accept Ahearne's trial offer of icing nine pros and then withdraw from competition until rules on using pros were officially changed.

On January 3, the Russians said they interpreted the International Olympic Committee's ruling against soccer using pros as also applying to hockey, and said they therefore refused to participate in the

1970 world championships. (To most countries, the IOC ruling was a moot point; they appeared not to object to Canada's intentions.) The same day, Hay was told by the IIHF directorate that an accommodation had been made which permitted Canada alone to use pros. "But the very next morning, the tournament was taken away from Canada and put in Sweden," says Lang. "It had been a unilateral decision, so Canada withdrew altogether." Lang says Ahearne's decision to move the world championships to Sweden was just his way of skirting the issue of using pros.

Hockey Canada had to pay expenses of $367,000 to Winnipeg Enterprises and the Montreal Forum for cancellation of the arenas. Father David Bauer's eight-year "noble experiment" died of national causes. Hay's rule that "every Canadian should be permitted a chance to play for his country" permitted Alan Eagleson, as head of the NHLPA, to eventually dominate all aspects of Canadian hockey abroad.

On January 4, Munro made public the decision arrived at collectively by the CAHA and Hockey Canada: there would be no world tournament in March. Canada, the host nation, was forfeiting projected revenues of $600,000 and opting out of world hockey.

During Canada's two-year hiatus from international matches, several important changes occurred in Hockey Canada's executive. Stafford Smythe (then board director) was arrested on June 17, 1971, along with his friend and business associate of twenty-five years, Harold Ballard. Smythe was charged with defrauding Maple Leaf Gardens of $249,000 and stealing $146,000 in cash and securities from the Gardens. He was also charged under the Canadian Income Tax Act with evading taxes on income of $289,372. Shortly before he was to stand trial on the tax charges, Smythe died of perforated stomach ulcers. He was fifty years old.

Smythe's nationalistic fervour had never waned, and could only be matched in degree by that of Hockey Canada president Charles Hay. Hay's early contribution with CAHA's longtime secretary-manager Gordon Juckes (later appointed lifetime IIHF member) in laying the groundwork for a "friendly" round-robin series in Leningrad and Moscow in 1969 with Russian, Czech, and Swedish authorities was to prove crucial to Canada's eventual use of NHL pros.

Hay took ill but, shortly before he did, Hockey Canada was granted status as a registered charitable foundation, and it was reported IIHF accepted Canada back into international competition. (Other reports say that Canada didn't officially return to the IIHF until several years later.) The foundation elected a separate board of directors and within a year raised just under half a million dollars in public donations. By August 1971, Hockey Canada's board announced its withdrawal from the '72 Olympics.

Before Hay took a brief leave of absence, he asked that Hockey Canada hire a management consulting firm from Edmonton, M & M Systems Research Ltd., to monitor the function of Hockey Canada and report to the board. In a study conducted between January 1969 and May 1972, called the "Organizational Development of Hockey Canada", M & M describes Hockey Canada's "marketing function":

> Because it is HC's aim to be financially self-sufficient as soon as possible, the HC organization must develop its marketing capability to a high degree. To be financially self-sufficient, HC must be able to successfully market international hockey, skills improvement courses, coaches' certification courses, university tournaments, and HC products (jackets, etc.) to domestic and foreign consumers.

If indeed it was the intent of Hockey Canada to become "financially self-sufficient", it is not difficult to understand why Eagleson assumed a major role from his position in what M & M called a "volunteer Board of Directors". While the firm warned the directors to "beware of conflicts of interest," it went on to describe the "management philosophy concerning the volunteer":

> ... Because the volunteer does not receive any direct form of financial remuneration a somewhat different management approach may be required. ... In order to gain his support it may be practical (and realistic) to assume that this support will only be forthcoming provided he can see certain returns accruing to himself or his associates as a direct result of his involvement. By assuming "everyone is in it for what they can get out of it", a management approach to the utilization of the volunteer may be developed.

M & M said the following suspicions were expressed in "formal and informal discussions with persons directly and indirectly associated with HC". Names were withheld, but during an interview former Hockey Canada chairman Doug Fisher filled in the blanks:

> [Fisher] is using HC to further his journalistic interests in the unfolding history of sports.

[Lang] is using HC to develop entrepreneurial opportunities and a science of sports management.

[Hay] is using HC as a hobby and as an alternative to retirement from business.

[Eagleson] is using HC to make personal contacts which will have social and commercial value.

[Regimbal] is using HC to pursue a career in hockey development and coaching.

[Lefaive] is using HC to pursue his personal dreams for the reformation of society through sport.

[Lefaive] is using HC to impose his values on others.

The [CAHA] organization is using HC to get government grants.

The [NHL] organization is using HC and its international connections as a front organization to pursue their own commercial interests in international hockey.

The [federal government] is using HC as a buffer to protect it from all the latent political problems and dangers associated with hockey in Canada.

The consultants are using HC to make a lot of money.

In short, the thrust of Hockey Canada's emphasis was on image and financial solvency.

One of Hay's last acts before taking his leave of absence was to name Harry Sinden as manager-coach of the proposed national team.* Eagleson was parachuted in to take over part of Sinden's job and given *carte blanche* in pruning the new national team — thirty-five All-Canadian pro NHL players.

The decision to make Eagleson *chargé d'affaires* of the September Series was never official. Had there not been a players' union, the major league owners would have held veto power over the series; but, as head of the union, Eagleson was in the most powerful position. Immediately after the announcement in April 1972 of an eight-game series that would see a team of NHL All-Stars pitted against the Soviet

---

*Before quitting his job as coach of the Bruins, Sinden helped the team win its first Stanley Cup in twenty-nine years; but when he asked the Bruins to increase his salary from $22,000 to $30,000, they would go no higher than $25,000. He quit hockey and left to go into business with an old school chum, David Stirling of Stirling-Homex, a company in the modular home field. However, before Sinden went to Hockey Canada, Stirling-Homex went bankrupt.

Union Selects, Eagleson started to call the shots. Although Hockey Canada formed a nine-man steering committee to run the first September Series, Eagleson cooperated very little with it. He hired trainers and a staff of fifteen "to keep the players going". His personal coterie was called Team Five: "Look, I can trust the guys who work for me — Haggert and Mike Cannon," he said. Bob Haggert was paid $5,000 and named administrative aide. Haggert had joined Eagleson a few years earlier as president of Sports Representatives Limited, a company handling endorsements and off-ice employment for players in public relations and advertising campaigns. Mike Cannon, who ran the players' association in Eagleson's office, was not paid, nor was Eagleson. Harry Sinden was approved by the steering committee as head coach and general manager, a job which paid him $10,000. He was assisted by John Bowie Ferguson, a retired Montreal Canadien, who was paid $5,000. Team Five ran the entire show, including selecting hotels and making travel arrangements.

Lou Lefaive was the top government rep on the steering committee. He was said to be somewhat bitter about being left out of the picture. "Once we had named Harry Sinden as coach and Eagleson became almost a self-appointed general manager, the rest of us really didn't see the bloody team until they showed up on the ice." Lefaive said he didn't speak to Eagleson more than a couple of times during the entire series: "The relationship between us and Alan was almost one of antagonism, constant antagonism, and part of this was that Alan was incapable of accepting constructive criticism. Anybody who suggested that there was something wrong was immediately labelled as being a Communist. So we could never sit down and discuss problems with Alan. ... If he saw a problem, he just went ahead and solved it."

It wasn't until 1974, when Lefaive had to deal with the Russians, that he appreciated Eagleson's efforts. Eagleson produced unprecedented gains in opening up communication channels with stoic Russian sports officials who, he reported, "had the diplomacy of a sledgehammer". The press idolized his performance, attributing his winning manner to an intrinsic ability to shoot first and ask questions later. They compared his decision-making tactics with those of Henry Kissinger, who was portrayed by the press as a lone cowboy who rides into town without guns and wins everybody over.

Chris Lang says it was "Eagleson's fighting the Russians" that caused the players to take an interest. " 'Christ, somebody cares!'

they said — that alone gave them a reason to care. . . . He puts all that time and effort in and with his skills, his negotiating skills as a lawyer and his reputation. . . . I'd argue he's left billions of dollars on the table by playing around in international hockey, and that's his contribution as a Canadian. . . . I think he's one of the most typical Canadians of all . . . he is what Canada is; Trudeau isn't, Eagleson is.''

Hockey Canada's Doug Fisher also felt Eagleson's role in shaping Canada's future in the hockey brotherhood warranted the All-Canadian medal: ''Mr. Eagleson is probably more the archetypal Canadian than men like Mitchell Sharp and Maurice Strong.'' The importance of Eagleson's influence cannot be overstated. Fisher says, ''We used Eagleson but we would never admit to it.'' It was Fisher's opinion that The Eagle used the series to ''push the NHL players to glory first, then money''. But at the same time, the government, through Fisher, used Eagleson. Fisher wrote to Eagleson:

> None of us is either all altruism or all chicanery, and often selfishness in purpose can be effective in aiding much grander principles. You know the principle I want advanced and entrenched because you share it, in your own fashion. This is that Canadians should have the chance on regular occasions to see the very best Canadian players play the very best of other nations — nation versus nation. And we've made great progress in the past decade to getting what we want for Canada, in the face of the Ahearne domination on the one hand [and] the deep-seated belief in pro hockey among owners, and to a degree among all executives and most players, that the best model for hockey at its best is not nation against nation but the best club teams against the best club teams. The leverage for what Canada has gotten has been largely provided by the NHL Players' Association through your presence and negotiations, aided by the clout of federal backing.

Selling a ''made in Canada'' product became Eagleson's one-man show. With federal dollars Eagleson was able to push ahead at any cost. Hockey Canada expanded in all lines of merchandising activity: hockey books, films, and jackets. Hockey Canada management operations were headed by Hay, Chief Executive Officer, and Allan Scott, Vice-President, Operations. Immediate plans were made to recruit a fulltime comptroller-administrator. ''This individual could be used immediately, and particularly when large amounts of money are scheduled to pass through the HC office in connection with the

September Series. This individual should have the capability to become a full-time administrator, allowing Christopher Lang to function more as a sports management consultant in the long run.''

In the ''long run'' Lang did just that. Christopher Lang and Associates is today a thriving sports-management consulting firm in Toronto.

Because of the cost of upgrading the pro's image abroad and changing the thrust of Canada's international involvement towards ''developing HC as an economically viable organization'', and since in essence Canada's representative team was now a joint NHLPA-NHL endeavour supplemented with federal dollars, the *raison d'être* of the CAHA was threatened. It still retained voting power in the IIHF because it looked after domestic amateur hockey, but had little pull now with the national team in either world championships or nation-versus-nation matches. This was a tremendous loss of face — and of federal revenue. The CAHA's attempts to play a role in the upcoming 1972 September Series were met with strenuous opposition from Hockey Canada management, and particularly from Eagleson. Most of the problem arose because the CAHA was cut out of revenues generated by radio, television, and film rights. Eagleson didn't fail to point this out in a letter to Joe Kryczka, a young, articulate lawyer and president of the CAHA at the time final details were arranged for the September Series. In effect, he told Kryczka: ''Keep off my turf!''

Eagleson's real success, however, was his dealings with the owners. At a time when their own expansions threatened to water down the quality of the product, he persuaded them to agree to a bill of goods which promised to severely undermine their box office by the pizzazz of an ''us-versus-them'' patriotic showdown. ''It was the support of the public in 1972 when we were putting together the first Canada-Russia series, the groundswell of public opinion, that forced the NHL to my side of the street to let the players play for their country,'' he says.

Having already wrested the balance of power from the patriarchy running the hockey cartel in 1967, and having brought security and wealth to his clients, aided ''by the owners' own greediness through expansion,'' Eagleson was now vulcanizing the powers invested in him. He successfully overturned a decision made by NHL President Clarence Campbell, who proclaimed that no player would be permitted to play in the proposed first nation-versus-nation match with the Russians. Eagleson told Campbell, ''My personal clients will play for Canada regardless of whether or not their club owners permit them to."

But before the Hay-Sinden team could gain momentum, Hay took his temporary leave, and Eagleson stepped in to top Hockey Canada's pyramid. A corporate flowchart places him just below the chairman's office. At the same time that the government representative, Doug Fisher, Hay, and the CAHA's Gordon Juckes were nudging Europeans for a "friendly" round of shinny with Canadian pros in 1969, Eagleson "ranged around Europe trying on his own to set up a series between the NHL players and the Russians," says Fisher. Not until a players' association semi-annual meeting in 1972 did Eagleson have enough signatures to guarantee that he could deliver the pros. After attending a meeting in Prague of Canadian and Russian officials in March, Eagleson announced there would be an eight-game series between the two countries in September. Eagleson describes his negotiations with the Russians as "clearly a test of will and having the courage of your convictions". He says, "I was a David fighting Goliath."

Eagleson was an ardent nationalist. He believed that hockey, as Canada's national pastime, deserved to make the same inroads soccer had, and that the ones to reap the profits — or at least to control the distribution of same — should be the players and not agencies such as the IIHF, CAHA, HC, NHL, the public sector or the federal government — all the constituencies forming Hockey Canada. Furthermore, Eagleson wanted to see his clients gain exposure and international prestige by playing a team outside the NHL, ultimately giving them more clout over their owners.

Certainly an injection of Canadian nationalism would unite the players. But he couldn't do it without the government, and his position as a director helped to ensure his success.

News of Eagleson's collaboration with the owners surfaced. He had drawn up an agreement between the players' association and the NHL executive which provided that neither group would participate in international hockey meets unilaterally. Doug Fisher suggests that Eagleson had to make a few compromises:

No sooner was the coup announced than it became apparent that the NHL owners, particularly the American ones, were much less enthusiastic about the series than was Mr. Eagleson. He used his bond with the players to dragoon the recalcitrant owners into line.

Eagleson was persuasive — to the point of promising that half of the net revenues would go into the NHL players' pension fund, thus taking the burden off NHL owners.

In *Hockey Night in Moscow,* Jack Ludwig writes:

> Not till this year, 1972, were we able to find a formula to bring together on one team the thirty-five best professional hockey stars who were still Canadian citizens.
>
> To do that Canada, the nation, had to deed a certain amount of power to Clarence Campbell, President of the NHL, and, with him, to Alan Eagleson, Executive Director of the NHL Players' Association.

Campbell, however, later suggested that the September Series couldn't have happened without Eagleson:

> ... There was no formal Collective Bargaining Agreement between the League and the Players' Association in 1972 at the time of the first Soviet series, so that his cooperation and support was paramount. Although he was not the leading participant in the original planning and organization of that Series, he certainly was the most dominating figure in the marshalling of the Team and the conduct of the Series — not only by his famous gestures in Moscow — but for genuine contributions to the overall success of the series financially through his business and professional contacts.

The apparent conflicts of interest were clearly set out. In spite of Campbell's deference to Eagleson's power, Eagleson, while representing players, while directing the players' union, and while expanding Hockey Canada's merchandising activities (and in turn those of his friends) was forsaking "pure" nationalism. The match couldn't be called "our best against their best" if some top-calibre amateurs were left out, or if some top Canadians were rejected because they had jumped to the World Hockey Association,* a rival league of the NHL. Yet NHL monopolistic endeavours were given priority. Ludwig writes:

> [When] with Eagleson's implicit blessing, [Campbell] decreed that players who "defected" to the newly-formed WHA would not be

---

* The World Hockey Association was incorporated in Delaware on July 10, 1971 (see p. 106). It operated without using the reserve clause (see p. 100) and had as its first officers Dennis Murphy, a California businessman, Gary L. Davidson, a California attorney, and Donald L. Regan, a law partner of Davidson's.

eligible to play for Team Canada, not even Prime Minister Pierre Elliott Trudeau could shake him. Bobby Hull was banned from playing with Team Canada; soon J.C. Tremblay was out — Gerry Cheevers and Derek Sanderson were never quite in. The guys on Team Canada made little protest. No team strike was threatened unless Hull, etc., were included on the National best: Prime Minister Trudeau issued a caveat against the privileged "option" clause (the WHA didn't have one) that keeps players tied to the team they've signed with, but Campbell ignored him — and prevailed. At the time nobody was really shook up by the exclusion of Hull and the others — except, perhaps, the Winnipeg Jets who looked for tons of free publicity from Bobby's play in the eight-game series. Conn Smythe not only didn't regret the exclusion of Hull, he went further: "As an old hockey man, I am proud that there are no contract breakers representing our country."*

In April 1972, when the eight-game Moscow-Canada series was formally agreed to at the world tourney in Prague, Canada had been out of international and Olympic hockey for two years, and yet the federal government, since Hockey Canada's inception, had so far invested $1 million into Hockey Canada. M & M reported that:

The Federal government ... desires the September Series to be a significant national and international event. Any controversy or mismanagement of this event which detracts from this objective will have serious repercussions.

The September Series presents an ideal opportunity to establish the national and international image of Hockey Canada. Thus, decisions must be made concerning exactly what image HC should convey.

An image which suggests that Hockey Canada is a "Federal Government agency" or a "tool of the NHL" is unsatisfactory. ...

Hockey Canada, through its Board and Governors, is supposed to represent all the major constituents of hockey in Canada. Anything which gives the appearance that the September Series is dominated by the interests of one or two constituents such as the

---

* Eagleson and the NHLPA had endorsed the recommendations of the task force to abolish hockey's reserve clause, yet apparently didn't make use of the opportunity of federal pressure to remove it. Not until 1981 would players' collective-bargaining units seek complete free agency.

NHL or NHL Players' Association is bad for the long range image and interests of Hockey Canada.

Fisher wrote in *International Perspectives*:

If the NHL owners wished some stability in their labour force during their war with the WHA they needed, at the least, Mr. Eagleson's neutrality. This he gave in a general way, and he did not antagonize the NHL by signing many of his own clients to WHA contracts.

The actual role Eagleson played in the September Series was later questioned by Robert F. McNeil, a Toronto freelance broadcaster and writer. In a long letter to Doug Fisher, McNeil refers to Fisher's article, suggesting that Eagleson's "us[ing] his bond with the players to dragoon the recalcitrant owners into line" was construed by McNeil as an act of "extortion":

Canadian players had individual contracts with individual club owners in the U.S., contracts which prohibited their playing for another team, including a Canadian national team. They had had the option of playing for a team representing Canada but they chose to enter contracts to play for U.S. professional clubs. In order for Hockey Canada to employ them as our representatives, they would have to be released from those contracts. The U.S. owners did not want to release them, but they submitted to extortion.

To this day, no one in Hockey Canada likes to admit how quickly it happened, but suddenly Eagleson was zooming past the entire hockey community with the press recording his every move. His dedicated efforts proved him a worthy snowbanker, and his reward was the power to call the shots in Canada's international hockey; just one more in an already impressive collection of crowns.

GETTING THE STEAK TO
MATCH THE SIZZLE

*It's a 90-10 business with Al. He gets
90 percent and we keep 10 percent . . . just
to make sure we have an easier time
handling our money.*
Bobby Orr

By his thirty-eighth birthday, Eagleson had completely reconstructed his image. He allowed his hair to grow longer, shaved his Keystone cop sideburns to above-ear-lobe length, bought wire-rim glasses, and began wearing fashionably flared trousers. The jewellery he began wearing then — Mike Walton's Stanley Cup ring, and the Canadian Football League Players All-Star Game pocket watch from client Jimmy Young — will likely become his grandchildren's keepsakes. Gold cufflinks on French cuffs and a diamond tie pin added a dash of panache to the Robert Alan Eagleson image.

But he wasn't there yet. He hadn't made the millionaire mark, and in 1973 he wasn't even listed in the *Financial Post's Directory of Directors*.* He said he didn't worry about becoming a millionaire, he wanted to see his client-friends well off. In 1967 he had promised to make Orr a millionaire by thirty; now he said Bobby would be there in one more year, "when he turns twenty-five". Money wasn't any problem. "If I ever need to become a millionaire I could easily ask Bobby to help me out, and vice-versa. I have access to more money than I need." He was talking about Orr's money. The Orr-Eagleson partnership was also a big brother-little brother relationship. After their contracts with him were signed, Eagleson's clients turned

---

* Eagleson was listed in 1975 and 1976, but did not appear again until 1980.

over their cheques to Sports Management Ltd., Eagleson's wholly owned personal financial consulting company set up in 1972 to handle his clients' financial affairs. The company will invest an athlete's money, set up estate plans, work out details of a will, develop insurance coverage, collect royalties, and establish trust funds. It promises to make living as simple as possible for those who do not care to be bothered by the intricacies of money management. By the end of fiscal 1972, Eagleson reported that he negotiated $7 million in contracts.

When contracts cover more than one year, Eagleson's fees are prorated. Some of the new contracts in 1973 were for:

- Mike Walton, Minnesota Fighting Saints: $100,000–$125,000 a year over three years, for a total salary of $405,000, plus a number of possible bonuses which could push the grand total to $440,000
- World figure-skating champion Karen Magnussen, Ice Capades: $500,000 for three years
- Paul Henderson, Toronto Maple Leafs: $100,000 for one year
- Darryl Sittler, Toronto Maple Leafs: $750,000 over five years
- Syl Apps, Pittsburgh Penguins: $750,000 over five years
- Bill Harris, New York Islanders: $300,000 for three years
- Rick Middleton, New York Rangers: $250,000 for three years
- Jim Evenson, Ottawa Rough Riders: $140,000 for three years
- Jimmy Young, B.C. Lions: $125,000 for three years
- Mike Torres, Montreal Expos: $35,000 for one year

Other clients he rendered services to that year included Mike Pelyk, Rick Kehoe, Marcel Dionne, Dale Tallon, Jim McKenny, Glen Goldup, Peter Martin, Steve Shutt, Steve Smear, and Bob Dailey.

In 1971 Eagleson had negotiated another deal for Bobby Orr — a five-year, $1 million contract with the Bruins. Orr's contract included a deferred-income clause. Canadian clients can purchase income averaging annuity contracts (IAACs). If Bobby Orr, for example, earns $200,000 in his first year he can then purchase an IAAC by paying $175,000 to an insurance company. He can deduct this $175,000 from income, leaving him with a taxable income for the year of only $25,000. This annuity pays a specific amount each month for the rest of his life; only the amount he gets in a particular year is taxable in that year. An athlete whose career lasts for ten years can thus pay his taxes like an ordinary businessman — there is no single year in which his entire income is taxable, and there are no peaks and valleys to his tax. The plan is not available in the U.S. There, the hockey player's only alternative is to tell his general manager, "Don't give me $75,000 all at once, defer it." An athlete would likely prefer that his money sit with an insurance company in Canada rather than with a U.S. agent.

More liberal tax deductions are allowed for an athlete in the U.S., but during his NHL career, Orr always retained residence in Canada by preference: he forfeited a sizeable tax saving by doing so. In Canada, the income of most athletes is considered income from employment; they may only write off against their employment income items specifically allowed by the Income Tax Act. In the U.S., Orr could have deducted Eagleson's fees, but he could not have done so in Canada. A Canadian athlete is taxed in Canada only if he is a resident; a U.S. citizen is taxed regardless of where he resides or works. For example, Mike Torres of the Boston Red Sox, another Eagleson client, is a U.S. citizen who came to Canada to play for the Montreal Expos. He lived in Canada all year round, and retained U.S. citizenship but earned money in Canada; he had to pay Canadian as well as U.S. taxes. The reverse is not true, however. The Canada-U.S. Tax Convention, 1942,* a treaty which prevents double taxation, allows a credit for one country against another, with the player paying the higher rate: if the U.S. tax is $20,000 and the Canadian tax is $30,000, Canada gets the extra $10,000.

Eagleson's practice of incorporating hockey players and then including their playing income in that corporation caused a major rift in his operations in 1970. Lyman MacInnis, an accountant with the firm of Touche Ross of Toronto, had a number of mutual clients with Eagleson until 1970 when the whole area of incorporating came under fire. One client they shared was Bobby Orr. "I think Bobby Orr included his playing income under Bobby Orr Enterprises [a private investment company set up in 1968] and most of Eagleson's other clients did, but none of mine did," MacInnis says. At the time MacInnis was a partner with the firm of Coopers and Lybrand. "I was the auditor and financial guide for Bobby Orr Enterprises and worked with a number of other clients of Eagleson's as well. In 1970 the incorporation thing came to a head and I finally said, 'Al, I'm not going to sign any more tax returns or any more financial statements

* An updated version of the Convention is in the works. In September 1980 the U.S. Treasury signed a convention (treaty) in Washington and both governments exchanged documents to be ratified.

that have hockey income in them because I don't think it's legal.'
At that point Al took all of his clients away from me and gave them
to another firm, Arthur Anderson." MacInnis says they remained
friends; it was just a "gentleman's disagreement". "He [Eagleson]
said in his opinion you could include playing income in a corporation
and I said in my opinion you can't."*

Orr was controlling shareholder of Bobby Orr Enterprises but had
little input into its day-to-day operations. By 1978, the company's
income was around $400,000, from real estate holdings, personal
endorsements, investments, and a 4.5 percent share in Pony Sporting
Goods Ltd. Other enterprises included his share in the (Orr-Walton)
Owaissa Hockey Camp in Orillia, of which Eagleson was part owner.
The company turned over annual profits of approximately $30,000 by
that time. Walkerheights Developments Ltd., a company in which Orr
held an 85 percent interest (Eagleson held 10 percent and Walton 5
percent), was valued at $350,000 in 1978. Orr also held a 40 percent
interest in Nanjill Investments Ltd. (Eagleson held a 40 percent
interest, and Walton 20 percent); it was valued at $200,000 in 1978.

Eagleson spent about half his week looking after Orr's affairs
personally, a job for which he was well paid, depending on the
services involved. One report estimated his fee at $40,000 a year.
Some, like Bill McMurtry, Q.C., a lawyer Eagleson helped bring into
the firm in 1969, felt Orr and the other clients were too dependent on
Eagleson.

McMurtry, a brother of Ontario Attorney General Roy McMurtry,
says, "I used to worry when Bobby was quite young, I didn't think he
was developing in certain areas. ... I remember spending time with
him. He has a strong personality, a native intelligence, but he was very
sensitive. ... I had a feeling he'd come of age, be his own man one
day." At the height of his career, Orr married Peggy Wood — a speech
therapist from Michigan. "Eagleson approved of the match, said she
was good for him." (The Orrs have two sons, Darren and Brent.
"Neither of them have ever been on skates," says Orr.) McMurtry
says, "Bobby just liked to play hockey ... he never lived, just played
... in that sense the association with Eagleson was very good for him
because Al took away all those responsibilities for him."

* Lyman MacInnis says the major point of contention in the Bobby Orr tax case
(1981) is the question of including playing income in a corporation. Revenue
Canada believes Orr owes approximately $500,000 in taxes on his salary from 1971
to 1976.

When Orr won his $1 million Boston Bruins contract in the summer of 1972, he was written up in *Sports Illustrated* as a superstar whose status matched that of Bobby Hull, Stan Mikita, and Gordie Howe. (At nineteen Orr was voted Rookie of the Year; in his second year he won the James Norris trophy as the league's best defenceman, and he won it again in 1969.) This provided excellent leverage for his agent, who was negotiating with the Bruins about injury compensation of $100 a week for a knee operation that restricted Orr from working during the summer months in 1972. Eagleson apparently sent a letter to the Bruins asking for the money due Orr. There was an alleged agreement between the players' association and the owners, stating that if a player is injured during the season he must be compensated if he can't work in the off-season.

Another report said that a batch of correspondence had gone out that same summer to general managers of twelve WHA teams, and that Eagleson was advising them, "When Orr's five-year contract with the Bruins expires in 1976 I would suspect Bobby Orr will sign for $2.5 million in the summer of '76." Giving Eagleson a free hand with his money was probably part of the reason Orr was a millionaire at twenty-five. Eagleson enjoyed nothing more than meeting a business challenge head on. Orr's reputation gave credibility to some unusual financial deals. Although Eagleson maintained that his client's investments were very conservative, he also, apparently, wasn't reluctant to back a deal when it came his way. One afternoon, for example, while relaxing on his yacht in front of his Mississauga home, Eagleson received a call from an old newspaper contact and family friend, Eddie Waring. "I told him about Esso using soccer players to promote cars at service centres," Waring says, "and did he want to lease the NHLPA licensing rights and Bobby Orr's name for the same purpose? The association stood to get $500,000 from Esso. By the time I got back to Esso about finalizing the details, Esso refused to say why, but had gone ahead on its own. I told Esso both Eagleson and Orr were partners in the deal, had made the agreement with Esso, and now the oil company was pulling out, trying to renege. Esso backed down and paid $500,000 in a settlement," says Waring. "Eagleson didn't have to do a thing!"

Eagleson's reputation in Toronto was rising, and his expertise was frequently called upon by many Toronto politicians.

Metro Toronto Chairman Paul Godfrey remembers first meeting Eagleson in 1963, when Eagleson received the nomination to run in the federal riding of York West. "He's a social as well as political friend," says Godfrey. "I cherish Al's and Nancy's company. . . . I also value his political advice: he's the type of person who makes things happen — closest thing to a human bombshell that God could create, vibrant, daring — God only makes an Al Eagleson once in every thousand years." Politically, Godfrey figures Eagleson is "pretty high up provincially and federally — could have any constituency in Canada he wanted to . . . he wouldn't have to run in Toronto, he would have me as a supporter in a riding anywhere."*

Evidence of the support Eagleson had in provincial party politics was apparent in 1973, when he was re-elected to the presidency of the Ontario Progressive Conservatives. The vote was 540 to 298. On the next day, a Toronto newspaper reported that he won by a "grudging majority". It was suggested that the reason his only opponent (Sharon Morrison, a twenty-three-year-old school teacher) won so many votes was that "it was the only time in four years any of the 1,400 members had a chance to protest the way the association had been run."

Another story illustrative of Eagleson's political clout concerns the time Toronto wanted to introduce major league baseball to the city in the early 1970s. Eagleson's connections with City Hall and the type of influence he carries in the sports market made him a valuable team player for John Labatt Ltd. of London, Ontario. The early bidding war to secure a franchise from the National League was between Labatt's and two or three other financiers, including Sydney Cooper, a former president and chief shareholder of Pitts Engineering Construction Ltd. of Toronto. Cooper set up Canadian Baseball Co. Ltd. in 1974; its sole purpose was to operate a major league baseball club.

It was during this period that Donald McDougal, Labatt's former president, formed his impressions of Eagleson. "The first person I spoke with about the possibility of our pursuing a league franchise was Al Eagleson," he says. "It is his outspokenness and frank manner most people speak about when they deal with him. His one problem — he tends to speak his mind and doesn't weigh the complications . . . he doesn't tolerate Mickey Mouse ways, is basically cautious, but because of his temperament he tends to bully his way through to win on his terms." McDougal remembers a phone call during one of the times he was in Eagleson's office discussing "the baseball thing". "A fellow invited Eagleson to play golf . . . this guy hadn't seen him

---

* On June 17, 1981, Godfrey announced Eagleson was hired by Metro Toronto to fight the Ontario government if the province allowed residents to remain on Toronto Island. Eagleson would be paid from a budget of $250,000 (see p. 219).

for eight or nine years and he was soliciting Eagleson's support for Queen's Counsel. Eagleson told him, 'No bloody way.'" McDougal holds that "people who do not like Al are people who do not know him".

The baseball dealings were an example of the type of behind-the-scenes power position Eagleson operated from. Eagleson's role was strictly as a confidant or consultant to McDougal but he was not Labatt's legal representative; the Toronto firm of Goodman and Goodman was.

"After a few meetings it became apparent Al played a key role," says McDougal. "We didn't need any of the other partners." The Labatt's group included two other partners, newspaper executive Howard Webster and the Canadian Imperial Bank of Commerce. At first, Labatt's tried to get the San Francisco Giants of the National League. The league's asking price for the Giants was $17 million, which included the cost of indemnification the San Francisco club would have to pay the city ($4.5 million for loss of revenue from concessions and parking over the nineteen years left on the contract) and a $500,000 loan to be paid to the National League. Horace Stoneham, who controlled the ownership of the Giants, had a 70 percent share in the club and was asking approximately $12 million for the franchise.

The picture changed significantly when, in late 1975, a San Francisco judge issued an order that the team was not to leave the city. Labatt's tried to persuade the National League to expand to permit a Toronto franchise, arguing that Toronto was the natural rival of the Montreal Expos.

But Labatt's lost the bid. Shortly after that Goodman and Goodman attended the meetings of the Western Division of the American League in Tampa, Florida, and made an application for granting a franchise at the meeting. "As the deal was grinding down to a close, the final bidding for a franchise with the American League was between Labatt's [and] Trevor Eaton of the Toronto law firm of Tory, Tory, who represented a syndicate ..." says Gordon Kirke, a lawyer with Goodman and Goodman.

In the end, Labatt's group won a new franchise and the city got the Toronto Blue Jays, who played their first pro season in 1977. The franchise cost $7 million. Labatt's owns 45 percent, Webster 45 percent, and a subsidiary of the Canadian Imperial Bank of Commerce 10 percent of the team.

In 1973, Eagleson was reputed to be "one of the most influential figures in Canadian sport'', and had become the most successful hockey attorney in Canada.

And where was the competition? At the time that Eagleson had made it to the number-one position in Canada as counsel, negotiator, and financial consultant to pro athletes, there was hardly a pro around who hadn't retained a spokesman to handle his affairs. Gerry Patterson was doing a profitable business in Montreal, based on the U.S. agency pattern. Two lawyers, Bob Whoolf in Boston and Mark McCormack in Cleveland, were reported to be in first and second place in the States in 1971.

Bob Whoolf Associates, with a staff of three secretaries, a book-keeper, and an accountant, reportedly handled contract negotiations and managed money and endorsements for 300 athletes, all under one roof. Whoolf's assistant Ken Fishkin said in 1977, ''We don't have a fee policy, but it is never more than a straight percentage of 5 percent ... on a $50,000 contract, we receive probably less than $3,000.'' The fee would vary considerably from the highest-paid athletes — basketball players who were earning between ''an average of $120,000 [1978 figures] to the highest ever paid, Lou Al Sinder [now Kareem Abdul-Jabbar], $600,000.'' Football players earn the lowest average salary; and ''Jimmy Connors [tennis] averaged an income of $800,000 in 1977.'' Fishkin explains that before baseball dropped its reserve clause,* ''pro baseball players were just pieces of property. ... Now they can bargain their talents to anyone.'' Only a certain percentage become free agents, however, because the key to free agency is determined by the number of years of service a player has. The *Toronto Star* ran a report saying, ''Whoolf's salary in 1971 was more than the combined wages of the eleven New England Patriot football players he represented.''

By 1973, Cleveland-based lawyer Mark McCormack's International Management Group was reported to be the largest sports agency in the world.† He started with golfer Arnold Palmer‡ in 1960, taking

---

* At one time, all major league sports used the reserve clause in player-owner contracts. It gave the club, which a player was currently tied to, exclusive rights to sign him again for the coming year. The player was held forever on the team's protected list. The reserve clause was virtually eliminated from hockey by 1973.

† In 1981, IMG Sports Management Group with 400 employees and 14 offices in 10 countries, represented 500 athletes, controlled several top-rated international tournaments including Wimbledon, and ran the major national sports events in several European countries.

‡ Golfer Arnold Palmer earns the all-time highest annual income of any athlete with a combined golf and business income of $60 million as of May 1981.

a fee of 10 percent of the purse. By 1970, his higher commissions caused golfer Jack Nicklaus to split from McCormack; his rates were as high as 50 percent, with the average around 25 percent. In an interview with the *Toronto Star*, McCormack explained that he worked on a sliding scale — so much on the first $50,000 and then downward from there. "... On the Gordie Howe contract with Houston, it probably worked out to less than three-fourths of one percent." Howe signed with the WHA's Houston Aeros club in 1973 for $1 million, and his two sons, right out of the juniors, signed for $400,000 each. All were long-term contracts.

When the WHA came on the scene in 1971, it was a players' market; there were too few top players to go around, temporarily causing a downswing in the talent curve, while at the same time pushing salaries up through auctions. "You can't replace a good player," said Eagleson, and quickly sold to the highest bidder.

With the WHA emerging quickly on the heels of the NHL expansion in 1967, followed in turn by the move towards improving players' rights [the WHA operated without the reserve clause], some of the diehards from the sponsorship days never quite recovered. "Before, you were paying for a service a guy can perform," says Imlach. "Somewhere down the line that's been lost ... now you're paying, I don't know for what. ... " Imlach says he remembers all too vividly his first encounter with the WHA. "I was in Buffalo and an agent came in to talk to me about a player. ... I had his record and I told him, 'This is what he did, I don't think he's worth any more money.' Then this guy starts hollering, 'Well, we can get that kind of money from the WHA.' Then things started to hit the fan ... he sat down ... never stopped talking ... $150,000 is what he wanted, but I said, 'That guy is not a $150,000 hockey player, not worth one-third of what you're asking.'

" 'Well, we think he is.' I explained to him about his record. He said, 'I don't care what he did or didn't do, the WHA has offered me X number of dollars for the player; if you don't give it to me he's going to the WHA — it's got nothing to do with how he played. ...' That was it in a nutshell. We had to sign a kid for $100,000 who couldn't even play; had to get them or else the WHA were going to ... that's what boosted salaries out of sight. ..."

It was only natural that agents started saturating the business at that time. During the salary wars a player needed a third party to go to bat for him, distancing the player from any bad feelings from the team's management. But when the agent's or lawyer's personality got mixed up in it, as happened with Eagleson, the player may have ended up worse off simply through association with that lawyer. There were times when Toronto wasn't big enough for both Imlach and Eagleson. Starting with Brewer, Walton, and Brian Conacher, the Eagleson-Imlach feud could always be counted on to liven up a poor season's performance by the Leafs. Imlach admits there were times when he went out of his way to avoid hiring one of Eagleson's clients.

In 1970, Imlach was hired as general manager-coach by an NHL expansion team, the Buffalo Sabres. "When I went to Buffalo, I swore I'd never draft one of Eagleson's clients. ... I didn't, either. I said to hell with it, I'm not getting involved ... it causes you problems so I won't have any problem with him at all. I ran the hockey club that way and it was a pretty good one." *

Imlach claims some of the problem stems from Eagleson's "special" relationships with players. "Eagleson is that type. I say sometimes some of the hockey players would have been better off if they didn't have him. If a player is an emotional and unstable character then he gets in with Eagle, who is an emotional character too, it's like mixing fire and oil ... you'd be a helluva lot better off if you had somebody else. But a stable guy like Sittler needs Eagle ... not Brewer, both of them are too jumpy. Worst thing was to get Eagleson with Walton. Eagle would probably encourage Walton to get into these situations because then it would become something that is front and centre for everybody. ... Eagleson loves the limelight, no question ... he's always fighting me. Again, he's on the other side of the fence, for Christ's sake. ..."

Are Eagleson and Imlach friends?

"No damn way. If [the front office says that], they are not telling the truth, I don't have him as a friend. If I see him someplace I'll sit down and have a drink, whatever ... as far as being a friend, who needs enemies!"

As for other agents, in 1980 Imlach said he thought that the world's biggest agency for hockey players was the partnership of Caplan and Kaminsky. Arthur Kaminsky, a New York attorney, operates A.C.K. Sports Inc.; Norm Caplan, a tax lawyer, runs R.D.S. Sports Ltd. in Montreal. Imlach says Bob Whoolf "doesn't seem to do a heck of a lot in terms of hockey anymore."

---

* Lee Fogolin was the first Eagleson client Imlach hired for the Sabres for the 1974–75 season.

Former Montreal Canadien Ken Dryden was an undergraduate student with Art Kaminsky at Cornell University, and became his first client. Kaminsky's reputation was etched in marble when he arranged a contract estimated at well over $100,000 a year — making Dryden the richest goalie in the history of the game.

Ken Dryden is often critical about what he calls "the dependency existence" most players have with their agents. To some degree he echoes Imlach's arguments. "Players don't learn how to handle money and there is often confusion about where the money went." He says young players are often tossed sales pitches like: "You're only a twenty-year-old kid, and all of a sudden you have a $50,000 signing bonus and won't know what to do with it." There's a pattern to what follows: "At first the kid thinks he's being responsible; 'Look, Mom and Dad, I'm not going to blow this money, I'm dealing with Mr. Eagleson, and he put me on an allowance ...'; gradually they get used to being told what to do; they never learn."

Besides running interference between a player and his boss, most agents or lawyers present prospective clients with a whole package of services: (1) contract negotiations — for a percentage; (2) estate planning; and (3) investment counseling and related services. The principal reason for hiring a spokesman is for the "creative contracting" service performed. On top of the basic salary and signing bonus commitments, much of the cash flow comes from the performance bonus or option system set up by the team's general manager. And it is usually complicated, only limited by imagination.

To begin with, a team prefers to start on the basis of salary plus bonus, because future contract negotiations start from salary only. For example, with a $120,000, two-year contract, in the first year a hockey player could get a $50,000 signing bonus plus $30,000 for his first year's salary, a total of $80,000. But his *salary* is still only $30,000. In the second year, he receives $40,000 straight salary. The next negotiations will be based on $40,000.

Dryden says bonuses are intricate problems, especially for goalies. "If a goalie is on a terrible team, yet has a good average, he doesn't get a performance bonus, it's weighted with the team." And then there is the problem of cash flow. Players are paid ten times during the hockey season, or every eighteen days (since a regular season is 178 days long). "But during the playoffs bonuses are paid differently; it is based according to how well you do," explains Dryden. "You will always hear of stories where a coach is throwing $1,000 on the dressing room floor ... 'if you do well here's what it means.'"

The number of clauses written into a contract largely depends on the lawyer's taste. Orr says he "never had a contract with a bonus", whereas his teammate Derek Sanderson signed a contract flagged with so many different clauses it resembled that of a movie star. The summer of 1972, Sanderson had signed what was reported to be a ten-year $2.5 million contract when he jumped from the Bruins to the WHA's Philadelphia Blazers. One clause guaranteed $100,000 to his parents.

"At the peak of things, Eagleson picked all the good ones ... ," says Imlach. "As far as he is concerned I put him in the same class as referees, a necessary evil. ... I just do what I have to do, sign the agents' contracts, bingo! Fight later. You win an awful lot that way, but you do get clobbered a few times."

But hockey players and their brothers and sons are not the only athletes Eagleson negotiates for. This was the year he paved the way in gold for world-champion skater Karen Magnussen. At a sports celebrity dinner at the Toronto Cricket Club, Eagleson saw Eddie Waring talking to Karen and dropped one of his trial balloons in Waring's lap: "This is probably the last time you'll be talking to Karen as an amateur."

"'When does Karen turn pro?' I asked," Waring says. "'I wouldn't say in the near future,' Eagleson hedged."

The next day all the wire services carried the story: Magnussen was signing a $500,000 three-year contract with the Ice Capades. "I got hell from Vancouver telling me how the announcement was supposed to be next week, when she would sign the cheque, having pictures taken and get handed the keys to a new car ... but that was Eagleson's way," says Waring.

A good illustration of the powerhouse position held by Eagleson in both the corporate and sports world is his promotion of Cindy Nicholas, who was voted Canadian Athlete of 1977. The twenty-year-old long-distance swimmer had six English Channel swims under her belt before she could find a sponsor. Soon after she became associated with Eagleson, he organized a Hollywood-style celebrity luncheon for her at the Hotel Toronto on January 9, 1978, with some sixty senior Canadian business executives, along with Senator Keith Davey, Metro Toronto Chairman Paul Godfrey, CTV's Johnny Esaw, and Jim Proudfoot, then sports editor at the *Toronto Star*. The companies pooled gifts and cheques for Nicholas totalling $15,000. A photograph taken at the luncheon shows Nancy and Alan Eagleson at the head table, flanked by Cindy and her parents on one side and Keith Davey and Paul Godfrey on the other.

It was Christmas all over again for the young Scarborough woman and Eagleson was Santa Claus. Two large tables were laden with gifts including a stereo set, two colour televisions, golf clubs, a sewing machine, and a silver tea service.

In his luncheon speech, Eagleson said: "I'm not flattered to say that, as a Canadian we have never recognized this young woman's achievements before this time. It's the sixth time she's crossed the channel, and this time, she broke the double channel swim record set by a male by 10 hours and 5 minutes. She was finally recognized as the Canadian athlete of 1977, and according to the country's press, was the outstanding athlete in Ontario."

Eagleson's credibility and fast talking aided him in arranging a "marriage of convenience": Standard Brands needed a client to promote a product and Cindy Nicholas needed someone to sponsor her next swim in August 1978. Standard Brands invited her to Nassau, where the company's marketing executives were planning a new advertising campaign. They paid Nicholas between $10,000 and $25,000 just to show her munching a chocolate bar.

In spite of Imlach's "sign now, litigate later" philosophy, he singles out Eagleson for making the biggest gains for players, particularly in the endorsement business. "If you are talking *agents*, Eagleson's done a lot of good for a lot of players. . . . I think endorsements would have come later, but nobody took advantage of it. Now everyone is prospering on merchandising . . . although I don't think they have been merchandised properly . . . the game has changed . . . Eagleson's done good for some people; Haggert has done pretty well."

Before endorsement and licensing companies such as Arthur Harnett Enterprises Ltd. and Bob Haggert's Sports Representatives Ltd. began operations in Toronto in the late sixties, most of the Leaf players' endorsements were handled through Maple Leaf Sports Production. The company was set up by Maple Leaf Gardens to handle all advertisers' inquiries for using individual players, or the team, to promote consumer products. Just prior to this, however, in July 1966, the player reps and NHL owners drew up an agreement whereby a player would be permitted to mention the name of his club and to keep 100 percent of the fee; if a team endorsement was involved, the players and the club would split the fee equally; if a player wore the

Leaf sweater or maple leaf insignia of the club, two-thirds of the fee would be paid to the player and the remainder to the club. But apparently the plan was never used. Within a short time, Maple Leaf Sports Productions' new endorsement formula superseded the player-owner agreement: rather than have the player or players involved get 100 percent of the fee, MLSP would give each player on the team a guaranteed $1,500 a year irrespective of whether he did any endorsements. Of course, the system left MLSP in control of the financial arrangements and commissions with the large advertisers.

In 1968, Bob Haggert entered this Toronto market and opened up Sports Representatives Ltd., which owed most of its success to referrals from Eagleson's office. "The company is 100 percent owned by Haggert," said Eagleson later on. But at that time complaints by the press of a "Haggert-Eagleson monopoly in Toronto" produced the explanation: "Lots of my clients have endorsements with people other than Haggert. ... It makes sense, though, to help a player. If he puts his future in my hands, sure I'll see if I can get him a summer job." (He was probably referring to the Orr-Walton hockey camp; Billy Harris, another Eagleson client, owned six summer hockey camps.) "And rest assured that players working for Orr are usually clients or friends of mine. I just wouldn't permit anyone who ever said anything anti-Orr or anti-Walton to work at the camp. You wouldn't call it a monopoly, but a referral system would fit."

If Eagleson is to be judged on the single criterion of boosting players' salaries then, according to at least one critic, he won't win the pennant. In 1979, *Vancouver Sun* sports columnist Jim Taylor wrote:

> When they write the history of professional sports in North America, they'll fight about where to put Gary Davidson. Builder or destroyer? He has to be there somewhere. More than anyone else — yes, more even than Alan Eagleson — he changed the face, the rules and the personality of sports. Eagleson took the whip away from the owners, but it was Davidson who handed it to the players. ...

The WHA was the brainchild of Dennis Murphy. The WHA was formally organized on November 1, 1971, with ten franchises: Chicago, Calgary, Dayton, Edmonton, Los Angeles, Miami, New York, St. Paul, San Francisco, and Winnipeg. Three weeks later, two franchises were granted to groups from New England and Ontario, bringing the WHA membership to twelve. Gary Davidson's law firm handled the groundwork and did all the organization behind the WHA. Davidson was a 35-year-old California lawyer and progenitor of three professional leagues, including the American Basketball Association and the World Football League.

It didn't matter that Davidson hadn't seen a hockey game before 1971. He knew he could collect a finder's fee of $25,000 for every franchise he sold (at the time they went for $6 million). Once the WHA was officially formed, players were needed and the NHL was raided for its stars. In 1972, the Winnipeg Jets locked up Bobby Hull* from the Chicago Black Hawks for $1 million up front, $1.75 million in salary over ten years as a player or player-coach as well as a goodwill figure for the league, and other benefits.

Hull's exodus from the NHL, plus other defections that followed, sent the owners running to the courts.† The NHL lost Sanderson; Gerry Cheevers (to the Cleveland Crusaders in 1972, at $1.4 million for seven years); Bernie Parent (to the Philadelphia Blazers in 1972, at $750,000 for five years); and Jim Dorey (to the New England Whalers in 1972, at $230,000 for four years). The Howe family jumped out the following year.

"There's so much money in hockey now you just keep raising your demands until your wife says you're crazy. Then you know you're asking for something you'll get," said Montreal Canadiens' Henri Richard in 1972. Minor leaguers turned major overnight: André Lacroix signed for $312,000 for three years; Larry Hornung for $130,500 for three years; and Gary Kurt signed a three-year deal to play goal with the WHA's short-lived New York Raiders‡ for a total of $107,500. Besides these unheard-of salaries, enormous bonuses were being appended to the contracts. Pat Stapleton signed with Chicago for regular bonuses of $50,000 a year for five years, plus bonuses for team performance, bonuses to match league bonuses, almost $100,000 in life insurance, and ten tickets to every game.

The press had a heyday during the salary wars. One report said: "John F. Bassett, Jr., president of the Toronto Toros, had $40,000 ransom money for Eagleson, who represented a number of players he

---

* The NHL succeeded in prohibiting Hull from playing the first fifteen games with the Jets.

† By mid-season in 1973, the two leagues settled out of court and the WHA paid $1.7 million in legal fees.

‡ The WHA took over the Raiders in its first season, and in 1973 the team was moved to Cherry Hill, New Jersey, and renamed the New Jersey Knights by its new owner, Baltimore real estate developer Joseph Schwartz.

wanted. ... Bassett and Bill Bremner, a shareholder on the Toronto franchise, were 'loaded for bear' in their quest for Darryl Sittler, Garry Monohan and junior picks like Peter Martin and Bob Dailey.''

Traffic in and out of Eagleson's office was wearing out the carpets. On one bright May day in 1972, there were eight of the thirteen WHA general managers waiting for him. In his capacity as executive director of the players' association, Eagleson reported that the average salary increase in the NHL during the 1971–72 season was 15 percent, ''but because of the competition from the WHA the average increase in the NHL for the 1972–73 season may reach 35 percent.'' That meant some players who played for $15,000 in the 1972–73 season had negotiated 100 percent increases in just one season. He translated this ''inflation'' factor: ''I guess the WHA has cost the NHL about $5 million in additional salaries. Normally they would have paid only $1 million to $2 million extra.''

Eagleson estimated the average payroll in the NHL in the 1971–72 season to be $620,000. ''Next season I believe payrolls for each club will be up to $900,000 or $1 million.'' NHL President Clarence Campbell reported that teams paid 25 percent of their budgets in player salaries in the 1971–72 season. The next season (the WHA's first) that figure rose to 32.6 percent; in 1973–74, it was approximately 39 percent; in 1974–75, 42.6 percent; and in 1981, 50 percent.

Eagleson succeeded in negotiating improvements in pension benefits and playoff guarantees.

Under the regular pension plan, players were getting $300 a month at age forty-five. Eagleson wanted to double it. ''The playoff pool last spring was $850,000. We want that increased to $1.5 million.'' There was quiet speculation that if Eagleson pushed for it he could get it, but not without doing grave injury to young teams such as the Oakland Seals, which would surely collapse under such demands. ''There are two or three hockey franchises I could make or break if I chose to be ruthless,'' he said at the time. One report said that Oakland owner Charles O. Finley lost $750,000 in 1971 and was expected to lose $1 million in 1972. But Eagleson figured no club was in trouble as long as the owners were still writing cheques.

While the NHL owners were having their stables raided and their payrolls inflated, Eagleson had to win support for his project, the '72 Canada Cup. To get what he wanted, he had to soften the edge of his sword: ''The demands of the association will be met by negotiation rather than strike.'' Owners had made it clear they didn't want Orr,

Brad Park, or Phil Esposito playing. So Eagleson countered further arguments on the ground of injury by acquainting the owners with the insurance policy he had arranged for the players if they played in the '72 series:

> In case of accidental death, the player's family is guaranteed $100,000 through a regular NHL policy. In case of accidental death, there is also $25,000 through a Players' Association policy and $200,000 through a Team Canada Policy.

All that was new. And disability insurance was jacked up as well:

> If a player is disabled and cannot play hockey, he gets disability insurance of $200,000. This does not mean total disability. If a player is injured and cannot pursue his career in hockey, he'll get a lump sum of $200,000. The premium on this item is $700 for each player for six weeks . . . every player's NHL salary is guaranteed. If a player is injured playing for Hockey Canada his contract is guaranteed for the life of his NHL contract.

Eagleson also won public support for his desire to have Hockey Canada pick up the insurance premium for the NHL; this was fancy footwork, but no one complained about hurt toes.

HIGH NOON IN MOSCOW

*I don't know of anyone else who could
have led us through this series as
well as Eagleson.*

Ken Dryden

Every hockey milestone creates new heroes, who, in turn, create new ways of spiralling the game into new directions. The 1972 Canada-Russia hockey series created a new hero who brought professional hockey into the twentieth century. Alan Eagleson single-handedly lifted professional hockey into the league of international world sport with all its rewards and problems. As an agent and union boss he took those lumps of muscle, guts, and talent and slowly turned them into highly polished, million-dollar skating machines; then he sent them into the international arena to test their performance. To Canada's hundreds of thousands of unidentified hockey players, it meant a chance to throw off the small-town image: they were now playing a sport that was gaining international influence and a world-wide reputation. Eagleson, hockey's Vulcan, brought hockey players into a new world.

"We're laying 100 years of hockey tradition on the line," said Dick Beddoes. To the press, everything else was peripheral. Nothing mattered except the outcome of the first of what was hoped to be an annual series. And Eagleson was the miracle worker, the producer-director of the first Canada-Russia series, hailed as the Game of the Century; he referred to himself humbly as "manager".

Manager? Hardly. The hype surrounding this occasion could only

110

be compared to an event as significant as Neil Armstrong's "one small step" on the moon. Sixteen million Canadians watched the series on TV, four million more than had witnessed man's first moon walk!

Why? Because there were more television sets? Perhaps, but it was also something else. Hockey is not only a Canadian metaphor, but a product, and Eagleson was its merchandiser. There was something in it for everyone: fans, players, owners, politicians, businessmen, and the media. Hockey is played by some 250,000 people in Canada; it is the common denominator of everything that is Canada. And there was only one man aware enough to bring it all together.

Word merchants pushing their prose on daily beats called him everything from "Commander-in-Chief" to "the Messiah", from "the benevolent despot" to the "arrogant dictator". Even the American press picked up on Eaglemania: "Hockey's self-appointed Pope" is how Joe Lapointe of the *Chicago Sun-Times* described him.

Hockey officials saluted him, owners were cowed by him, players called him affectionately "Uncle Al", and the press idolized him and introduced Eaglemania into the seventies. The Eagle was their new folk hero, the Mao Tsetung of the hockey revolution. He was giving Canada a chance to recoup its losses in the international forum. Fans had waited for this since 1959 when the Russians first sent a team to World Cup Hockey, splashing across the headlines, defeating mediocre Canadian amateur intermediate teams and ending Canada's thirty-year domination over international hockey.

Eagleson had to win the confidence of tight-fisted club owners who wouldn't make a cent from the series. Yet he did it. He sought the blessing of the top caretakers of the NHL and got it.

He also had to convince the hockey players they should cut short their already brief vacations by one month — not for money,* because there wasn't anything in it for them — but for "a chance to play for their country." That was how he sold it, that was how he justified it for them. He coaxed them: "If we are masters at the game, and yet haven't proved ourselves, then we are masters by default"; and he challenged them: "Our pros are miles ahead in hockey and now it's up

---

* Players weren't paid anything for the Canada-Russia series. However, each player received $500 a game for six exhibition matches — three in Toronto before the series, two in Sweden against the Swedish nationals, and one in Czechoslovakia after the series. In addition to the total wage of $3,000, players received $17 a day for expenses, plus travel and accommodation for their wives.

to our guys to prove it.'' So, ready or not, here was Eagleson, single-handedly propelling Canada into its national manhood.

Yet Eagleson had confidence in himself most of all. Besides expanding his own business into more lucrative territory and making his clients a little wealthier, he was getting the treatment usually reserved for ambassadors and dignitaries. All this was evidence of only one thing, Eagleson watchers proclaimed: he wants to be prime minister of Canada one day, and he's paving the way.

While making international deals that would determine the fate of hockey for many years, he was also testing his power on another level. Here was the players' agent and union boss, playing footsie under the table with the team owners. Where else could seemingly opposed forces like a union boss and a company owner make financial deals?

But Ballard was happy. "It's my rink and Eagleson's team," he said. Whatever Eagleson wanted, Eagleson was getting.

Eagleson held the balance of power in the Toronto Maple Leafs' dressing room as well. Since the majority of the Leafs were his clients, his decisions percolated down through the team, swinging the vote his way.

Eventually, the owners would find themselves backed into a corner, where the only way to win back control of the team was to rid themselves of Eagleson's clients. Unions had become big business and the NHLPA could not easily be undermined. It wasn't until several years later that Punch Imlach started to trade several Toronto players who were also Eagleson's clients, thus splitting up Eagleson's power-hold on the team.

But there were more immediate catastrophes to contend with. It was because of Eagleson's "shoot first, ask questions later" style that there was even a series at all. A couple of days before Game One, a Montreal judge issued a court order to seize the Russian hockey equipment as compensation in a personal damage claim filed by a Czech living in Montreal. The story goes that the young man had lost his personal possessions in 1968 during the Russian takeover of Czechoslovakia. Eagleson didn't hear about the case until the day before Game One, at which time he called an emergency meeting with Hockey Canada. It took a few hours to realize that going through the proper diplomatic channels was futile, so he said, "I'm going to spring the equipment and give the Czech $1,500 or whatever it takes." Lang recalls Eagleson met with the lawyer involved the next morning, handed over his personal cheque for $1,500, and picked up the equipment. News of his patriotic deed filtered back to Toronto, and by the time he arrived on home turf again for Game Two, Eagleson had mustered so much influence and popularity that when a decision had to be made as to who would drop the puck at the ceremonial face-off for the game in Toronto, Eagleson got the nod over Trudeau. "Can you believe it?" piped a young reporter. "Eaglemania beats Trudeaumania."

At Maple Leaf Gardens Eagleson entered a power play in Conservative politics. Obviously caring little about a sense of national presence at this "historic" time, he said, "Give Trudeau and the Liberals free TV exposure time, no bloody way*. . . . To hell with that. My idea is for Ontario's [Conservative] premier, Bill Davis, to make the ceremonial face-off in Toronto."

Now take a quick glimpse immediately behind the Team Canada bench. Virtually the entire row of box seats was filled with Conservatives getting free TV exposure every time the camera panned the bench. The Eagle had arranged that the six seats be filled only with prominent Conservative Party supporters. Robert Stanfield, then leader of the Conservative Party, and his wife, John Diefenbaker and his wife, Eagleson and his wife — true-blue Tory bench strength.

Would this, just maybe, bring Eagleson a federal riding or a chance at the provincial leadership? All bets were on.

In Game One, the Soviets dumped the best of the NHL 7-3. Canada went on to win Game Two in Toronto 4-1 and to tie Game Three in Winnipeg 4-4. The Vancouver match would set the tone for Russia.

Eagleson entered Vancouver's airport at his usual fast clip. The Vancouver game was to be played the next evening. This was truly his finest hour. He was just as well packaged as any of his millionaire clients. He kept himself in good shape, standing erect so that you noticed the nice cut of his three-piece, hand-tailored suit, breaking at just the right place on his shoes. He looked like a polished advertising executive, with his close-cropped hair and carefully trimmed sideburns. His fashionable gold-rimmed glasses complemented his rawhide attaché case.

His destination was Vancouver Airport's Stardust Show Lounge. He had a date with the world hockey series elite — executives of the Soviet Union Selects, Team Canada, and External Affairs department officials.

*Prime Minister Pierre Trudeau had just called a federal election for October 1, 1972.

At the other airport pubs the fans chattered excitedly: "There's Eagle" and "Hi , Uncle Al," they yelled as The Eagle passed, as if there were a personal bond between them. Lately his face had appeared on the front pages of major Canadian newspapers above stories of his great deals, his clever manoeuvres, and his struggles with the Soviet government, who finally bent a few rules for him to bring the game that would eclipse all others.

Hockey was always a good investment to the fans. It represented part of their heritage, something fathers passed on to their sons. But it was so much more than just a feeling of continuity.

Hockey was a game small boys in Saskatchewan learned to play on cold winter mornings. They could skate long before they could ride bicycles, and they could jabber away about the game before they could write their names.

"Hockey is Canada's national passion, as well as its national pastime," Trudeau said. But it is also Canada's national pride.

The Team Canada-Soviet Union Selects hockey classic was to run for many years to come, and there was a rumour that it could be held annually, instead of every three years. Let Italy have soccer, Britain cricket, and America baseball — but give Canadians hockey, their long-standing symbol of white male supremacy. It was a powerful act of male chauvinism. No women's group could disrupt the Saturday night ritual of *Hockey Night in Canada*. To a Canadian, hockey's appearance every fall was as certain as the arrival of winter snow.

When Eagleson entered the Stardust Show Lounge, it was international sportsmanship's finest hour. They were all there: Tony and Phil Esposito; the consumer crusader, Ken Dryden, who played goal for the Montreal Canadiens; and, of course, the wonderkid from Parry Sound, Ontario, superstar Bobby Orr,* his popularity unprecedented in hockey or sports fame. Eagleson stood sipping $200-a-bottle champagne. The scene proved one thing: in hockey there is a land of the rising son who, with the right agent, can go on to become a hockey hero, immortalized in the NHL's Hockey Hall of Fame.

After giving them a final once-over to make sure the players of his empire were on their best behaviour and dressed in proper attire — no hairy chests, love beads, or sandals — Eagleson slipped away to his

---

* Orr underwent surgery to remove cartilage from his left knee in the spring of 1972, and although he was selected for Team Canada, he had to miss the series.

meeting. He had developed a compulsion for double-checking every-thing, a carryover from his university days as team manager. This time it was making sure Team Canada's equipment had arrived as planned in time for Game Four in Vancouver. He runs a taut ship, on a very straight course. Everything has to be done right the first time. Disci-plining minds as well as bodies produces winners.

Suddenly, his quick temper flared. Team Canada's equipment had arrived but had been rerouted: "For delivery to Paris! What the hell?" He personally saw to it that the equipment was relabelled for Stock-holm. Once again Eagleson had saved the day.

As he swept back to the bar that September evening he could sense victory in the air. The year 1972 was full of winners. American swimming champion Mark Spitz, the dental student from California, had taken seven gold medals at the Summer Olympics in Munich. Derek Sanderson, a gritty-edged, fast-talking kid, won a ten-year, multi-million-dollar contract with the Philadelphia Blazers of the WHA. Bobby Fischer, the youngest ever to win the U.S. chess championship, became the first American to win the world title when Russia's Boris Spassky quit. "They [the Russians] were killing the art with their dull methods, dull matches, and dull country," Fischer quipped to one reporter.

Now it was Canada's turn at bat, and all eyes were riveted in her direction. "Beat those Commies," fans chanted. Before the series, most North Americans thought Russia meant only vodka, *Doctor Zhivago*, spies, and arrogance. Russia was the only country to refuse to hold the Olympiads for the Handicapped: the Kremlin denied having any handicapped athletes and refused to go along with the ruling that every country which stages the regular Olympics must hold the Olympiads the same year.

But Canadians had had a preview of things to come a week before the fans were to go over. An international electronic newsgathering service which feeds most of the daily and weekly newspapers with the bulk of its stories had sent an item over its wires about a Soviet spy ring in Canada. All across Canada, newspaper headlines ran the story on the front page: "Soviet spy reveals career of blunders in Canada".

Nothing could steal the thunder from the greatest Canadian resolu-tion: Team NHL will win the series.

When Eagleson returned to the Stardust Show Lounge, Ballard was busy making an offer of a "measly" $1 million to Soviet hockey forward Valery Kharlamov. Soviet coach Vsevelod Bobrov, as usual, made no comment.

Eagleson was sidetracked for a moment. He had to work out the details of whom to send to Prague as advance men for Team Canada's exhibition game against the Czechs after the Soviet series was over. There had to be a Czech match; the Czechs were pegged as the number-one team to beat because they had won the World Championships the previous spring.

What colour jerseys would they wear? Then Eagleson started arguing with the Extenal Affairs man about who was supposed to pay air-freight charges on the three hundred steaks Hockey Canada had bought from Canada Packers to be shipped over for the team.

A reporter interrupted, asking for an interview. "I'm giving the players a chance to play for their country," Eagleson said. He knew how to handle the press. Give them motherhood — or controversy — and they will return it in spades with columns of print. And Eagleson had found his niche in promoting winners. It was easy: everyone needed winners, and needed to win. In Phil Esposito's words, "I don't care who my linemates are, whether I play with Roy Rogers and Trigger, just so long as we win."

And Eagleson, because he works not only for hockey's highest-paid pucksters, but for their bosses as well, uses the limelight to increase the ante. It is the controversy as much as the game that sells tickets.

But, suddenly, the wind changed course; now there was a distinct mist of anti-Canadianism charging the air. Canada was defeated 5-3 in Game Four. Public sentiment began to turn against Team Canada. The Selects were ahead with two wins, one tie: Canada, with only one win, had lost the home series.

While Eagleson was pushing earlier for an all-or-nothing victory, saying, "Anything less than an unblemished sweep of the Russians would bring shame down on the players and the national pride," others carped that Eagleson was perhaps doing too much too soon.

Canadian Amateur Hockey Association president Joe Kryczka, who had voted in favour of the series, said, "Things are in such a mess, either Hockey Canada will fold or it will be operated in an altogether different manner." He even threatened to prepare a "pretty severe" evaluation of the entire situation, and eventually he did. He took it to the pinnacle of Canada's sport authority, the Fitness and Amateur Sport Directorate at the federal level.

If there wasn't pressure on Eagleson from the amateur wings at the time, it was now apparent that Team Canada was undergoing a public debunking: the great Canadian myth was being exposed.

Canada's invincibility was shattered. The team was a national disgrace. Only Richard Nixon could lose so much face so fast. Very quickly, a stance was taken: "I'm ashamed to be a Canadian," Eagleson said. Team Canada was getting whipped. Brawlers! Bums! The hecklers were having a field day.

Even the players themselves tried to quell the uproar. Phil Esposito wasn't about to let it all go down the tube: "The thirty-five guys here gave up their short off-season break to play for Canada, and that cost all of us considerable money. But we did it because we're Canadian and I for one wanted to play for my country ... everybody sacrificed to be here."

Perhaps the articulate Ken Dryden put it best: "What happened was this. We were going to have a big party and the Russians spoiled it."

Eagleson, as usual, turned everything around. Ultimately it would be the fans who were to blame. "Because of the fans' poor behaviour, there will be no further series played in Vancouver," he snapped.*

Red Fisher explained it firsthand: "What is happening in the media is a case of an overload of confidence suddenly turning into defensive backtracking. All of us in the media predicted this series would be a sweep. Well, it didn't turn out that way and we are taking it out on the club, and, by extension, Eagleson."

When Eagleson returned to Toronto for the mid-series break prior to leaving for Moscow, he learned that some of the Canadian players were at the point of calling it quits. Sinden says he remembers receiving a call from Eagleson at his home in Rochester with the news that Frank Mahovlich's nerves were shot, and his doctor forbade him to continue playing.†

On the day of the exhibition game in Stockholm, Canadian players were on the verge of mutiny. Out of earshot of Sinden or Ferguson, Eagleson listened to several players' complaints for two hours, then emptied the musket against the down-in-the-mouth players. "I have enough troubles without losers," he told them, suggesting if they

---

* Eagleson's promise held. Vancouver, a city which boasted a major-league franchise, never figured in any future international series — junior or senior — except in the Canada (WHA)-Russia 1974 September Series which Eagleson had no control over. Vancouver was left out of Canada Cup II in September 1981.
† Frank Mahovlich did finish the series.

didn't believe the team would win the series they were to board the next plane back to Canada. Team Canada won the game that night, 4-1. However, they only managed to get a 4-4 tie in the second and last exhibition game against Sweden.

All of this behind-the-scenes drama was unknown to the fans, however. On September 14, 1972, some 2,700 Canadian hockey devotees were assembled from all corners of Canada. Two charter groups — one in Montreal, the other in Toronto, were about to take part in the largest single airlift of Canadians since the Second World War.

This bond of strength emerged not through a common wanderlust, but by dint of a double devotion: hockey and patriotism. For the first time, live, centre ice, the best of the National Hockey League would be pitted against the best world nationals, the Soviet Union Selects. This world spectacle would be transmitted via satellite to televisions in the homes of millions of Canadians and Russians. It would be the greatest show on earth — the Super Bowls and the Big Top rolled into one. Canada versus Russia! Hockey Night in the World.

The hockey fans were the crusaders of the twentieth century, and the Canada-Russia hockey series was their holy war. Decked out with beanies, buttons, banners, and bullhorns, they looked more like Grey Coach tourists than dignified ambassadors. Statistics on goals, averages, and points were memorized through daily readings from the columns of sports writers. But unlike the missionaries of holy wars of the twelfth and thirteenth centuries the intention of these hockey mercenaries was not to leave behind the word of God, but rather the wrath of God: a few bloody noses, broken teeth, broken limbs — and, of course, defeat.

Each fan had paid in excess of $2,000 for travel, lodging, meals, and tickets to see top-flight athletes play top-quality hockey. Their presence seemed vital to the morale of Team Canada, but it was their willingness to part with hard-earned dollars that kept the spirit of Team Canada alive.

By the time Team Canada arrived in Moscow for the last four games of the series, Vic Hatfield, Rick Martin, and Jocelyn Guevremont eventually had left, complaining they weren't getting enough ice time.

This was definitely affecting Eagleson's nerves. His patience was wearing thin. For the past three months he had lived under extreme tension. "Big decisions are made alone," he had told his son, Allen. Now defeats were also being shouldered by him alone.

Suddenly the lights were going out all around The Eagle. He had risen alone, and would topple alone.

Team Canada was like a newborn baby. The teammates had never played together as a single unit. Maybe they had been overreaching or counting too much on outdated, ill-founded rumours that the Selects were supposed to be an unlikely match, labelled as inferior in shooting, goaltending, and skating. Certainly now the whole question of "us versus them" was sorting itself out a little more clearly.

The socialist-versus-capitalist dialogue was aired time and again. The Selects were cleaning up and their players had absolutely no monetary incentive; that much we recognized. No player made any more money than the average Soviet citizen. It must have been bad — why else would some athletes run huge risks by defecting to the U.S.? The big question was, how did they come up with a winning team? At stake were decades of belief in the free enterprise system. "Only one thing was certain," said Dick Beddoes, "things will never be the same again in Canadian hockey."

The media had applauded Eagleson as the shining star; now, before the series was half over, they were depicting him as a fallen angel.

Because it was the first time Soviet officials had permitted a Western touring team inside their walls, virtually everything was left up to Eagleson to manage. Most frustrating was that every time a deal was made, the Russians would change their minds. This happened again and again, until, just before Team Canada was to leave for the two exhibition games against Sweden's national team, Eagleson was on the edge of a nervous breakdown, or so it appeared to people close to him.

"He called me several times at two and three in the morning just to talk," says Fisher, "because everybody was dumping on him about how lousy the hockey club was doing. He just wanted a shoulder to cry on. I'm not a doctor but the signs were there, he was just about to go right over the edge, and he told me himself he was heading for the meadows. And he was shaking all the time. You say 'good morning' to him and depending on how he felt you'd get into an argument with him."

After Eagleson arrived in Moscow, the media bore the brunt of his wrath. He even came close to slugging Vancouver sports columnist Eric Whitehead. Eagleson had replied to a question Whitehead had asked concerning whether two West German referees would be pulled from the series.

"Well, what you are really saying is ... " Whitehead gave his interpretation of Eagleson's answer.

"No, that's not what I said."

"But what you mean is ... " Whitehead inquired.

"Now wait a minute, don't put words in my mouth, you've been trying to put words in my mouth for the last five minutes," charged Eagleson. "And you're the one who wrote in a column for your paper that the behavior of some members of Team Canada on the plane coming over to Europe was despicable and yet you weren't even on the plane."

Whitehead mumbled something, and Eagleson grabbed him by the throat, rammed him against one of the marble pillars in the lobby of the Intourist Hotel, and threatened to beat the hell out of him right there. Just in time, Herb Capose, who owns the Vancouver Whitecaps soccer team, restrained him.

"Don't do it, Al, he's not worth it," pleaded Capose. Eagleson backed off, leaving Whitehead pale and shaken.

Eventually tempers cooled and interest turned to what was happening in the game, for there was little else as colourful or exciting going on in Moscow.

Fans from Canada, who were staying in the players' hotel, the Intourist, found that while no one would move a finger for an individual, groups were served fairly efficiently. The only sign of undeserved harassment on the part of the authorities came during the customs check before departure for Canada, when nearly everyone was subjected to an exhaustive examination lasting nearly two hours. It was conducted in an atmosphere of hostility.

Still, the most amazing phenomena were the Games. The Russians took Game Five with a 5-4 win, gaining a 3-1-1 standing in five games. To win the series, Canada had to take the last three games. Team Canada won Game Six with a 3-2 score and also Game Seven, 4-3. Game Eight would prove the champion. The controversy surrounding the final game of the first Canada-Russia series still rages as to whether Canadian conduct was disgraceful. Eagleson was, to no one's surprise, smack in the centre.

In terms of power, influence, and control, it was here at the Sports Palace (capacity 15,000) that Eagleson reached his peak. He told a friend that when the Russia series ended, he'd have accomplished in hockey all he ever wanted to do.

It was in the third and final period of Game Eight, somewhere around the twelve-minute mark, that Eagleson turned the game upside down.

At 12:56 Yvon Cournoyer took the puck from Phil Esposito and tied the game 5-5, or so it was thought; but the goal judge's light had failed.

Eagleson lost his cool. He was sitting in a box seat, centre ice, as always, and he leaped up over his seat straight out towards the promenade, heading directly for the scorers' bench to start his own game of grudge. In leaping over his seat he fell against two Soviet police, who caught him by the elbows and pulled him to a full stop. When one of them turned around and shoved Eagleson, he shoved back, whereupon half a dozen more grabbed Eagleson and started dragging him to the nearest exit.

Eagleson was shouting loud enough to draw the attention of Pete Mahovlich, who made a beeline to his rescue. Within seconds the entire Canadian team had left the bench and, with those already on the ice, went over to the boards to rescue Uncle Al.

The police released Eagleson, who was as white as a sheet. Team Canada propelled him gently across the ice.

The tension inside the Sports Palace grew to riot proportions. The Canadian fans, stamping and cheering, lifted the roof, waving the red Maple Leaf, cheering after their fallen leader. Hail to The Eagle! Like a Roman emperor he was carried from the arena.

While the house was still standing, Eagleson had to have the last word. But he was speechless. The episode had knocked the wind from the thirty-eight-year-old warrior. To make sure everyone knew he had been the victor, and his honour preserved, Eagleson blessed the event by turning around and giving the Russian police vanguard the street-fighters' genuflection — the one-finger salute. Then, thinking it might be an understatement, he followed it with the whole-arm command.

Eagleson was truly a David among a whole network of Goliaths, one man challenging the very foundation of the U.S.S.R.'s authority. The goal was granted, and an unwritten law was made: Eagleson was untouchable. Never before had there been such a show of solidarity for a non-player.

As the house was busily calming down after its frenzy of flag-waving, one woman leaned forward in her seat and naively asked, "Who was that guy?" Unknowingly, she had spoken within earshot of Chris Lang, who was sitting next to Eagleson and Doug Fisher.

"It's Alan Eagleson," said Lang.

"What does he do?" she pressed.

"He turns chickenshit into chicken salad," he blurted out, "and I know of very few people who can do that."

Team Canada went on to win for their country, for Eagleson. They won the series with a goal by Paul Henderson with only thirty-four seconds left to play, a final triumph on this V-E — Victory for Eagle — day.

NEKULTURNY

*He has an extra special picture of
what he wants to be; I think that
is one of his drives. Few people
have ego big enough to have a
preplot of their lives;
most just live it.*

Morley Kells

When Eagleson set foot on Canadian turf again everything had changed. Before the 1972 Canada-Russia series he was known to only a handful of loyal hockey fans and sports journalists. Now he was a bona fide personality.

As Eagleson led a victorious Team Canada off the aircraft at Montreal's International Airport on September 29, the emotion of the past twenty-seven days instantly disappeared when he caught sight of 25,000 fans singing "O Canada" in French and English. In an official welcome-home tribute, Prime Minister Trudeau shook his hand while cameras clicked on the memorable occasion. Hours later, Eagleson and Phil Esposito marched Paul Henderson around on their shoulders before a Toronto civic reception of 80,000 raging fans. It was the largest demonstration the city had ever witnessed.

Canada has few celebrities to boast of, and they come in two categories: sports heroes and politicians. Eagleson was a special hybrid, a synthesis of both.

Public appreciation of both sports and politics was at a low ebb when he returned. Everyone was feeling post-partum depression after the summer's tumultuous Munich Olympics, and Trudeaumania, with its love beads and sandals, was "old hat". Eagleson's boyish enthusiasm and his impeccably tailored post-hippie three-piece suit made him perfect for a new kind of Canadian folk hero. His rise to fame and fortune grew with the increasing number of millionaire skating superstars.

It was actually Paul Henderson who had salvaged the series, saving face for hundreds of thousands of hockey fans who had bet their money on the one match that would wipe clean from the slate the eighteen-year blotch marring Canada's world-champion reputation. Ever since the Soviet national team had trounced Canada back in 1954, rarely a day had passed without someone in Canada whining that, until Canada's best confronted the Soviets' best, nothing had been proved. Now Canada was Camelot: Henderson had turned Canada again into the hockey centre of the world.

Eagleson's gesture* had been seen by millions of television viewers in Europe and North America. Henderson's winning goal was almost anti-climactic compared to the impact Eagleson had scored. Future generations would hear as much about Eagleson's confrontation with Russian cops during that series as about any particular shot or goal.

The players' rally during the final Moscow game was the feather in Eagleson's cap. He cherished it as ''the greatest moment in my career''. This acceptance by the players was instrumental in his decision to pull out of his law practice in 1975 to take on the responsibility of organizing the first World Cup of Hockey in 1976. What happened in Moscow was important because it was the first time the players had publicly shown any loyalty to Eagleson.

The public and press had supported Eagleson in the past, calling the formation of the players' union ''the best thing that was ever done for the players'', and praising him for successfully courting the Russians into a might-for-might match. The players, however, had cared only about higher salaries and ''playing the Russians''. Eagleson's public recognition had, until now, come through his clientele — an Orr or a Mahovlich — rather than to him personally. There were no wild cheers from the players when Eagleson brought them into a union in 1967: it was one of Eagleson's inside men, Bob Haggert, who induced the players into presenting him with a plaque for what he had done.

''Haggy went out and bought the goddamn thing, had it engraved, then told the players, 'Here, go give this to Al and tell him thanks for being the executive director of your union,' '' said one close associate.

But even after Eagleson's triumphant return, hockey purists re-

---

* Eagleson insists he never gave the Russians the finger: ''Because in my vintage we gave two fingers, not one!''

gretted the transformation of "their" game of hockey — the symbol of Canada — into a three-ring circus.

Hockey was unique to Canadians. It was private cultural property. Hockey was part of the definition of their character and their drive. Canadians gave more time and devotion to hockey than to God, and they defended their freedom to play the traditional game, the game their fathers' fathers had played, with a religious fervour. Naturally they perceived a blow to this freedom in any change to the game from the way it was when the NHL was nothing more than a six-team house league. Every expansion since 1969 had been interpreted as a threat to the purity of hockey. The NHL had increased the league to sixteen teams by the end of 1972; this watering-down had clearly jeopardized The Game. The ingredient being watered down was The Hockey Player: he was the high priest who justified their faith.

But to the hardened hockey purist, Eagleson was more an anti-hero, the guru associated with the new hockey order. When Eagleson entered their world, winning higher salaries for hockey players, he tainted the priesthood. Why should a hockey star play his heart out when his salary was guaranteed for life? The players' quest for money was a break from the old faith. A player was supposed to be a chosen disciple who played not for money (as was the case before the union) but for the love of the game. The urge to win had been replaced by a quest for contracts, bonuses, and pensions. Eagleson was the culprit who had degraded the game and the players, and through them, the fans.

The irony was that Eagleson, the son of a poor immigrant, was also an archetypal Canadian working-class foot-soldier, weaned on Canadian hockey culture like any other survivor of the Depression and the Second World War.

Eagleson's drive to "get at the meat" turned a Canadian myth into a profit-making industry. He combined his connections in business and politics and his association with the sport with numerous successful business ventures. His impact on the natural state of The Game was as devastating as rust is to steel.

He tapped the rich resources of the field for every penny and every advantage he could find, and he left the indigenous hockey fans with nothing. Eagleson and expansion had taken The Game from them. Players couldn't go back to the six-team, house-league structure and the simplicity of playing to win. Yet they couldn't continue their sport as a top entertainment industry either, because escalating salaries would push franchises into bankruptcy. Eventually, The Game was priced out of the market. Here was a classic case of a multinational corporation (the NHL) exploiting a "third world" country (hockey).

Growing numbers of corporations buying up large blocks of season's tickets to give away to clients made tickets scarce. The average hockey fan can no longer afford scalpers' prices to watch the game live in its chilly temple. Hockey has become a grey-blue blur emanating from a little box in their homes.

Hockey ceased to be the symbol for Canadianism. The national spirit which cut across political and regional borders and had a strength and will of its own died when idealism was sacrificed to economic ends.

The press were the first to see Eagleson as The Spoiler. Controversy is part of being a celebrity. In the eyes of the great Canadian public and press, The Eagle had fallen from grace. Under the pressure and strain of Moscow, Eagleson had lost his cool. He personally needed Team Canada to win because it was his chance to prove Canadian players were just as good as the Russians. He needed to prove Canada could be Number One again. But in those last few moments of play he panicked.

After the first flush of excitement subsided, and a post-mortem of the series was taken, Eagleson was held to be no better than the "classless boobs" he had been ranting against. "The Russians have only one system," Eagleson had told everyone before the series, "and that's the muscle system.... I'd rather be a bum in Toronto than a major general in Russia!"

Now he was. Newspapers across the country told of his fall from diplomatic grace. His finger salute put him in a class by himself, throwing North Americans on the defensive in an ideological war when the real battle should have been decided on the ice.

Decorum and how the game is played still mattered to Canadians. "I saw us being led by a man who qualifies as a walking diplomatic disaster," wrote John Robertson in the *Montreal Star*. "Eagleson's badgering the Russian Army when he felt hassled by them was making us one and the same as them," wrote another reporter.

Eagleson had done a soft-sell job on the press, convincing them his was the way of the "gentleman's handshake", until his true colours were shown to millions of Canadians on television.

"Only a bum uses muscle on an unenlightened opponent," the press complained. The Russians were suddenly the underdog.

At the victory party held at the Metropole Hotel for Team Canada immediately following Game Eight, after presentations were made, Eagleson gave a talk. He spoke about how many things happen in the heat of battle, but hoped the series had been a friendly one. Air Canada's international sports representative, Aggie Kukulowicz, was present at the time, and recalls that in response to his remarks, Alexander Gresko, Russia's official representative in international hockey, stood up and said, "I made a friend of Eagleson in July and that friendship died two days ago. ... As of today, and tonight, I feel very sorry for Alan Eagleson."

"Bum! Brawler! Boor! *Nekulturny!*" the Russians quickly labelled Canada's ambassador, and the Canadian press were quick to translate. Trent Frayne, a Toronto sports columnist, defined *nekulturny* as "yahoo or boor or simply a pain in the ass".

Frayne reported an earlier incident in Sweden. He caught up to Eagleson's giant stride one day in the lobby of the Grand Hotel in Stockholm, where Team Canada was billeted during the 1972 Olympic Games.

"I've never seen a team pass the puck as impressively as the Russians," he said to Eagleson.

"Jesus," Eagleson said, incensed, "you must be a Communist."

Frayne noticed that Eagleson was very tense, his face pale and drawn. "All I said was that the passing knocked me out," he repeated.

"We lost, you know," Eagleson reminded him.

"Yeah, I know we lost."

"We lost, and you're telling me you like their passing."

"That's right."

"Anybody who thinks like you do has to be a bloody Communist."

Letters to the editor in newspapers across the country suggested Eagleson was poking fun at a country where, until the last decade, ice hockey was a game played only by a few eccentrics on racing skates.

Eagleson, Canadians realized, was suffering from acute hardening of the ideological categories. Until now he had enjoyed a fruitful and cooperative relationship with the sports writers, who got a lot of print out of his succinct and colourful remarks. But once Eagleson's image showed the first spot of tarnish, the press and the public were quick to look for more. It was easy to find, both in his relationship with the press and in his business dealings.

A member of the press who challenged him was usually dealt with personally. Christie Blatchford, a sports columnist for the *Globe and*

Mail, encountered this when she later attacked Eagleson's empire in 1977. "I was convinced he wore too many hats, and I was sure the guys working for him were getting all the plum jobs,"she says. Eagleson didn't like what she wrote about him (although she later said she didn't find anything on him). He boasted, "I got her off that paper." Blatchford denies this, saying she left the paper for a better situation.

Another *Globe and Mail* reporter says Eagleson used to "drop a lot of trial balloons on me. .... I'd write it up then he could gauge what his next move would be, if any, from the type of reaction it got." The writer says he refused to deal with Eagleson on that basis again. "It was too bad the way some sports writers would cross broken glass on their hands and knees for Eagleson and would never say a negative word about him."

In short, the myth surrounding Eagleson was much larger than the man. As his relationship with the press deteriorated, the interpretations given to his actions became less favourable. Dick Beddoes was part of the press entourage that had been responsible for creating the cult of Eaglemania. Now he waged a battle against him. In one of Beddoes' columns, the *Globe* ran a distasteful mug shot of Eagleson with his jaw jutting out in bellicose defiance.

He liked playing the role of the godfather, and openly admitted this in a CBC interview when he was asked, "Is there really an Eagleson mafia?" "Sure there is," he replied casually.

The Eagleson "mafia" is headed by three major players. Eagleson, at the top, is flanked by Haggert on one side and by his chief accountant, Marvin Goldblatt, on the other. Eagleson's first involvement with Goldblatt dates back to the mid-sixties when Goldblatt worked for Blaney, Pasternak. Through his association with Eagleson, Goldblatt acquired many private clients in the sports market. Bill McMurtry describes Goldblatt as one of the many "sycophants" surrounding Eagleson.

As Eagleson's empire grew to include more than player representation, he set up athletic merchandising and sports endorsement companies to mitigate the charges of conflict of interest, which "were well-founded," says Morley Kells, one of Eagleson's former business associates.

One such company was Sports Representatives Ltd., with Haggert at its helm. Eagleson maintained that "Bob Haggert's company is 100 percent owned by him, whatever he makes belongs to him, I don't want any part of that money."

He said this about all the companies he set up for his friends, the spinoff operations that grew through the industrialization of hockey. "We have separate companies everywhere because I don't ever want to find myself being depended on, totally, by others."

Yet Harold Ballard and others close to Eagleson claimed that the basis of the conflict-of-interest accusations was true. Ballard says, "I know Eagle runs the endorsement agency of Mr. Haggert's.... He started Haggert in the business."

After Haggert left his job as Leaf trainer, he took over the administration of the Orr-Walton hockey camp, and still kept his job with MacLaren Advertising. But his association with the ad agency didn't last long. Handling the advertising in the hockey programs for both the Montreal Forum and the Gardens had been quite lucrative, and the loss of that revenue was a tremendous financial blow to Haggert. He told one writer that he lost the job "because of my association with Eagleson". Eagleson had introduced trade unionism into hockey, and MacLaren Advertising* considered him "bad blood".

Eagleson swore he'd get back at MacLaren's for firing Haggert. "I've got a great memory," he threatened. And he didn't forget. He made a deal whereby Harold Ballard and Bobby Orr owned all of the TV rights to the first Canada-Russia series. When MacLaren's announced that it would handle the series, a meeting was called between the ad agency and Hockey Canada. Eagleson and Harold Ballard, as HC directors, were also there. Just before the meeting, Eagleson received a call from a CBC friend who briefed him about MacLaren's offer. "I'll always be indebted to him," he says. "Then when MacLaren made its offer of $500,000 for the controlling advertising rights to the series I said it wasn't enough money. Ballard and I huddled, made a few phone calls, and figured we could outbid them. We returned and offered $750,000," Eagleson says. Most media people considered this a steal.

Half of that money was Orr's. Orr didn't know it, because Eagleson hadn't been able to reach him. Eagleson admitted it was a gamble, but he took it for granted he would have Orr's approval. Orr's comment on this? "I have a lot of faith in Al.... if he did something with my money and lets me know later, I would say it's okay."

Eagleson claims that neither Orr nor Ballard made a cent from the deal. "... If they made any profit they would turn it all back to

---

* MacLaren Advertising has always been the agency for the federal Liberal Party.

Hockey Canada, that was the deal. So they gambled over three-quarters of a million dollars against a zero chance, all they could do was lose. They trusted me and made the deal."

"We set up a company called Ballard-Orr Enterprises to look after the deal and turned that $750,000 into a $1.2 million profit," Ballard says.

Ironically, Ballard was supposed to be sentenced on September 7 — between Games Three (Winnipeg) and Four (Vancouver) — for stealing from his own company, Maple Leaf Gardens Inc. The court, in a display of generosity, postponed the sentence in order to avoid embarrassing Team Canada. On October 20, 1972, the *Globe and Mail* reported that Ballard was sentenced to two three-year terms — one for "defrauding the company of about $82,000," the other for "participating in the theft of about $123,000" from Maple Leaf Gardens. The two terms were to run concurrently.

Why would Ballard risk over one-third of a million dollars if, in turn, Eagleson couldn't find sponsors, without a chance of making a personal profit? Was it a debt owing?

"People think I am hard-boiled and greedy for money," Ballard said later. "I did it for the good of hockey." Eagleson claims, "He did it because I asked him to." Gross revenues from radio and television broadcasts of the eight-game series were approximately $2.19 million. After commissions and expenses, a net profit of $1.19 million was realized.

Even the formation of the players' association proved ambiguous in the wave of anti-Eagleson feeling touched off by his famous gesture. Many people came to suspect it was the owners and not the players who wanted Eagleson to form a players' "association", because the Teamsters were putting pressure on the owners to organize a union. When the NHLPA was put together, it was the owners who eventually got what they wanted, and not the players. Certainly, by comparison with other craft unions and other professional sport-league organizations, the NHLPA was a sham. "It didn't even come close in benefits for the hockey players that other pro sport leagues have," says Bruce Kidd, an assistant professor in the Department of Athletics at the University of Toronto.

Ballard, on the other hand, couldn't say enough good about his supposed archenemy. "I think Eagle's a great man for hockey. He is a good businessman and I always try to promote him. I tell my boys who don't have lawyers to go to The Eagle."

When Bill Watters, Eagleson's first lieutenant and president of Sports Management Ltd., who looked after preliminary negotiations and the day-to-day operations of Sports Management, broke from the Eagleson empire in 1980 after fourteen years, he described Eagleson's financial base this way: "I think Al's powerhouse is the NHLPA." The next largest portion of his business? "Publicly it's the agent business [law firm]; privately it's the Harnett business. . . . It's strictly international hockey. . . . It's my opinion that international hockey is what made him, gave him his power. . . . putting everything into international hockey by bringing it to the pro status from the amateur status."

Arthur Harnett was news director of Toronto radio station CFRB when he became a campaign worker for Eagleson during the sixties. After Eagleson was elected president of the Ontario Progressive Conservatives, Harnett became the party's executive director, a post he left in 1971. At that time he joined Ontario Place as acting general director. But it wasn't a permanent appointment, and there had been a chance he wouldn't get it — again for "political reasons". "Either it was because I was too political," said Harnett at the time, "or not political enough."

One account says that on a particular Friday afternoon in early July 1971, while Eagleson and Harnett were drifting around in Eagleson's boat near his lakefront Mississauga home, The Eagle hired Harnett as president of Team Canada Products Ltd., and "assured his future with Bobby Orr Enterprises Ltd. in the field of closed-circuit television sports." Later in 1971, Harnett was set up in Arthur Harnett Enterprises Ltd., which became a flourishing sports endorsement business.

Eagleson's empire was a major industry. Through it he was making valuable real estate purchases, setting up hockey schools, selling television and product licensing rights, and beginning to mold a new breed of athletes. They became Hollywood-style superstars promoting products and buying fast food franchises. (Mike Walton set up a chain of Bobby Orr Pizza Parlours in Ontario.) Arthur Harnett Enterprises was a major recipient of business associated with the communication aspects of international hockey, domestic hockey, and boxing.

"As a radio-TV person, we slotted Harnett into a company to handle all communication aspects . . . so that when we go into a deal for international hockey or domestic hockey, we call Harnett; or when we go into the boxing business we work with Irv Ungerman. His company comes in and fills that role. But again, that's 100 percent owned by him. I don't want any part of it," says Eagleson.

Boxing was a sport Eagleson was able to vulcanize for his friend Irving Ungerman in 1971.

"Ungerman was typical of the . . . small businessman who gravitates to Eagleson," explains Kells, who was part of the empire then.

The friendly business relationship with Ungerman began in 1971. By that time Eagleson was better known as a deal maker than for any particular area of legal experience. "Companies would hire Eagleson to appear before the Transport Board. . . . Eagle doesn't know anything about it, but nevertheless, the law is like that . . . like Broadway they need a star," explained one associate. This was particularly so in corporate law practice. Corporate clients were the bread and butter of any law firm, and Eagleson eventually specialized as a corporate lawyer in the sports market. There were few people with as much expertise in this area, and Eagleson carved himself a comfortable niche as a power broker whose connections could open any door. So when former Torontonian Jack Kent Cooke (owner of the L.A. Kings) decided to stage the first Muhammad Ali-Joe Frazier fight in 1971, Cooke came to Eagleson.

"Do you want Toronto? That's your market and you have to put up the money for it," Cooke told him. Cooke always wanted cash up front; the practice had made him millions in the lucrative Los Angeles sports market.

Eagleson knew it was a gamble. He called Ungerman, who had made some money in real estate and from promoting local fights. "Irv, do you want a piece of this action?"

Ungerman decided to go for it and as a result got the larger share of the $1 million gross receipts in Canada from selling closed-circuit television coverage of the fight. Eagleson, who seldom used his own money, financed the deal at the Gardens through another Bobby Orr–Ungerman partnership.

Through Eagleson's contacts, Ungerman grew from a small promoter of local fights to a big-time promoter of New York-style championship fights, managing stars like George Chuvalo and Clyde Gray, now Ontario's boxing commissioner.

Hundreds of these friendly business associations sprouted in Canada as a result of Eagleson's reputation as a deal maker in the international hockey market. When the Canadian market wasn't big enough in terms of size or expertise, he moved the product south of the border.

One area where Canada fell drastically behind was in the licensing business. When Kells left *Hockey Night in Canada* in 1969 "because I was so goddamn bored" and went to work for an Eagleson enterprise called NHL Players' Hockey School, an offshoot of the NHLPA, he was confronted with a major decision.

"One of the big things Eagleson sold was the licensing rights to the NHLPA logo. He went to an American because there wasn't anyone up here who understood what to do with it," explained Kells. "It wasn't his fault he had to turn to the States. I didn't have very good experience."

But after that Kells and Eagleson parted company. Kells describes what it was like working within the Eagleson structure: "[Eagleson] can only operate as long as he's the boss and everyone else is below him. If you've got any ego of your own you can't deal with being dominated. . . . anyone who works with Eagleson has been dominated, but he looks after them." Kells' experience with this love-hate relationship was very typical. "I only like him as long as I'm detached from him. I wouldn't want to be involved in any other enterprise that Eagleson has anything to do with."

·11·

WHITE MAN'S TRINKETS

Why don't you go the hang-out route now?
When an inquiry is finally called, you won't
be able to stonewall it forever. Eventually
you are going to have to admit Eagleson
received the power to do those things in
exchange for acting as your agent of
extortion. You won't be able to say,
"I didn't know" because three years ago
I warned you that there was a cancer
growing around Hockey Canada.

Robert F. McNeil

Eagleson's tireless quest to bring power and affluence to his private clients and associates, and to build a strong players' association to protect the futures and rights of professional hockey players, had won him many victories. Then, driven by his desire to make the most of his own abilities (for the benefit of others), he volunteered in June 1974 to become the Canadian government's lone missionary in staging the first World Cup of Hockey for 1976.* To win, Eagleson depended on the same strings he had pulled in his other trailblazing pursuits: media contacts and client-player support were all important to the success of his mission.

Eagleson had already proved he could be a powerful catalyst: in orchestrating the 1972 win over the Russians he had fulfilled the desire of the Canadian public and the federal government to win back Canada's place in world hockey, expanded Canadians' knowledge about the Russian style of hockey, and provided opportunities for interested investors to develop business contacts and pursue activities in the entertainment field.

Canadian hockey players who played for American teams, and who

---

*The Canada Cup '76 was referred to as the World Cup of Hockey because it resembled the World Cup of Soccer in using a country's best players.

otherwise would not qualify for international competition, were given an opportunity to play for their country. They were not directly paid for winning the series, but the NHLPA pension fund was given a healthy injection of approximately $500,000 from the proceeds of the '72 tournament.

In part, Hockey Canada's mandate had already been fulfilled. Eagleson's "summit" series produced an immediate improvement in Canada's status in international hockey, but it did so by subverting Canada's national sport to the controls of the private sector, namely the NHLPA and the NHL. Hockey Canada's mandate, as first outlined by Munro, had been to improve Canada's hockey image abroad and to improve domestic (amateur) hockey by training coaches and improving players' skills. The government recommendation in setting up Hockey Canada's board carried with it the warning, which Doug Fisher (the government rep and newly elected IIHF committee chairman) explained at the outset: to avoid domination from any one sector. Yet such domination was the eventual result: the private sector took over the rights of the players to play on international turf. Eagleson and his hand-picked crew had shut out Hockey Canada.

Given that the NHL corporation would not be dictated to by the government or an international body such as the IIHF, and that the players selected to represent Canada held long-term contracts with NHL clubs, Eagleson's power as chief mediator was academic. The clincher was the "long-term contract". Since there was no collective-bargaining agreement at the time of the 1972 series, it was easier for Eagleson to manoeuvre between Hockey Canada's needs and the NHL's stronghold. Concessions had to be made. The biggest concession was turning over half the profits ($500,000) from the sale of TV revenue, which, ironically, Ballard helped raise, to the NHLPA pension fund; Eagleson was saving the NHL money. NHL players played in the annual All-Star games to replenish the pension fund; now the same players were carrying the load for the rest of the league. In addition, the payment of $500,000 to Hockey Canada, which in turn paid $100,000 to the CAHA, created a double dependency (HC and CAHA) on the private sector in the form of tied aid.

Tying Canada's future in domestic hockey to the private sector, the American-dominated NHL, was held to be more damaging in the long run to the overall state of the art than any short-term improvement in Canada's image abroad. Canada's hockey became "underdeveloped." Hockey players delighted in higher salaries, better pension and medical plans, and the protection of new rules for drafting juniors — the white man's trinkets — all won at the point of a strike threat. But there were huge gaps in levels of development as well as remuneration among the players. Enticing eighteen-year-old players with multi-million dollar, long-term contracts, then tossing them into emotional pressure cookers, killed the natural maturation process of a player's mental and physical development. McMurtry had worried about Orr's dependency and maturation. Many others held the opinion that if Orr hadn't done too much too fast in spite of his knee problems, "he'd still be playing today". The upshot of Eagleson's magic was rampant inflation within the industry. As salaries took one step forward, the quality of performance took two steps back. The inflated cost of salaries forced consumers to pay $12 a ticket, yet because of expansion consumers were watching fringe players.

By 1974 global hockey was a boom industry. Plans were announced for an annual World Junior Tournament (to follow the national junior championships in Winnipeg at the end of 1974), as well as for bantam and university matches abroad. The CAHA reported that "in the current season alone, the federal government through the CAHA has arranged more than 100 international matches in Canada". Already the industry was generating revenue in the millions of dollars from selling TV and radio rights, gate receipts, and an assortment of merchandising spinoffs such as commemorative coins and albums. The exhibition games and European–Soviet tours were providing stiff competition for fans' dollars to the regular club games.

Traditionally in Canada, hockey had been legally considered a sport, not a business, and therefore had stood outside normal business laws. In December 1974, an amendment to the Combines Investigation Act was being considered. The amendment would have expanded the act's coverage to include sport. On December 11, Eagleson, as the executive director of the NHLPA, made a submission to a Banking, Trade and Commerce Tribunal at a Senate committee hearing.* He argued that it was a necessary condition of sport to combine together

---

* As a result of these hearings, the Combines Investigation Act was amended in 1975 to include Section 32.3 which states: "Anyone who conspires to limit unreasonably the opportunity of any other person to negotiate with and, if agreement is reached, to play for a team or club of his choice in a professional league is guilty of an indictable offence." There is room for judicial discretion, however; the act refers to taking into consideration the "desirability of maintaining a reasonable balance between teams and clubs participating in the same league".

into a league or monopoly and that therefore, hockey should be exempted from the Act. (André Ouellet, then Minister for Corporate Affairs, had sponsored legislation to exempt amateur sports from combines regulations the previous January.) In a forty-three-page brief, complete with case citations and a long appendix, Eagleson pointed out the consequences and dangers of allowing professional hockey to become subject to the Combines Investigation Act, and suggested an alternate measure that he felt would be more appropriate for the multi-million dollar concern:

> Professional sport is a business. This fact is indisputable, as witness the commercial contracts negotiated, the people employed, the profit and loss statements calculated, the advertising sold and the general economic structures of professional teams and leagues; but sport is unique, and therefore could not draw on other businesses for ideas in organization and structure. Instead, it had to develop its own system. The commodity it sells is entertainment, and the vehicle it uses to promote that commodity is competition.

Throughout his presentation he agreed that hockey was guilty of several business misdemeanours and should undergo investigation, but also pointed out certain shortcomings in Canada's laws:

> ... this country has established certain concepts, by legislative authority and by judicial pronouncement, to guarantee and protect the rights of individuals against monopolies, restraints of trade, and restrictions on freedom of choice. In certain areas, however, these concepts have not been fully developed, and I will expose the ways, some subtle and some not so subtle, in which professional hockey has exploited the undeveloped parts of these concepts. I recognize the fact that the proposed amendments to the Combines Investigation Act are intended to strengthen those concepts; but I submit further that they may not, by themselves, eradicate the injustices and inequities that exist in professional hockey. There may be other alternatives that require consideration and I will also undertake to discuss at least one.

He suggested that because hockey is almost an essential ingredient in the Canadian lifestyle, it is

> almost capable of judicial notice that the calibre of and the competition in the game we have made famous has been reduced im-

mensely so that there is now, more than ever, an urgent need to reverse this deterioration. As long as the only ones who control the sport are motivated by economic factors, there is no guarantee that professional hockey in Canada will return to its original level of skill and excitement.

Continuing in that vein, he declared:

. . . hockey is a big profitable business. As such it should not be exempt from controls other businesses are subject to . . . unless it could establish three things:

1 that it is essential to the existence of the league structures that legislative authority not be extended to hockey;
2 that they [the NHL] are capable of organizing hockey in a judicial and equitable manner without government assistance or control; and
3 that such freedom is in the players' and public's best interest.

He concluded:

. . . On past record alone, the organizers and owners of the professional hockey teams will find it impossible to establish any of these three criteria.

Yet on November 13, 1974, NHL President Clarence Campbell, a Rhodes scholar and distinguished lawyer who had presided over the league for thirty years, told the hearing that any government interference in pro hockey would dangerously threaten its survival:

No professional sports organization could possibly continue to function under such a law, because the object of the legislation is the elimination of the weak and the less efficient in skills or material resources. Such a philosophy would simply eliminate the competitors to the point where there would be no one left to carry on the competition, which is the major objective of all professional sports. The major portion of all professional sports legislation and regulations consists of the establishment of rules to ensure balanced competition, not to eliminate it. It is hard to conceive of a single regulation or rule in professional sports which is not basically in direct contravention of the literal text of the Combines Investigation Act. . . .

If there is any single piece of legislation I have read for a long time that is designed for the protection of the individual, as distinct from the welfare of the public, this has to be it, because everything in it relates to the removal of any limitations on the part of the individual player, and goodness only knows he has ample recourse to redress any difficulties he may encounter in the course of negotiating his contract.

Campbell later said his fear was that the proposed Canadian combines law might be similar to U.S. anti-trust law. "I had been watching the devastating effects of that legislation on the conduct of organized sports (all except baseball) in the U.S. for over twenty-five years. These include the attack on the 'reserve clause', the attack on the 'drafting' of players, and hockey's 'equalization by-law',* which was and is still not finally resolved."

Campbell was happy the Canadian constitution placed some restrictions on the federal jurisdiction: " ... the only way that its intervention in this area can be supported at all is to treat it as a matter of criminal law — not property and civil rights. ... no one engaged in sports wants to be treated as a criminal."† He admitted in a letter: "In retrospect it can be said that my answer [at the combines hearing] indulged in hyperbole — not entirely warranted by the results."

Although Eagleson told the hearing that he disagreed radically with Campbell's interpretation of the situation, he did agree that hockey should be exempt from the proposed legislation. In short, he felt the league must operate as a monopoly, yet he claimed the organizers and owners were incapable of running the NHL in an "equitable" manner.

---

* A player becomes a free agent by playing out his option year. During that year any member club is free to sign the player, but must, in return, give the first club some form of compensation or equalization for the purpose of leaving the team as competitive as it was before the player left. The equalization provision agreed to in the NHL-NHLPA Collective Bargaining Agreement, 1975 (revised in 1981) introduced a final arbitration rule: Judge Ed Houston of Toronto is the arbitrator. If the two teams cannot agree on compensation, each club submits a sealed proposal to Judge Houston for what it thinks is a fair equalization settlement. Houston must select one proposal; he cannot structure one of his own (see p. 178).

† On February 8, 1980, a Quebec Superior Court fined seventy-year-old Campbell $25,000 and imposed a one-day jail sentence for conspiring to bribe Liberal Senator Louis Giguere in the Sky Shops affair. Campbell and businessman Gordon Brown were found guilty of giving Giguere $95,000 between 1971 and 1972 in exchange for his influence in obtaining a federal lease extension for Sky Shops Export Ltd., a duty-free store in Montreal's Dorval Airport. Campbell received only a token day in jail because Judge Melvin Rothman, who presided over the case, felt his asthma condition too severe for a long-term imprisonment. In March, the NHL executive committee gave Campbell $50,000 to cover part of his $100,000 four-year legal bill and $25,000 fine.

As an alternative, he suggested "a government commission or tribunal to which players and owners could take their grievances and
problems. This tribunal could have the force and power to act as an
ombudsman in effect." He argued that a player's life in sport is a short
one, and he could get tied up in lengthy court cases, whereas if a
government-appointed arbitrator settled disputes, the government would
still be involved in sports, but only as an ultimate decision maker. He
felt the proposed legislation of the Combines Act to be too severe for
application to hockey, and believed the problems would be resolved
without making anyone liable to "an indictable offence".

By not opposing tighter government controls on hockey, Eagleson
supported the *status quo*. Since hockey was not subject to Canadian
competition and trade rules, the new colonialists, the WHA, and the
new NHL-American expansion teams which sprouted after 1967, were
afforded an opportunity to exploit the Canadian hockey system. In
1974, the NHL sold new franchises for "unrestricted profits", inflat-
ing the price of a new club to $6 million, a huge leap from $2 million
in 1967. American owners were permitted to concentrate the majority of freshly developed Canadian hockey players in U.S. cities, which
achieved maximum profits and employment for Americans. Unfair
operating practices such as equalization, which limits player movement between leagues or clubs, and unequal distribution of talent
through midget and amateur draft concepts, acted in opposition to the
principles of competition and free trade. No mechanisms within the
structure supported quality control or balanced competition.

The WHA was free to attack the CAHA "farm system" to the same
degree as the NHL, and yet the WHA ignored the stipulation set out in
the 1974 agreement between the NHL and the CAHA that development
fees (averaging $20,000) were to be paid to the junior hockey clubs for
each draft pick. Although it is a small sum in comparison to the huge
profits reaped by the NHL, it was the only attempt made at perpetuating the source of supply.

By 1974 the threat that the WHA would be eliminated from the
competition was quickly becoming a reality. Inflated salaries had
already caused franchises to fold, leaving behind a wasteland of
deserted hockey arenas and unpaid promotion debts. The much-
debated NHL-WHA merger would allow the NHL to resume its oligopo-
listic power to restrict trade, competition, and players' freedom to
change teams or to play amateur or international hockey.

The state of the art in the mid-seventies saw the professional hockey business peak with 32 top pro clubs — 18 NHL teams with 400 players and 14 WHA teams with 300 players. While franchises were mostly American-owned, approximately 90 percent of the players in the pros, plus thousands of players who earned salaries at minor-pro and semi-pro levels, were Canadian. The domination of a Canadian national resource — its hockey players and provincial hockey organizations, which depended on development fees from pro teams, and a share of the profits from international pro matches — by American multinationals was what the Liberal government had hoped to end by setting up Hockey Canada in 1969. After six years, the federal hockey tribunal had failed. Not only had it been ineffective in influencing major league policy, it also failed to fulfil its mandate to improve domestic hockey development. The entire responsibility for amateur hockey was tossed back to the CAHA.

Then Hockey Canada completely restructured its objectives, concentrating only on developing a national hockey team or teams using a total pro format or combining pros and semi-pros to represent Canada internationally. Hockey Canada, however, continued to receive regular federal grants (approximately $200,000 for 1974) and employed a full-time executive director. There was one catch: the CAHA continued to exercise its power in the international arena by retaining its role as the official spokesman for Canadian hockey abroad. The CAHA returned to Hockey Canada in March 1975. In December 1974, the CAHA withdrew from Hockey Canada. This was the situation at the time Eagleson was suggesting to the Senate committee that all Canadian hockey players should be eligible to play in international competition if they wished, regardless of ownership. He was also paving the way for the day when professional players' participation in international competition would become a condition of their employment.

As a direct result of Eagleson's enlistment of the aid of the pros to boost Canada's sagging image abroad, another door on Canadian culture closed. His suggestion to stage the first World Cup of Hockey, called the Canada Cup, with pros from both the NHL and WHA, was possibly the final blow to any attempt to save Canadian hockey. At the conclusion of their book *The Death of Hockey*, authors Kidd and Macfarlane made a final appeal to nationalism:

If we cannot save hockey, we cannot save Canada. .... As problems they are remarkably similar. Canada is becoming a colony of the United States. We supply the Americans with raw materials and energy, they supply us with the finished product making us dependent on them not only as a market for our exports but as the source of our consumer goods. The people who run the country rationalize this dependency by telling us we do not have the resources to develop the country ourselves — a lie — and that therefore it makes more sense to sell it for what Prime Minister Trudeau calls "good hard cash". The same is true of hockey. A game nurtured by generations of Canadians has been sold to Americans. ... Why should the NHL be allowed to harness this community investment for private profit — profit reaped mainly in another country?

If it was the Liberal government's desire in 1969 to erect a Canadian hockey federation to decentralize hockey, develop a truly national team to better represent Canada in world matches, and end American multinational domination of Canada's game, the effort failed on all three counts. The "nationals", a team of amateurs and semi-pros used in the annual IIHF World Championships, had been run independently out of Winnipeg, and was now controlled by Hockey Canada. Hockey Canada in turn was tightly controlled by the Eagleson network running between Ottawa and Toronto, where its headquarters were set up. And because of the embarrassment caused by Eagleson's rudeness to Russian authorities, it was debatable whether Canadian pride had been restored or eradicated. The immediate short-term gains from the hockey summit in Russia were obviously financial ones and since all the profits were raised by Eagleson, he wanted complete control over distribution. Only in time would the effects of this quick fix take their paralysing toll.

People such as Walter Bush in the U.S., who had always been active in amateur and college-level hockey, started up an American national team of Canadian pros who became naturalized Americans through the NHL. (There were only thirty American citizens playing pro hockey at the time.) A few years later a memo from Doug Fisher's office suggested that Eagleson was contributing his personal entrepreneurial skills to this end: "Eagleson had done extremely well in getting a U.S. team off the ground; it has splendid coaching and management and is likely to be very competitive. ...." It was. Team

U.S.A. took the gold medal in the 1980 Lake Placid Winter Olympics, while Canada finished sixth.

The most immediate problem Hockey Canada faced was that the 1972 Summit Series would become in retrospect another Woodstock, a one-time fling. The first series was a trial run, and because the Russians suffered embarrassment from Team Canada's management, namely Eagleson, at the 1973 meetings, Bunny Ahearne was expected to influence IIHF rulings against using pros. To muddy the waters further, the NHL was aware of the tremendous public exposure the first series received and club owners were concerned the public would grow less excited about the product they were supporting through television and by attending league games at home. The NHL had little choice but to compete for profits from the international hockey market. Sam Pollock, managing director of the Montreal Canadiens, suggested that a team of non-Stanley-Cup contenders be pitted against Russia. Also, the NHL and (particularly) the WHA were aware of the potential for huge profit to be made from selling television rights to future series, and figured they could work separately with the Russians.

Proceedings across the Atlantic proved unfavourable. Just prior to the April 1972 meetings in Moscow, Hockey Canada had elected a new IIHF Committee. Selected at a Montreal meeting were Gordon Juckes, CAHA executive director, Lou Lefaive, and Allan J. Scott, newly appointed chairman of Hockey Canada's executive committee. These same three were to attend the 1973 Moscow meetings. Doug Fisher was elected chairman of the new IIHF committee, a body representing the CAHA, Canadian professional hockey, government, the Canadian Intercollegiate Athletic Union (CIAU), and Hockey Canada. The committee was the spokesman for Canada in international hockey matters, and suggested that Scott take out a CAHA membership card to legitimize Hockey Canada's presence. (CAHA still casts Canada's vote at the IIHF meetings.)

Before leaving for the 1973 official IIHF conference in Moscow, Scott sent a memo to Hockey Canada's honorary chairman, Charles Hay, suggesting that HC continue its push for "open competition". After the meeting Scott, however, reported that during his private talks with the Russians, Andrei Starovoitov, Russia's number-one hockey man, hedged slightly about a second nation-to-nation series on the basis that the behaviour exhibited by the Canadian team and its management was an embarrassment to the Russians, happening as it had "in front of the very top people of their nation", but did say that he himself would be interested in seeing another series. From what was called "the political side", Lefaive received more positive response from the number-three man in Soviet hockey, Alexander Gresko: " ... 1973 was out of the question ... some time should elapse to 'allow the sharp edges to dull' but as a matter of principle, another series could be organized from [the Canadian government's] end; then he [Gresko] would be willing to talk further."

At the same time, European pro leagues were starting up, and wanted the Canada–Russia format turned into a soccer-style World Cup event. Three other nations were to be added to a round-robin format: Czechoslovakia, Sweden, and the United States.

Meanwhile, the sale to the North American public of another series was already underway. While it appeared that Fisher and other Hockey Canada members resented Eagleson's domination of the series, their public statements never reflected this. Fisher and Lang held a press conference in January 1973 for the dual purpose of explaining the high levels of profits generated by the September series, and praising Eagleson's inventiveness in ensuring that "no one made an end-run with HC's money". (Hockey Canada ultimately received $500,000, one half of the profits.) Hockey Canada directors and executives tackled the problem of gaining the NHL support necessary to release the players for another exhibition. There was still no collective-bargaining agreement — and Eagleson still held the trump card with the owners, as the player spokesman. In spite of the adverse publicity he received in 1972, once again he was publicly wooed by Hockey Canada.

Eagleson was still seen as the biggest single factor in launching another summit series. Bill McMurtry was close to him in 1972 while events were unfolding: "Because of the great deal of power Al had in the public eye, in the media and marketing, he single-handedly did create Team Canada. Don't ever accept the fact he didn't do it in 1972." McMurtry says he remembers hearing from the players as early as 1970 how much they wanted to play the Russians: "I remember having lunch with Normy Ulman, he said the same things other players did, but I specifically remember Ulman saying, 'God, I would *pay* to play the Russians!'" McMurtry says the same three groups opposing the 1972 series — the politicians, the owners, and amateur hockey — remained opposed to Canada's continued participation. The government was against the series, McMurtry thinks, because "it was extra work and something politicians wanted control of but didn't have the connections to carry it out; and down to the last NHL governor and owner there was not a taker anxious to participate." McMurtry was in Eagleson's office when Eagleson took on the owners over the telephone just before the first series: "He was talking with Jennings of the Rangers. Jennings was saying, 'No way, we have contracts and contracts say you can't do it.' I remember Al saying, 'Well, I don't care what your contracts say.' There was Campbell who said he couldn't do it and there were two lawyers who said he couldn't do it. So Eagleson told them: 'Okay, I'll tell you what, Mr. Jennings, you have Clarence Campbell play centre and put the two owners on the wing when you open up the season because that's what's going to happen.'"

McMurtry said it was a question of Eagleson's simply having made up his mind to do it: " . . . a lot of it was no more complex than sitting around chatting with a few players at lunch, like a group of Canadians anywhere, Canadians off the shift saying, 'Goddamn it, why . . . it is just so obvious . . . why shouldn't our best play their best' and it was that simple. Once our best wanted to play and Al was our rep, he wasn't going to take no for an answer."

McMurtry says that scene in Eagleson's office summarized "what I admired about him . . . he had total tunnel vision and he wasn't concerned about contracts or anything else, just knew intuitively he was right . . . that's an example of what he can do when he puts his mind to it." (Later, McMurtry attacked Eagleson for failing to apply his reserved, disciplined forcefulness in drawing attention to his one-man investigation of violence in amateur hockey.)

Many close associates describe Eagleson in a similar way. But not everyone wants to give Eagleson credit for masterminding Team Canada. In a letter to Canadian writer and political essayist Walter Stewart, Doug Fisher wrote:

An aspect of Alan I found astounding, and I still wonder at, is his inability to do any synoptic thinking or planning ahead. Despite his quicksilver, he's not reflective about the long-range future. . . . I don't think he's ever come up with any [idea] on his own, beyond the general idea he had, almost a suspicion, in 1970 and 1971 that in international play on a nation vs nation basis lay a ramp his association could climb for money and a unique independence from the owners. . . . I'd say Chris Lang, Gary Aldcorn [a former NHL player and vice-president of development for Hockey Canada in 1970–74] and myself developed the overall strategy, the tactics, and the long-range plans for Canada and the pros in international hockey back between 1969 and 1971. . . .

Eagleson was particularly useful to Fisher, however, when Hockey Canada needed a liaison-broker-diplomat to develop its international hockey goals. In 1973 the second seduction of Alan Eagleson began. After the January press conference Fisher and Lang held to explain the "huge profits" generated by the series, Fisher wrote in a memo to Eagleson: "I let fly a trial balloon deliberately for your speech . . . that we are ready to help do it again, to do it better, to fit future matches into a World Cup of Soccer-type of arrangement."

A month later Hockey Canada voted in favour of the NHLPA being represented on the Board. This would mean that Eagleson, as the NHLPA spokesman, would have direct influence on Hockey Canada policy. Lang later described the effect this had: "Besides the national organizations affecting policy, we have pro organizations — the NHL and WHA — which are multinational corporations. We have the Players' Associations which are multinational in nature; the two governments — Canada and the U.S.A. — and we have the educational associations — the National Collegiate Athletic Association [NCAA] in the U.S. and the CIAU in Canada." With this input, Hockey Canada became another wellhead for American expansion. Perhaps Lefaive, the federal government's rep, who became Hockey Canada's full-time president in 1980, was the first to draw attention to this in 1973. Lefaive's statement was included in a memo sent to Fisher in June of that year:

> We have not been entirely honest with the members of our constituents, and especially, the Board members of Hockey Canada. A core group has had the advantage and opportunity to resources and to a degree, has out-stripped our associates and counterparts of other associations, particularly the CAHA. A privileged position has been assumed by many of us, and this to a very large extent has caused the friction between our organizations.

By August, however, complaints of "opportunism" were suppressed and the CAHA's position altered further by a ruling covered in a telegram from Vienna wherein IIHF's secretary Walter Wasservogel told the CAHA's Joe Kryczka: "The Executive Committee of the

International Olympic Committee decided unanimously to permit games between amateurs and professionals, whereby it does not make any difference whether these games [are] between clubs or international games or an open World Championship. Players who play against professionals at such tournaments do not lose their qualification for Olympic Games. ...''

By December plans were underway to revoke the charitable status of the Hockey Canada Foundation; a decision was made in October 1973 to change the fundamental thrust of Hockey Canada and to reduce staff and involvement in hockey development programs.

The CAHA, however, still retained pseudo-power. In Wasservogel's official statement it was declared that any international meet must be "under control of the IIHF". The amateur association had been Canada's official voice in global hockey talks since the country's first international competition at the 1920 Antwerp Olympics. On December 9, 1974, the CAHA informed the new federal health minister, Marc Lalonde, of its proposed withdrawal from Hockey Canada, and outlined details for a CAHA International Council. The federal government would now have a two-tier system for handling international hockey matters. The new CAHA committee would be composed of two reps from the CAHA; two from the federal government; one each from the NHL and WHA; one each from the NHLPA and the World Hockey Association Players' Association (WHPA); and one from the CIAU. A chairman would be appointed from the CAHA. The letter to Lalonde further stipulated that neither the pro leagues, the players' associations, nor the CIAU would have input in the subcommittee concerned with international junior hockey competition. Nor would the amateurs' representatives deal with competition among pros. While the CAHA would continue to depend on federal financing, Hockey Canada was moving towards self-sufficiency.

Part of the CAHA's reasoning behind its decision to pull out of Hockey Canada was discussed at a joint meeting between CAHA and HC officials in December 1974. CAHA vice-president Don Johnson (a personal friend of Eagleson's) indicated that CAHA members looked upon Fisher as "not a hockey person". CAHA president Devine and executive director Juckes called Lefaive and Lang "non-hockey people" and maintained that there had been many additions to the Hockey Canada board of "non-hockey people". Fisher admitted that perhaps Hockey Canada had taken too low a profile in steering the organization away from controversial and debatable issues, including the junior and midget drafts, the new junior contracts, and violence in hockey.

Juckes was critical of Hockey Canada's failure to raise more money, "especially in the private sector". A report (*Corporate Plan Hockey Canada*, dated June 18, 1973) says: "HC is broke and the Treasury Board wants answers prior to approval of further funding." It is surprising to note that, in a letter sent by Scott to NHL president Clarence Campbell on May 25, 1973, Scott has turned down funding from the NHL: "Our current budgeting anticipates no requirements for financial support from the NHL." Much later, Fisher would summarize his feelings about Hockey Canada's decision to move the domestic responsibility from HC back to the CAHA in his "record of substantial failures and real successes".

> When I said "substantial failure" it related to the optimistic plans Mr. Munro had for HC, especially in the domestic side. He wanted a revolution in organization, attitude, coaching and playing style in Canadian hockey. Not only did this not happen and HC fail as a catalyst and leader in domestic hockey ... at the demand of Mr. Munro's successor, Marc Lalonde, HC abandoned any domestic role, leaving the field as it was before to the CAHA and its affiliates.

He then noted how, without the impetus of the real funders, domestic hockey failed to follow through with development and coaching programs.*

> The withdrawal was not from total, but relative failure. HC's work in initiating coaching schools, levels of instruction, indeed a systematic approach to hockey development, from individual techniques to team training became the inheritance of the CAHA, and those programs are carried on after a fashion, although not as thoroughly or with the stress on analysis of hockey at which HC had aimed and never really achieved.

Fisher later said there was only one occasion when all of the Hockey Canada directors met as a group. He described the hockey federation as an example of another "favourite device of government to create empty councils. ...." He said, "Once we lost Charley Hay,

---

* In 1971–72 Canadian community colleges certified 450 coaches at a cost to Hockey Canada of $20 each; 1,300 were certified in 1972–73.

there was a big failure to change HC back to the initial idea to improve hockey.'' He pointed out that Hockey Canada failed to distribute the coaching development programs across Canada, and added, ''HC remains a centralized organization, failing to link up with the western provinces.'' He made several proposals to Eagleson over the years to get players involved in hockey development, but without success. ''I had one idea that would enable the NHLPA to become a force in coaching development and Ken Dryden and Bobby Clarke were interested, but it didn't get off the ground because Alan never pushed it.'' Another of Fisher's ideas was to ''use funds from international hockey competitions to set up programs whereby retired hockey players develop minor hockey in terms of skills''. Fisher felt this would be ''a real cachet for the players — great public relations across international airwaves ... everyone would see them as pros doing their share ... paying back hockey at the basic level ... but Eagle didn't push for this either.'' Overall, Fisher sees Eagleson's long-term association with Hockey Canada as a drawback rather than a contribution.

It appears that Hockey Canada's success depended entirely on Eagleson's largesse. ''Once he liked an idea he would begin to run with it. But if he didn't push for it ... it never happened.''

In April 1974, the Soviets agreed to a second September series.

At the NHL and NHLPA joint meetings (held in Bermuda in May) both parents formally informed the Hockey Canada board that they could not participate in the proposed series because ''it was the wrong time of year''. One report said the NHL declined because it wasn't willing to share TV revenues with the IIHF. More likely, the strife between the two leagues prohibited any fraternizing. Davidson of the WHA had proclaimed the reserve clause and option clause illegal and signed more than 70 NHLers. The NHL (which operated under the reserve clause until 1973) said it would take the new league to court. Lawsuits multiplied, costing approximately $4 million, between the two leagues. Any series between the WHA and the NHA would have hurt their legal status. At the Bermuda meeting, the NHLPA also voted unanimously against playing the WHA in exhibition games in the fall. By this time, the WHA and the NHL settled out of court. These games were scheduled as part of the settlement package the WHA won, and by playing the NHL, it hoped to gain instant credibility; for each exhibition game not played, it was reported the NHL had to pay the WHA a penalty of $10,000. The Players' Association's support of the NHL was seen as a stab in the back by the WHA franchises, which had helped boost NHL players' salaries.

The NHLPA also wholeheartedly endorsed the NHL decision to decline the Soviet invitation, and Eagleson resigned from Hockey Canada that same month. By mid-May, however, Eagleson was being actively pursued by Hockey Canada and was formally invited to rejoin the board. In a personal note, Fisher appealed to "our mutual interest", asking Eagleson to do what he could to prevent the hockey world from being controlled by the private clubs:

It is my appreciation without your help, indeed without your leadership, we are not going to have a world hockey situation that isn't dominated and determined by the interests of the professional owners, particularly the American owners of the NHL and WHA franchises. ... Despite the reality that for the foreseeable future (say 10 years) the large majority of hockey players will continue to be Canadians, the weight of the proprietors is so heavily American that our national interests are going to get the short end of consideration. It is clear that Ahearne has become convinced that the time has arrived to play cahoots with the NHL through [Jim] Norris [owner of the Chicago Black Hawks] and that Western Europe should become tributary through minor professional leagues to the NHL interests. ...

Then Fisher went directly for Eagleson's weak spot:

The only organization and the only individual with the clout and the energy to keep developments open and fluid for a time and to link in clinching something like the World Cup competition and Inter-City competition (as in soccer) is you.

Eagleson accepted the invitation to join the board on May 23, 1974. At that time, Hockey Canada closed its offices on St. Clair Avenue in Toronto and reopened in the Administrative Centre for Sports and Recreation in Ottawa, under the watchful eye of a new full-time executive director, Derek Holmes. (Holmes had played European hockey from 1969–74 and was given the post upon his return. He was paid an annual salary of $24,000 in 1979, the year he resigned.)

The NHL's earlier refusal to acknowledge the WHA in exhibition games, however, was turned around when the NHLPA forfeited an opportunity to make profits on the 1974 Team Canada–Soviet Series,

giving the rival upstart league the international exposure it desired.*
By August, Fisher's diplomacy was heavily taxed by his role as
mediator between Eagleson and his WHA counterpart, Ron Roberts.
Excessive name calling directed at the NHLPA and its leader by the
press forced Fisher to attempt to put the matter straight in a three-page
memo to Eagleson:

> ... I tell Roberts you are a spectre he must either allay or produce in
> as quick and decisive a way as you have. Now — I don't know what
> Hockey Canada spokesmen criticized the NHLPA. I didn't. Lefaive
> says he hasn't. I doubt Lang has. I might add that I asked and
> didn't get the co-operation I thought was assured from [Ben]
> Hatskin [WHA Counsel] (and through them Harris) in leaving any
> question of seeking any NHL players for this series such as Orr and
> Esposito. ...
>
> However, I think you should remember that the reason we got
> this particular series triggered at all was because of you. You and
> I agreed that it might be possible to put a series together this
> fall. Remember that you even worked out possible playing dates
> in September and October. We also agreed that we could not have
> another Hull case; therefore the WHA must be brought in. What
> followed was fairly straight-forward. I approached both the NHL
> and the WHA. The former said Nay, the latter, Yea. ... Was it
> worthwhile to clinch it? It depended on how the WHA reacted to the
> terms we felt necessary. They did, including an understanding that
> NHL players were not to be involved. ...†

Fisher's memo attempted to save face for Hockey Canada and keep
Eagleson as an ally:

> It is easy to kick the stuffings out of an ... organization such as
> Hockey Canada. By its very nature the organization does not place
> its key, on-going people in a high-profile or fight-out-in-the-open

---

* The WHA won only one game during the series. The outcome of the 1974 September
Series was: Game One, Quebec City, 3-3 tie; Game Two, Toronto, Canada 4-1;
Game Three, Winnipeg, Soviet Union 8-5; Game Four, Vancouver, 5-5 tie; Game
Five, Moscow, Soviet Union 3-2; Game Six, Moscow, Soviet Union 5-2; Game
Seven, Moscow, 4-4 tie; Game Eight, Moscow, Soviet Union, 3-2.

† Later, Roberts publicly proclaimed the WHPA "would look forward to working
closely with the NHLPA" on world championships.

position. And hockey, as you know — indeed you are the classic illustration of it — has a host of fast-moving, quickly opinionated, levering, strenuous personalities. That doesn't mean that we in Hockey Canada are dummies or incompetent most of the time.

In an odd way in this '74 series we really miss an Alan Eagleson, and yet the very record of Alan Eagleson makes it harder for us all.

Eagleson didn't attempt to defend himself in his response, but merely suggested "hearsay is a dangerous area of comment", and affirmed his continuing support of Hockey Canada: " . . . I would like to offer any assistance whatsoever that I can give Hockey Canada in that the only motive I would have in this offer would be to assist Hockey Canada in its aims." His willingness to swing with the punches from the press and from Hockey Canada was evident; these were not the last blows he would endure for that cause.

Hockey Canada also had its problems with the media. Fisher later had to defend HC and its board publicly in the pages of the *Globe and Mail* in reply to a columnist's characterization of the international committee as "bush league" and suggestions that some members were "free-loaders, along for the trips, the booze and the glory of media attention". In his rebuttal, Fisher defended the work of the international committee and singled out Eagleson for praise: " . . . without Alan Eagleson the series in '72 would not have happened — in my opinion. It is really not publicly known that Mr. Eagleson played a strong part in achieving the '74 series." Hockey Canada treasurer Chris Lang and chairman Doug Fisher approached Eagleson in desperation before the WHA-Russia 1974 series hoping to enlist his help in selling TV rights for the eight-game series. Hockey Canada was roughly at the break-even point (the advance sale of gate receipts would cover all expenses), but the publicly funded corporation wanted a cushion. "Jimmy Patterson in Vancouver wasn't having much success in locating buyers, so we called Eagleson in desperation," says Lang. Eagleson was successful in getting Standard Brands to commit to buying the TV rights. He proposed that if gate receipts were high then all profits from the sale of TV rights should go to Hockey Canada and not the WHA. Both HC and the WHA voted against accepting his proposition. As a result, the 1974 series did not make a profit.

"The disappointing financial performance of the 1974 Series was not due to a great overrun on expenses . . . in fact, the expenses of the

1974 Series were more tightly controlled than in 1972. Rather, the disappointing financial performance of the 1974 Series was almost wholly attributable to the failure to properly market Canadian TV rights. In 1972, $2.1 million in gross revenues were realized from the sales of Canadian and U.S. TV rights; in 1974 only $190,000 in gross revenues were realized from this source," says M & M Systems Research Ltd.

The reasons M & M gave as a possible explanation for this failure were (1) a lack of lead-time to successfully market a TV proposal; and (2) "inexperienced marketers, lacking 'other levers' available through NHL and NHLPA in 1972 to pressure would-be purchasers."

Not all the press Eagleson received was harsh. Eagleson attended the 1974 series in Moscow as an observer. One headline said, "Eagle is given royal welcome by Soviet hockey brass", and mentioned that he was treated like a "visiting head of state" with a chauffeured limousine awaiting his arrival at the airport; he demanded and received a deluxe two-storey suite in the "best" Moscow hotel, the Intourist; and after conferring with Alexander Gresko for five hours, he was presented with the best seats in the house for the remaining games of the series "in front of Brezhnev and Kosygin".

Eagleson was outraged later by Gresko's alleged spying:* "It's a joke. ... The RCMP have known about Gresko's suspected activities for a long time, but he's had an easy access to this country. ... Gresko had easy access to Pierre Trudeau's office on November 14 when he accompanied Professor Ed Enos of Loyola College who gave Trudeau a Team Canada practice jersey."

Eagleson accepted the media applause, claiming that his keen reception in the U.S.S.R. was "their way of saying they want me to arrange another match with the 1976 NHL Stanley Cup winners."

In June 1974 Marc Lalonde offered Eagleson the job of arranging a six-nation tourney to mark Canada's official return to international world hockey. Eagleson says, "One of the conditions I made before I took the job was that I'm not interested in a lot of red tape. I want

---

* In December of that year, a report surfaced that Gresko, formerly the third secretary of the Soviet Embassy in London, was expelled from Britain on Sept. 24, 1971, along with 90 other Soviet diplomats alleged by British Intelligence agents to be involved in espionage. At the time Gresko met with Eagleson and other HC officials, he was head of Russia's Winter Sports Committee, and had actively promoted the 1972 and 1974 series. As well, he was the official attaché to the 1976 Summer Olympics in Montreal.

somebody to say, 'there's the target, you supply your own tools, namely the players, and we'll clear the path.' " Eagleson knew about TV lead time requirements, and even if announcing this tourney threatened the 1974 series by competing for fans' attention, he quickly promised the "best ever" performance in hockey history; dropping the names of Bobby Orr and Esposito added sizzle. "It'll be better this time for several reasons. First, both leagues will be represented. Second, the players will be chosen, not invited. ... "

Toronto Sun sports columnist Jim Coleman gave Eagleson the new title: a "singularly wise and enlightened autocrat". In just two short years, Eagleson had come full circle, from *Nekulturny* to bespectacled Superman: "the Incredible, the Invincible". He was riding high. His fall prior to the 1974 series had been wiped clean; by swinging the media around to his side he had again clearly shown his power. He was widely praised: "Eagleson's decision [to organize the World Cup of Hockey] is one which, in the years to come, undoubtedly should be remembered with gratitude by every Canadian sports enthusiast," continued Jim Coleman. Coleman took the opportunity to suggest to the Canadian government that it should make Eagleson "the Czar of all sport in Canada".

THE SINGULARLY WISE AND ENLIGHTENED AUTOCRAT

*Al Eagleson? I think he is smart, and from
what I know of his background, honest. But
he's in the fast buck area too, you know,
he's got to make it.*
Conn Smythe

By the mid-seventies, Eagleson's career had found its safe harbour and dropped anchor. He was now a millionaire. His fall from grace in Moscow had been erased when the federal government appointed him Canada's official czar of hockey in arranging the first major-league World Cup of Hockey to be held in September 1976. This time Orr would play. He had drafted the longest-running collective-bargaining agreement in sports history. The NHL was close to winning a national television contract. And he had the chance to make a political come-back.*

This Sammy Glick of Canadian sport, law, and politics was walking a tricky tightrope: he ran the agency for 150 hockey players, headed the NHL Players' Association, represented general managers in their dealings with the owners, and assisted owners in setting up international hockey matches. His wheeling and dealing had the press on a constant high, showering him with praise. At forty-two, Eagleson had developed a keen sense of self. The dark pin-striped suits and startling white shirts accentuated his even tan and robust trimness won by sailing, skiing, and playing squash and tennis year round. He

---

* Eagleson confirmed he would not seek leadership of the federal Progressive Conservatives on January 5, 1976. "... a lot of people have approached me but I'm committed to Brian Mulroney," he said. Eagleson and Metro Toronto Chairman Paul Godfrey were in charge of the campaign in Metro for Mulroney.

155

mixed a low-church sense of superior morality with the arrogance of never permitting anyone to forget he is self-made.

Eagleson bragged to his friend, University of Toronto coach John McManus, about how good business was. He had just moved from Mississauga to a stately ravine-lot Tudor mansion in Rosedale, owned a condominium in Florida at the exclusive St. Andrews Club, held a dozen private club memberships, owned a Rolls-Royce, and kept a Cadillac in the driveway: " 'I could fit four in my living room,' he would say to me whenever he took some of the U of T's athletic department out for a freebee lunch at Hy's Steak House," McManus recalls. At the time, Eagleson says his list of best friends included: "Paul Godfrey, Don McDougal, Ross Johnson, Senator Keith Davey, Bobby Orr and Nancy."

His wealth hadn't necessarily changed him. He used to drop by McManus' office occasionally at lunchtime when he was at Queen's Park. "One time he was in my office talking on the phone. I had a copy of *Sports Illustrated* on my desk. After lunch I came back to my office and noticed the magazine was gone. I called up Al and said, 'Did you swipe my *Sports Illustrated*?' 'That's right,' he replied, 'that's why I'm rich and you're poor.' Instead of calling him an arrogant son of a bitch, we shrug our shoulders and say, 'That's Eagleson.' "

One close friend who has spent hundreds of hours with Eagleson in "messy" hockey deals attests to his resilience and his cunning. Others comment on his loyalty and generosity to those he sees as being "with" him. He's known to be vindictive to someone who breaks a promise, and he won't tolerate anyone who patronizes him on class or social grounds. He is proud but no Citizen Kane; if there is a special luncheon for Ontario Premier Bill Davis, Allen Eagleson, Sr., gets head-table seating. He is anti-intellectual to the point of being crass with anyone he suspects of being an "academic" (excepting legal scholars). But otherwise he's balanced in mood and temperament and looks forward each day to "having a hell of a good time".

Other acquaintances prefer to maintain a business rather than a social relationship with him, calling him "the rudest, noisiest, most inconsistent man I've known ..." saying, "he can outrage almost every sensibility I have" ... and, "Thank God he doesn't drink, and if he plays around with women I don't know about it."

He believes hard work is rewarded and that the rewards show in one's lifestyle; yet his natural tendency towards tight-fistedness permits him few luxuries outside of indulging his family. His marriage, which endures, appears to be the touchstone of his security. "I prefer to deal with him when his wife is far away because they seem to compete with each other. Each has drive, stamina, and always wants to win. They stimulate each other," says one close friend. Eagleson openly says "I like my wife" and says that Nancy is his favourite travelling companion. "I'm happy to have my wife with me when I go to Europe, which is not something that applies with a hell of a lot of my friends." He is proud of her and likes to show off her collection of art and antique Canadian furniture which adorns his offices.

Nancy accompanied her husband on European hockey junkets in the early sixties, and combined the trips with visits to art galleries. (Eagleson possesses a retentive memory, and quickly became familiar with and developed a taste for contemporary art.) Nancy never liked being interviewed as "the little woman behind the man" when he was in politics. "I'm not domestic, I never cook breakfast, and sometimes we take the kids to eat at McDonald's or the Ponderosa," she says. Like her husband, she can't tolerate smoking, doesn't drink, and dresses stylishly but conservatively. There's a story, perhaps apocryphal, that they went to church on their first date. She says they often watch hockey on TV, "then Al runs down to the Gardens for the final minutes of play." New York is Nancy's passion: "I could move there tomorrow," she says. Her knowledge of New York's antique shops, art museums, and galleries is extensive: she can orchestrate a shopping-sightseeing tour complete with dinner suggestions ("there's no time for lunch") and hotels on five minutes' notice.

In 1975 Eagleson set Nancy up in business as sole owner of Rae-Con Consultants Ltd., and hired Marvin Goldblatt as treasurer. Rae-Con is the vehicle for Nancy's interior design business. One of her tasks is looking after her husband's office decorating and furnishings, a job for which she is paid a monthly salary of just under $1,000 (1978). Rae-Con also owns the ten-room family ski chalet in Craigleith, Ontario, which in 1978 was worth $100,000. Goldblatt estimates Rae-Con's gross annual billings in that year to have been $250,000.*

* As an employee of Rae-Con, Goldblatt would seem to compete indirectly with Eagleson's company, Sports Management Ltd., by offering financial-planning services to sixty pro athletes, including Sharif Khan, a leading pro squash player. Goldblatt was simultaneously paid $40,000 a year (1978) as Eagleson's comptroller.

As a result of the sudden rise in interest in sports as entertainment at home and abroad and the rapid growth of hockey franchises, Eagleson's personal financial power base skyrocketed. At the end of the boom period of the early seventies he was administering no fewer than nine separate business enterprises, which generated a gross income of $14.5 million in 1977. Today, R. Alan Eagleson, Q.C., the crown jewel in his hockey czardom, is the largest law firm for professional athletes in Canada, with a full-time staff of eight. Eagleson combines directorships and consulting fees from private legal work for twenty-five corporate clients such as Coca-Cola Ltd., Standard Brands Ltd., Gray Coach Lines Ltd., John Labatt Ltd., and Taft Broadcasting Corporation. These giants usually hire his services in connection with sports sponsorship or athlete product endorsements. Eagleson is retained by some 150 hockey players who are paid an average (in 1980) of $95,000 a season. His law firm's gross annual billings in 1978 for negotiating contracts were $500,000. His combined directorships and consulting fees from his various businesses bring him a salary of more than $100,000 a year.

Sports Management Ltd. is Eagleson's wholly owned personal financial consulting company. Founded in 1972, its staff of eight now manages the financial affairs of some 180 athletes. Athletes are charged up to $100 an hour. In 1978 this company's billings were more than $500,000.

Eagleson's real estate interests are primarily held by Nanjill Investments Ltd., a company he started in the late sixties and in which he held a 40 percent interest along with Orr (40 percent) and Mike Walton (20 percent). Interests in industrial properties in Markham valued at $350,000 (1978) and Bramalea, Ontario ($200,000 in 1978), plus a 3 percent interest in Pony Sporting Goods Ltd., accounted for most of the company's assets of approximately $500,000 by 1978.

By 1980 he was personally grossing $1 million per annum, which included the $70,000 a year he charged the NHLPA for his role as executive director; after taxes he expected to net well over $200,000. At the time he estimated his net worth at "less than $2 million and more than $1 million". (Harold Ballard says, "Eagleson's worth $5 or $6 million in cash.")

His success has largely depended on the long-standing friendships he has made over the years through business, political, and, of course, sports contacts. To stage another of his profitable hockey ventures, he need only pick up the telephone to get the sponsors and financial backing. That dependability is a measure of the goodwill Eagleson has earned over the years.

One way in which he develops these special close relationships is by referring clients and friends to members of his network, such as the Orr–Walton hockey school and Lang's, Haggert's, and Harnett's companies. He cuts his friends in on deals when they come his way: for example, the partnership with Irv Ungerman for the Ali–Frazier fight, or the sale of TV rights for the 1972 series to Ballard and Orr.

One friendship that has endured over the years is that with Ross Johnson, president of Standard Brands, probably one of the most successful Canadian businessmen operating in the U.S. The two men met in 1958, when they were just starting out, at a time when neither one could manage the $600 membership fee for the Lambton Golf Club. Since then, the Standard Brands family of companies has become one of Eagleson's largest clients. Conversely, Standard Brands has hired a number of Eagleson's athlete clients to endorse and promote products, which opens up business for his friend, Bob Haggert. "If Sittler has an endorsement opportunity I want to throw it to Haggert, let him do all the work on it. I'll read the contract, I consider that part of my fee, of what I charge Darryl, but if there's a 15 percent agency commission that goes to Haggert's company. I don't want the trappings related to that kind of discussion ... but I read every word of each commercial and I make sure nothing is going to offend the public or their appreciation of Darryl or Bobby Orr," says Eagleson.

Whom does Eagleson pay? Who pulls *his* strings? Those questions inevitably accompany success that cannot be attributed to a silver spoon or an established family crest. The answer? It seems Eagleson does pay with favours. His influence opens most doors.

One favour he attempted involved the department of the Secretary of State. George Crombe, regional director of the federal department, remembers receiving a phone call from Eagleson in 1977: "I told him, 'We've never met but I've heard of you.' He told me, 'I want to meet with you to get a Canadian citizenship for Vaclov Nedomansky [a Czech hockey player who played for the WHA's Toronto Toros, a club which became the Birmingham Bulls]* and the wife of the president of Coca-Cola' whom he believed to be the wife of Canadian president

*Nedomansky now plays for Detroit.

Neville Kirchmann. So we set up a meeting for 2:00 on July 25, 1977. A half hour before the meeting Eagleson calls to cancel. Then we set it up for 11:00 on July 28. A half hour before, the same thing ... 'I'm off to New York and can't make it but maybe you can process it through.' The next day I see in the paper a photo of Eagleson and Billy Harris playing tennis at some club. I wrote him a letter enclosing the picture saying, 'I know you are busy but so am I' ... I never heard from Eagleson again.''

Crombe says he still remembers Nedomansky's papers and his citizenship ceremony in 1978. ''Nedomansky kept his home in Canada but I found out the wife [of the president of Coca-Cola] never was a Canadian, yet wanted dual citizenship without having lived in Canada.''

Eagleson sums up his business philosophy in one word: independence. He says Harnett's, Haggert's, and Ungerman's companies are 100 percent owned by them. ''I don't want any part of it because I feel one day I want to pack this all in. I want to know I'm not going to pull down a whole batch of people, just because I retire I'll know they won't be forced elsewhere. They are now so strong in their fields that they are generating a lot of business outside of my clients which is good, so they can remain on their own two feet.''

With his player clients he demands total dependence. For ten years he has said, ''I have one philosophy, if the player doesn't like the way I do work he doesn't pay the bill.'' It's not a friendly philosophy. The first key to his success, he says, is ''the relative importance in negotiations — [it is] the client's ability, not the lawyer's, the client's ability that is supreme.'' At another time, he said, ''It's the big star, not the fringe player, that brings the owners to their knees. Second is credibility. If I make a deal with an owner he knows that my client's going to back me up. He's not going to come back with a last minute jiggle. He knows I can commit to a deal. The final requirement is the team, how badly that team needs that player.''

Eagleson maintains that the type of relationship he has with a player ''separates me from the others. I try consciously not to let anybody down. I think that's important. Players trust me. The minute that trust ends then there's nothing. That goes for everybody. That's what impresses them most, I treat them equally whether they are Bobby Orr or Nobody Jones. That's the reason our players' association has been so successful. I do it all without any written agreements. Others sign those things. ... If a player doesn't trust you it doesn't matter if you have a contract or not.'' With no contract there is some risk a player won't back him on a deal. "If I ever hear back from a manager or a player: 'I was just talking with my wife, or friend, and he thinks I should get $5,000 more,' I have one simple rule, there you are, there's your paper — no bill, do it yourself. . . . My credibility is more important than any individual client. On the other hand, if I say to a manager there's what I think, but I have to get back to you, he knows that I'm going back for approval. But if I shake hands with the general manager then that handshake commits my client; if it doesn't, then the client has to find another lawyer."

Harold Ballard has maintained a close and continuous referral association with Eagleson over the years in spite of the enormous controversy surrounding the Leaf management. "In any business I have had with Eagleson, his word is his bond," he says. "I always try to promote him, I tell my boys who don't have lawyers to go to the Eagle. . . . The last one I sent was Lanny McDonald. I always recommend any boy who wants a good solid counsel judgment and I have never heard that anybody that works with Mr. Eagleson quit." Of enemies, he says he doesn't think Eagleson has any, but "he did give [Ontario Premier] Davis's wife a low shot when he said 'she was the worst dressed woman in town' . . . and it made the front page of the *Globe and Mail*."

That was his prime job, getting as much money as he could for his clients through income-averaging annuities, the players' pension plan, and, of course, higher salaries. He did the job well, but it brought him little public sympathy. Eventually he was attacked by hockey owners and people in the press for putting a lot of "fat" into the system.

Eagleson had no problem finding money to back his ventures in merchandising sport on television. Eagleson hurriedly set about tapping his resources when he was first asked to stage the World Cup of Hockey. When he heard that the 1976 Canada Cup series was not generating the television revenue he expected, he asked for some time to see what could be done. Within twenty-four hours he is reported to have persuaded Wilmat Tennyson, former president of Carling O'Keefe, to offer $2.3 million for 50 percent of the TV time, along with a guarantee to sell the remaining half at the same price. The net profit for Hockey Canada and the NHLPA pension fund came to more than $2.5 million.

As long as there are buyers of franchises, a continuing supply of players will be necessary. The more franchises there are, the more frequently lower calibre players will be used. In the mid-seventies there appeared to be no limit to the buyers' available cash. One of Eagleson's top clients, Marcel Dionne, had turned in a dazzling performance for the Detroit Red Wings in the 1974–75 season, but, because he was unhappy with management, he wanted to leave. On June 1, 1975, when he became a free agent, he had already been to Edmonton, on a "fact-finding mission", something the press picked up as advance publicity for the bidding wars. But he ended up being traded to the NHL's Los Angeles Kings instead.

"When I got to L.A. we signed a *verbal* agreement," chuckles Dionne: "Jack Kent Cooke [owner of the Los Angeles Kings] says to me, 'I've known Al for years' then Al says the same thing and makes Cooke an offer. I said, 'It's fine with me.' I played for L.A. the next season without signing a contract! So you have to trust a person like that. I didn't sign my contract until around December 31. I was playing for three months and I didn't have a contract because we were working on an agreement for tax reasons. But Campbell calls up and says, 'Listen, you've got to sign, you need it as a record.' I signed when it was all finalized."

In 1975 it was time for Eagleson to sever ties with Blaney, Pasternak, to say goodbye to a relationship founded on principles of friendship, trust, and loyalty. Most of the original six partners had met through their mutual interest in sports and been called to the bar together. They attended each other's weddings and the christenings of each other's children. The firm had grown with its clients. By the time of the first Canada Cup, the business had expanded sufficiently that they could all go to Russia together. Eagleson's partners had supported him through the first contract negotiations between Orr and the Bruins, and they had backed him on the Springfield crisis. His partners wrote many of his political speeches, they stumped for him in every campaign, and, while he was at Queen's Park, they even paid for his trips while he was setting up the players' association. As head of the Real Estate Division he had been a leader *in absentia* for almost ten years. When Eagleson gave up his partnership he was saying goodbye to a close family. He was pulling up the roots of his power — and putting twenty-five-year friendships on the line.

He wanted to do things his way. "I was forty-two and I wanted to change my style," Eagleson says. Publicly, his excuse for leaving the firm was to stage the 1976 World Cup of Hockey. "The reason for leaving the firm came when they asked me to run the Canada Cup without pay. I knew it was going to take two years and I wanted to do it ... and I wanted to do it my way, without any obligations to anyone.''

Privately, however, the partners claimed there were other reasons for his leaving the firm, and that Eagleson used the World Cup only as an excuse. Bob Watson, one of the six founding partners at Blaney, Pasternak, claims, ''There were certain lawyers in the firm that Eagleson didn't relate to very well. He approached us and said because of this he was quite prepared to leave. He said he would stay on with the original group. But by that time we had expanded and were getting quite a good reputation and we couldn't see ourselves going back to the original six just for Al, so he broke with us.''

Although Watson says he couldn't pinpoint its source, ''there was certainly a great animosity; [Eagleson] just felt [the new partners] didn't have the philosophy we had and our philosophy, you must remember, was the desire of being a friendship as much as being a legal partnership. But as you get larger that's harder to accomplish and Al felt there were people in the firm who weren't of the type who'd fight for you to their dying day. Al feels very strong about loyalties, felt some didn't have the strong loyalty other partners did. He felt it was only worth working day and night for people he really cared for.''

One aspect of the firm's *modus operandi*, Watson explains, was that much of the revenue went back into developing the business. ''We certainly weren't drawing $100,000; we were earning about $50,000 in 1974, because we were putting money back into the business to make it grow. What we thought was wrong about his leaving was it was at the time when the department [which] Al headed [still called real estate] had finally developed into a lucrative specialty and everyone had worked very hard towards this. ... I think that was what was wrong.''

The firm was broken up into separate branches: litigation, corporate, and real estate, a cluster of specialties each of which referred clients to the others. Watson says the partners felt that they had contributed to building up Eagleson's real estate department: ''[We] spent a lot of time making it happen when Al was going to meetings with the players' association; there would be months when he wasn't doing much legal work, in fact, when he wanted to go somewhere we paid for it, so when he left he more or less took a debt with him.'' The partners operated on a total trust basis. ''[We] didn't know what each other was billing, no one really went into it so we were very vulnerable. Whereas if we knew he was leaving we would have made sure we had continuing contact with his clients. That's where the hardship arose because we felt we'd been very supportive in developing Alan Eagleson."

Watson says the six partners had covered for Eagleson. "During the early years Al could have been a very large business getter in other areas which would have been much more lucrative [than the one he was interested in] ... when he left, his department was finally growing and anyone would just have to look to see it was a very lucrative area ... and for whatever reasons he didn't feel he wanted us to share in it ... that was really hard to accept."

Eagleson says he felt a great deal of pressure while he was with the firm: "In those days [the mid-seventies] at Blaney, Pasternak it was easy for me to slide salaries. We had about forty lawyers, and I was at Queen's Park anyway so I was pretty well on a half-assed leave of absence. The decision to branch separately wasn't really because of the financial aspect, because I had a nice situation where I was and a lot less pressure really in many ways. The difficulty was my time was being drained so extensively for these purposes ... it was tough describing to my partners the reasons because it is a funny business ... the amount of hand holding and time consumption is not appreciated unless you are doing it yourself. In the case of Bobby Orr I would have to go to Boston for three days just to solve what would on the surface seem to be a minor problem, or I would have two or three players in from the Leafs for a whole day just to structure a few things ... the partners felt I was spending a lot of time on that aspect of the business without realizing the time I was spending was much more rewarding financially to everybody else."

He gave the partners a choice: count him out, or return to the original six partners. "We felt it was not really a choice. When you get to the size we were at, we really had a close commitment to the other partners so we didn't think it was a choice at all ... it was an impossibility," says Watson. "... I think Al should have stayed ... he had success ... but I think having a solid firm behind him was very important. I think it still is today ... he'd have greater credibility today if he had stayed ... if he'd been a partner of a large firm rather than Alan Eagleson, Q.C., with a junior or two in his own business."

Bill McMurtry, Q.C., is counsel for Blaney, Pasternak and also heads the firm's ten-man litigation department. McMurtry says Eagleson's break with the firm left him (McMurtry) torn between losing a twenty-five-year friendship and compromising his principle of loyalty with the other partners. "[Eagleson] might have been producing half of what others were over the years — but was very equally paid ... he started to see things taking off and he left, taking all his clients with him." He suggested the difficulty between Eagleson and some members of the firm stemmed from the question of loyalty: "I'm in the middle. ... I never felt Al used me and I certainly didn't use him. He's a unique guy. Al did a lot of things other people couldn't have done, but even Al couldn't have done them without the support of the firm. It was betrayal the others felt more than the money issue."

But Eagleson's definition of loyalty was unique. "If he has a difference of opinion with you, he'll almost treat you as being disloyal. ... I get the feeling the only people who can really survive with Al definitely are sycophants ... who will never criticize the emperor's clothing ... it was my feeling the only way to please him was to keep agreeing with him. ... I always liked Al, always respected him but disagreed with him half the time ... sometimes he didn't show the best judgment," says McMurtry. He says he discovered that he was one of the personalities on the list Eagleson couldn't tolerate. McMurtry feels this stemmed from one particular incident: "Eagleson sabotaged my report on hockey violence ... called it nonsense."

On June 27, 1974, Bill McMurtry had been commissioned by the Ontario government to report on violence in amateur hockey in that province. His report to René Brunette, then Minister of Community and Social Services, was entitled *Investigation and Inquiry into Violence in Amateur Hockey*. McMurtry says he gave Eagleson an advance copy of the report. On August 22, the day after the report was officially released, the *Globe and Mail* quoted Eagleson's comments on the study:

> It is not nearly so bad as Bill suggests. The NHLPA's overwhelming reaction was "here we go again". I think the NHL and the NHLPA are going to be everybody's favorite whipping boys in this thing.... There is a great deal of difference between pro and amateur hockey. In amateur hockey there is no reason for violence; in pro hockey you take certain risks. There is nothing wrong with the report's suggestions for amateur hockey but the fans will dictate what changes are necessary in pro hockey.

Eagleson saw no link between violence in pro ranks and violence in amateur hockey. He went on to repeat, "I do not think it is as bad as Bill suggests. If it were, there would be a lot fewer players anxious to earn their living in the NHL."

McMurtry blamed the sorry state of amateur hockey on the commercialization of pro sports, an attitude which, by the nature of the hockey hierarchy, is limited throughout the amateur leagues by the people running them — coaches and parents:

> When the evidence strongly indicates that there is a conscious effort to sell the violence in hockey to enrich a small group of show business entrepreneurs at the expense of a great sport (not to mention the corruption of an entire generation's concept of sport), then one's concern turns to outrage.

McMurtry concludes that hockey is sick, and

> ... is perhaps the only sport, professional or otherwise, that encourages the use of physical intimidation *outside* the rules as a legitimate tactic.
>
> It was apparent that the TV networks did not like the inordinate delays caused by the interminable fighting which once consumed over three and one half hours of prime time. The TV networks represent money and their wishes were to be fulfilled.... What was the solution? To take measures to prevent fights? No! Fighting will still be tolerated — but there will be a team penalty if any player delays after a penalty or a fight in proceeding directly to the penalty box!

McMurtry says Eagleson wouldn't even let him meet with the players' association during his research. "It is my feeling," McMurtry says, "Mr. Eagleson could have done a lot more as head of the players' union to help out and clear up violence ... he really ... quietly sabotaged the whole thing. ... I gave him an advance copy [of the report] and he never even read it."

Eagleson left the practice shortly after the report was released. He took with him Goldblatt, the comptroller, and law student Howard Ungerman, the son of Eagleson's friend Irv Ungerman.

The way Eagleson dealt with the report on hockey violence is an excellent example of how he manipulates owners, players, and the news media to advance the interests he represents. Roy McMurtry, Q.C., was appointed Attorney General of Ontario by the Davis government in 1976. Shortly after he took office, he started a campaign to clamp down on the proliferation of violence in professional hockey.

By June 1976 criminal charges had been laid against five NHL players. McMurtry called in Toronto police to monitor games at Maple Leaf Gardens. "We fully intend to prosecute where there is a clear breach of the Criminal Code," he said. He informed lawyer Ben Hatskin of the WHA of his intentions and said he felt the increase in violence was due to the expansion of hockey into U.S. cities. The incident caused an uproar from the Gardens' owners and one of its patrons, John F. Bassett, Jr., president of the Toronto Toros of the WHA. Bassett objected to McMurtry, calling him "the dirtiest hockey player who ever played ... he's using his power of office to become the Messiah for his little brother's cause." Harold Ballard attributed McMurtry's stance to politics, saying "He's [McMurtry] just been given a new job by Bill Davis and he has to get his name in the paper — get some ink so people know who he is."

Eagleson sided with the owners, trivializing the issue by saying "hockey is everybody's whipping boy." He felt "cases of vicious assaults on the ice are dealt with adequately by players and the league." This time he used the example of the Russians to back up his position: "If the government of Ontario feels it can persuade the government of Canada to change the rules so that we get the Russian style of play, then we may have fewer assaults but more spearing, which is worse."

However, the week before McMurtry's statement, Bobby Hull of the Winnipeg Jets had refused to play in a game, protesting the increasing violence in pro hockey. He attacked both the coaches' encouraging "goons" in hockey and the failure of league officials to police them.

By this time, Davis had brought pressure to bear on the Ontario Hockey Association as a result of McMurtry's report, but only in relation to leagues below Junior A level. In the meantime, the Forbes–Boucha case had come up. Henry Boucha of the Minnesota North Stars received an injury from Dave Forbes, a Boston Bruins player. Boucha was left with double vision and there was a chance that he would have to forfeit his career in pro hockey. Forbes was charged with aggravated assault with a deadly weapon — a hockey stick. The trial marked the first U.S. court case brought against a hockey player for violence. The case was eventually dropped when the jury failed to reach a decision. Had Forbes lost, the penalty would have been five years in prison, or a $5,000 fine, or both. By NHL rules, Forbes' penalty was a ten-day suspension!

Canadian jurisprudence in this area dates back to 1969, when Ted

Green of the Boston Bruins and Wayne Maki of the St. Louis Blues were charged following a stick fencing duel which resulted in a skull fracture for Green. Maki was charged with assault causing bodily harm and Green was charged with common assault. While courts ruled in both cases that charges were to be dropped on grounds of self-defence, Green's injury brought about the decision to make helmets compulsory.*

In 1975, the *Washington Post* published a succinct report by Burling Lower, an English professor, which compared the violence in hockey to a film called *Rollerball*: "The playing field is a privileged sanctuary where ritualized crimes can be committed by citizens in the role of athletes without their being subject to the laws of the land."

Lower, like McMurtry, thought that the force behind perpetuating violence was evident in *Rollerball*: "... the relationship between corporate tyranny and sadism as public entertainment, one being absolutely essential for maintaining the existence of the other."

By the spring of 1976, violence in pro hockey was out of hand. A hockey Watergate developed when Roy McMurtry suggested that some NHL tapes of previous hockey games played at Maple Leaf Gardens had been doctored. "If it can be proven, the charges could be conspiracy," he said. During one playoff game at the Gardens, some players had swung sticks at the police. It wasn't until that spring, two years after Bill McMurtry's report had been tabled, that Eagleson finally acknowledged the issue publicly. He said, "The NHL Players' Association had so far failed to persuade the owners to crack down on fighting ... but we might have to insist on it now or we'll have more of our players in court and behind bars."

He was also quoted as saying that it was his "strong impression" that most of the players would welcome stricter rules against fighting. He compared it to wearing helmets: "no one wants to volunteer to wear them; they want the league to make the decision for them. ... "

Eagleson finally endorsed putting an end to "goon hockey", but only when it served his purpose, to draw attention to his proposed new deal, the first NHL collective-bargaining agreement. One newspaper headline quoted Eagleson: NOW THAT THE NHL PACT IS SIGNED, PLAYERS TO TACKLE VIOLENCE. The story went on to say that "The

---

* It is compulsory for new players coming into the league to wear helmets. Older players have to sign a release if they choose not to wear them. Eventually, everyone will be wearing a helmet.

only way to put an end to violence in hockey is by suspending repeated offenders for life. It would also rid the NHL of players who have no business being in the NHL and are getting $25,000 for one purpose only — the goon type of hockey.''

Eventually Eagleson told Bill McMurtry that his report was the best thing he ever read on sports and that the players backed it. ''That's his loyalty for you,'' McMurtry says. ''It suited his purpose to be loyal after the fact ... pretty funny for a friend and a partner.'' Then he softens. ''I guess my criticism of Al is not a reflection of Al's potential ... the fact is ... he could have done so much and he just chose not to do it. It was unfortunate because I saw what he could do in an area when he tried.''

WHERE EAGLE DARED

*Canadians are too goddamn modest
because we've always kept everything in the
country, instead of going out in the world
... instead of beating the world. ... We
should start thinking we are a lot bigger ...
we should start thinking like Al Eagleson.*

Steve Shutt

In early 1976, while Eagleson was beset with the problems of steering pro hockey into the world market, Ted Lindsay, the fifty-year-old former star left-winger with the Detroit Red Wings, attempted to evict Eagleson from his throne. Lindsay's form letter to some NHLPA members urging them to replace Eagleson with a "hockey man" was interpreted by an *Ottawa Citizen* columnist as "a strident cry to break up the Players' Association, unhorse Alan Eagleson and get back to realities".

Alan Eagleson, who believed in action, not rhetoric, sardonically replied: "My letter of resignation is permanently on file with the NHLPA", which he runs out of his law office. Looking back to Lindsay's unsuccessful attempt to organize the players in 1957, it seems safe to assert the type of craft union he envisioned for pro hockey would in no way have resembled the monolithic NHLPA of today.

The opening shots in Eagleson's campaign to stage a world championship of hockey that would include pros in the style of soccer's World Cup began in 1969, the year that Canada's national team came in fourth in the international tourney held in Stockholm.

In hindsight it is easy to see that Eagleson was attempting to turn hockey from a small regional business of no great importance into an international cartel, modelled, again, after the world-wide proportions of soccer.

170

By expanding the business of hockey, of course, Alan Eagleson, now forty-two, was bringing prestige and wealth to members of the National Hockey League Players' Association, and especially to his own hockey clients and business associates. Other clients connected with Eagleson's network who received a slice of the pie were the corporations that bought hockey TV time and arranged endorsements with the players. And by helping everyone — players, owners, sponsors, and fans — and uplifting the game itself, Eagleson was also benefitting himself: an enjoyable situation all around. Not that there was any hint of impropriety in all this; hockey was then, as it still is, free from most stringent anti-combines controls. Eagleson's ability to juggle his roles as union boss, financial advisor (to his 150 clients), and leader in his country's effort to restore its hockey dignity attracted resounding applause; what's more, his ability at the same time to score high profits for the game was an unparalleled entrepreneurial feat. Assisting him were Doug Fisher, chairman of Hockey Canada, CAHA president Don Johnson, and Paul Woodstock, deputy minister in Lalonde's department. The federal government gave a $40,000 grant towards the tournament to Hockey Canada, of which Eagleson's Canada Cup '76 Tournament Corporation was a part. Sports Canada, a federal directorate of fitness and amateur sport, contributed $20,000. There were many difficulties to be overcome, but the pieces were falling into place.

Soccer was the only team sport that outdid hockey both in revenue and in the scope of its nation-versus-nation play. There were two problems that stood in the way of hockey's breaking through into a larger format. The first was the lack of a rich American TV network contract. Baseball and football receive from TV an annual windfall of around $3 million each. Without a TV contract — and the U.S. market for hockey was at its lowest level ever — hockey still had a long way to go to shed its regional (northern U.S.-Canada) image.

The second problem was the IIHF's domination of European hockey, which contributed to the game's image, at least in North America, as a poor cousin to other major-league sports. The IIHF insisted, among other things, on using amateurs; by 1974 they were still insisting on an annual world championship that would admit a Canadian team of amateur, WHA, and NHL players. Nor would the IIHF change the date of its annual World Championships (April) to favour one country, Canada; because of NHL scheduling, Canada would never be able to use its best players.

Eagleson, however, was persistent. On July 14, 1975, he and

long-time CAHA secretary-manager Gordon Juckes embarked on a ten-day European mission to win support for his Canada Cup concept. They visited each of the invited countries three times — the Soviet Union, Sweden, Finland, Czechoslovakia, and the U.S. Eagleson suggested it would be a "trial" tournament and impressed on all parties the need for a cup independent of the IIHF, whose authority the NHL clearly would not accept. He pointed out, too, that while fifteen of the league's eighteen owners were American, the tournament was still stamped *Made in Canada* because 90 percent of the pros were Canadians.

To sweeten the pot, he said, Canada was willing to pick up the tab plus share the prize money of $465,000. The purse was divided: first prize, $100,000; second prize, $75,000; third, $65,000; fourth, $55,000; fifth, $50,000; and sixth, $45,000. In addition, the winning team and the loser in the final games would receive $50,000 and $25,000 respectively. Canada also agreed to pick up travel, accommodation, and meal expenses, including:

- air travel for each team to Canada to a maximum party of 30 from Moscow, Prague, Stockholm, and Helsinki;
- expenses of $30 a day for 30 players for a minimum of 12 days, and for an additional 15 days if the team reached the finals;
- accommodation expenses up to $30 a day; and
- a free TV and radio feed to the U.S.S.R., Czechoslovakia, Sweden, and Finland.

Other payments included the sum of $25,000 to the IIHF's from proceeds of North American TV sales in return for the IIHF's releasing Canada from any and all other financial obligations arising from the tournament. In return, each participating club agreed to play a minimum of two exhibition games on the conclusion of the tournament against Canadian, U.S., or CAHA teams for a fee of $5,000 a game plus expenses. Finland, the Soviet Union, Sweden, and Czechoslovakia guaranteed to pay the IIHF 5 percent of net TV revenues from televising the games in their countries.

In September, Hockey Canada's board approved Eagleson's plan for a completely open six-nation tournament to be called the Canada Cup. The Cup was to be contested every four years in September, which would not conflict with NHL schedules.

The basis of the Canada Cup received IIHF approval in return for the promise that Canada would participate in the annual world championships, which are played every year except during Olympic years.

Two further irritants remained that required Eagleson's attention and presence in Europe. One was an objection raised by the U.S.S.R. on the matter of Canada's keeping back 15 percent tax on the prize money; the other was the insistence by IIHF president Dr. Gunther Sabetzki that Canada put up a $100,000 bond to guarantee Team Canada's presence at the 1977 world championships in Vienna.

Finally, Eagleson was able to report back to Lalonde: "We've received a wholehearted endorsement."

Of course, the IIHF wanted its cut of the Canada Cup profits. So did the other participating countries, particularly the Soviet Union. This they were given in a substantial pool of prize money. The operating budget of $2.5 million for the 1976 Canada Cup also included a one-time grant to the IIHF of $25,000 from proceeds of North American television sales. (The 1981 Canada Cup up-front payout to the IIHF had increased substantially to $1 million, paid from TV sales. To cover this amount, the total 1981 budget was increased to $3.5 million.)

The final deal Eagleson put together, which helped stretch hockey's income-generating capabilities to several foreign markets, included a complex set of agreements and reciprocal arrangements. The cycle of hockey activity included the 1976 Cup and Canada's return to the IIHF annual championships in 1977. In addition, Canada was to host the world junior championships in December 1977; there were to be exhibition games between European teams and the NHL pros; and there was to be another Canada Cup in 1980. (This one was cancelled when the NHL players declined to participate because of the Soviet Union's incursion into Afghanistan. It was rescheduled for 1981.)

Credit for arranging the 1976 Cup is usually given unconditionally to Eagleson. It seems clear the competition would never have happened without him. As hockey's chief wheeler-dealer, Eagleson's ambition, decisiveness, and ability to manipulate enabled him to carry out several powerplays at once. His ability to juggle all these roles was constrained only by his popularity, by the players' willingness to support him. While they did, his influence over events — and over the participants who really mattered, the professional players — was formidable.

When Eagleson resigned from the social and financial security of the law firm of Blaney, Pasternak in 1974, he said he resigned to take a two-year job without pay. (Without pay, but not entirely without remuneration. Eagleson did have a contract with Hockey Canada for every international meet — junior and senior — in which it was agreed that a percentage of his law firm's operating expenses could be charged to the federal body. The 1976 Canada Cup expenses included rent, secretarial services, travel, accommodation, and telex as well as staff and services incurred under his financial consulting company, Sports Management Ltd. These payments amounted to some $87,200 in 1976.)

Why was Eagleson so keen to do it? For one thing, he is an ardent nationalist. For another, he believed that Canada's national pastime deserved the same secure financial base soccer had elsewhere. He also believed that the people to reap the profits — or at least to control their distribution — should be the pro players and not agencies such as the IIHF, the CAHA, Hockey Canada, or even the NHL. Profits, in turn, accrued from corporate sponsorships and the sale of TV time (the gate receipts covered costs); it was primarily Eagleson's longtime corporate clients Carling O'Keefe that put up the largest chunk of money to secure the TV rights.

Eagleson negotiated the largest TV contract for a sports event in Canadian history on May 12, 1976. Carling O'Keefe Ltd. signed a contract for $2,530,000 to televise the first Canada Cup Hockey series in Canada. The brewery bought rights to 50 percent of all the commercial TV time in the series (ten commercial minutes in each of the eleven televised games in Canada); a guarantee of the other 50 percent of commercial time if unsold; and a first option to a similar share of any future international Canada Cup tournaments.

The cost of Carling's contract was $23,000 a minute — believed to be the highest price ever paid for commercial TV time in Canada. Unsuccessful bids for commercial time were submitted by J. Walter Thompson, representing Labatt's Ltd., at $2 million for Canada TV rights, and the Montreal-based firm Productel Inc. at $2.025 million.

There were no unsold minutes. Additional television advertising contracts totalling $1.96 million included Bombardier Ltd., which purchased 8$\frac{1}{2}$ minutes for $238,000; Ahed Music Corporation Ltd. bought 11 minutes for $308,000; Standard Brands Ltd. purchased 17$\frac{1}{2}$ minutes for $490,000; Lotto Canada bought 11 minutes for $308,000; STP Scientifically Tested Products of Canada Ltd. purchased 7$\frac{1}{2}$ minutes on the English network only for $155,400; the Department of National Defence bought 5$\frac{1}{2}$ minutes for $154,000; and Canadian Motor Industries Ltd. (Toyota) purchased 11 minutes for $308,000, payable as $252,000 in cash and $56,000 in automobiles.

Other Canada Cup contracts signed were for specific commitments. The Canadian Broadcasting Corporation, for example, contracted to televise the series over affiliated stations in jurisdictions not covered by CTV or TVA at a cost of $228,320. Productel purchased TV rights for the world, except Canada, Philadelphia, and participating European countries, and the exclusive film rights for one year following the tournament for $187,500 plus approximately 25 percent of gross film revenue over $187,500.

Hockey Canada's agent on the Canada Cup TV sales was Arthur Harnett Enterprises Ltd. Harnett bought the TV rights from the IIHF, then sold them, receiving a commission on gross sales at a rate of 5 percent, for approximately $50,000 compared to $118,750 in 1972.

In addition to television advertising rights, the Canada Cup '76 corporation sold licensing rights to Licensing Corporation of America for all rights other than radio and television time, and Telmed Communications Ltd. for radio broadcasting, for a total of approximately $340,000.

Eagleson had already consolidated his place in the official hierarchy through his official appointment by Lalonde. That was the first of the four contracts necessary to secure the Cup. The second was his success in securing international agreement. Two tasks remained: to persuade the NHL owners to go along and, just as important, to talk the players into playing.

Hockey Canada had demanded that any pro player selected should be released by his club for the Cup. In fact, Hockey Canada had no influence or power over the pros. Furthermore, it was depending on the series' earnings for its financial survival.

It was the NHLPA, and by extension Eagleson, who had leverage over the NHL owners and could veto any decision they made concerning international play. Having already wrested the balance of power from the patriarchy running the hockey cartel in 1967, and having brought security and wealth to his clients, aided, as he put it, "by the owners' own greediness through expansion", Eagleson had spent some years consolidating his powers.

Before he could put his prestige and influence to work, he had to secure the beachhead. The next two contracts he drafted were crucial. One bound the players to a five-year collective-bargaining agreement (later extended to 1984) whereby players would be willing to endorse the continuation of the equalization or compensation clause for a cut in the revenues from international games. The second contract, perhaps more tragic because of its irrevocability, was for the services of Bobby Orr, "who risked his career and $3 million [the total value of his contract with Chicago] to play for his country," says Eagleson, who needed this show of loyalty to encourage other players to participate.

As hockey's chief curator, the cornerstone of Eagleson's strength, particularly over the owners, was his ability to keep players' salaries growing. While violence in hockey was being debated, business aspects of the sport were also being dealt with. In October 1975 Darryl Sittler was getting $150,000 a season; the average player contract was then valued at $55,000. The growth was threatened by new anti-inflation legislation introduced by Jean-Luc Pépin. Pépin, the chairman of the Anti-Inflation Board, looked into the inflationary effects of these huge contracts. Eagleson fought back, pointing out that the average career of a professional hockey player lasts only six years: "To limit him to a $2,400 increase for half his career can only be a joke." He added that Canadians couldn't work under controls when U.S.-based teams didn't.

The NHL players' salary was exempted from the wage and price controls, but the Canadian owners were not. In 1978 the AIB froze Maple Leaf Gardens season ticket prices at 1975 levels to "return some of the excess revenue as a result of profit margins wider than permitted under the controls".

By 1975 the state of the art had changed dramatically. Gone forever were the days when it was a "buyer's market", when owners ran a monopoly and could dictate low salaries. The rich players were getting richer. In 1966, when there was one six-team league and twenty-five minor pro teams, there had been a shortage of top talent in the NHL. By 1975 there were two leagues and a total of thirty-two teams.

Significant raiding of the minor leagues resulted in fringe players' obtaining top salaries. At the end of 1975, however, when WHA franchises started bailing out from unpredictable fan loyalty and an overall economic slowdown, there would be 250 players, nearly 42 percent of a total of 600, facing unemployment. The Central Hockey League still had five or six teams, and the American Hockey League seven or eight. The Western Hockey League had folded.

Eagleson continued to fend off owners' requests to scale down high salaries, and fought the merger of the WHA and the NHL. "If there's a merger, all bets are off and we go the anti-trust route," he warned them. A few WHA teams declared bankruptcy and others fell into receivership, bringing the total number of players down to 400. One of the fastest exits from the WHA was made by Ray Kroc, the owner-founder of McDonald's Restaurants. In his green and growing salad days he bought the San Diego Mariners of the WHA. "I felt the city deserved to have pro hockey as well as baseball and football," he writes in his book, *Grinding It Out*. He says it didn't work out and fans didn't seem ready to support hockey: "I wound up selling the team back to the league."

"The rich will get richer ... that's as it should be," argued Eagleson. "Owners never balk at paying a great hockey player what he's worth. What really upsets them is paying an average player an inflated salary. The players who are out of work are players who in some cases should never have been employed."

Meanwhile, Eagleson was wheeling and dealing with the team owners on another matter. When the NHL was firmly committed to a Soviet Union series in January 1976, Eagleson publicly refused to release the players until the NHL met his demands for increasing players' pension plans by $250 (an extra $22,000 a year from each club), to bring the monthly maximum pension contributions to $750. In addition, he wanted full owner approval of the 1976 World Cup tournament. "Eagleson's bargaining position was a little irritating," NHL President Campbell said. After twelve days of negotiations with the owners, Eagleson announced in October that an official "peace treaty" (the 1975 collective-bargaining agreement) had been approved. "We have confirmation with respect to no merger with the WHA and that justifies our withdrawing the threat of an anti-trust suit," Eagleson said.

The unique five-year pact, the longest in pro sports history, was to last from June 1, 1976, to June 30, 1981. For the first time, "equalization" or compensation had been recognized by players and achieved through collective bargaining. Under section 9A of the NHL agreement, the owners have the right to "equalization" or "compensation" from another NHL team which acquires the services of a player who has played out his option.

At the same time, the National Football League Players' Association was engaged in a court battle to eliminate equalization. A

St. Louis court ruled that the "Rozelle Rule"* unduly restricted the freedom of movement of players. "We haven't accepted the Rozelle ruling, we've accepted independent arbitration for equalization whereby each club submits its proposals to an arbitrator who would choose what he considers the fairest deal," confirmed Eagleson.

The role of arbitrator was assigned to Ed Houston,† a county court judge in Ottawa who had been NHL salary arbitrator for the previous four years. Players were granted the privilege of terminating the agreement in the event of a merger between the two leagues; they then would be entitled to reopen negotiations in regard to equalization and free-agent status. (This happened when the merger occurred in 1980.)‡

Charles W. Mulcahy of the Boston Bruins negotiated on the owners' behalf, across the table from Eagleson, who headed the players' negotiations. Terms of the historic agreement included:

- An increase in the players' pension plan by 50 percent to $750 a year, bringing a player with ten years' service a pension of $14,000 a year at age fifty-five;
- Throughout the life of the agreement players and owners would share equally in the proceeds of international hockey games. Players agreed to pay out of and to the extent of cumulative proceeds from international competition 50 percent of the increased cost of the new pension plan;
- Players agreed to participate in international games without additional compensation for the following schedule: the joint NHL–WHA World Cup 1976; and the anticipated eight-game series with the Soviet Union in January 1976, whereby the winners of the NHL Stanley Cup of the preceding season would represent the NHL;
- In addition, there would be allowance for games that would involve both cup champions and All-Star players. While no player was entitled to extra compensation for these games, it was

* The Rozelle Rule in the NFL differed from the equalization rule in hockey in that the NFL's commissioner (Rozelle) could have told the club that signs a free agent which players have to be forfeited to the original club.

† In June 1981, York County Court Judge Joe Kane was named alternate arbitrator of the NHL to assist ailing Judge Ed Houston.

‡ In May 1981, the NHLPA and the NHL voted to terminate the agreement as of September 1982. However, the equalization rule would apply until September 16, 1984, at which time a new agreement would be in effect.

agreed they would not have regular salary deductions made;
- An option clause of one year, or longer if mutually agreed, or the possibility of a no-option contract;
- The extension of the current arbitration agreement, and an independent arbitrator for disputes between a player and his team;
- The selection of two player representatives to attend all meetings of the NHL rules committee in a non-voting, advisory capacity; and
- An increase of per diem expenses from $23 to $27 during the life of the agreement and an increase of just under $500,000 for award money provided by the league for individual trophies, All-Star games, final standings, and Stanley Cup playoffs.

The official document was signed in May 1976, almost a decade after the NHLPA's inception. In the fall of 1975, Clarence Campbell's response to the proposed contract had been: "It was a great day for our sport." By the time of the official signing in May, however, his remarks were tempered somewhat: "The NHLPA has the best of both worlds. The matter of equalization is not going to be resolved during the length of this agreement. And it will probably go to the U.S. Congress eventually. So players get the best of both worlds by letting someone else do the litigating. But 'peace for five years' was a palatable answer." Then he cautioned: "The league is afraid that if the case goes to court the players' agreement could be found in violation of U.S. anti-trust laws. ... We don't want to reach the stage where we're not the masters of our own fate. Lord knows where you end up once you go to court," said Campbell.

Eagleson was apparently worried about going to court as well. "As one of the designers of that agreement it would put me in a very embarrassing position. ... Once in the courts this agreement might be torn apart by someone who does not have a complete understanding of what it's all about and the people who will suffer are the owners," he said. Campbell maintained that "[Eagleson] wants all the players' reps to sign it; he's doing it for his own protection." The document was signed by the player reps, who represented their teams; therefore, it was not necessary for 100 percent of the membership of the NHLPA to sign.

June 1, 1976, was another hockey milestone. On that day Bobby Orr became a free agent.

Some NHL presidents and managers claimed the delay in officially signing the five-year collective agreement was linked to troublesome negotiations between Bobby Orr and the Bruins. If Orr was traded without compensation, one argument ran, as a free agent he would receive a bigger dollar deal if the new team didn't have to forfeit a player. Others felt Eagleson deliberately delayed having the agreement signed so Orr wouldn't be affected by it. Under the new agreement, if Orr signed with another NHL club the Bruins would have to be compensated to their satisfaction.

"I get the feeling he [Eagleson] is putting his own interests ahead of the leagues'," said Dennis Ball, vice-president of the St. Louis Blues. One report said that Philadelphia had already expressed interest in signing Orr, and had been told by Boston management that Flyers' captain Bobby Clarke would be appropriate compensation. The $10 million deal Eagleson had tried to make with the Bruins a year earlier dragged on towards the June 1 deadline. During his last season with the Bruins, Orr underwent his fourth and fifth knee operations. As a result, he only played ten games that season. Fearing that his injury would keep him off the ice, the Bruins would not meet his salary demands. Eagleson flared up, saying the Jacobs brothers (the new owners of the Bruins) "are not hockey men . . . they've thrown Bobby to the wolves with their attitudes." In the next breath he was telling the press. "So far ten teams are pitching for [Orr]. I've had ten calls since Monday from the NHL and WHA teams wanting to talk business. . . . No doubt, Chicago's offer is a serious one," he said.

Then suddenly the rivers divided and a solution presented itself. In a last-ditch effort to save the situation, Eagleson reread Orr's contract with the Bruins. Appended to it was a letter of agreement which in effect made it a no-trade contract. "I don't even know whether the NHL knows about the letter of agreement, but there is precedent for its legality," Eagleson said.

He cited the 1960 case of Sam Etcheverry and the Canadian Football League. "[Etcheverry] had such a letter and the courts ruled the trade breached a contractual agreement," Eagleson pointed out. This special clause meant that no compensation was due the Bruins if Orr signed with another NHL team — the opposite of what the owners and players had just agreed to. Eagleson immediately said the agreement didn't apply to any player holding contracts prior to 1972. Orr's contract had been signed in 1970. Even the other players began to question the intent. "It's possible for any player to have a clause negotiated into his contract," Eagleson explained.

Shortly after Orr's free agent status was announced on June 1, the Minnesota North Stars of the WHA were reported to be offering Orr $6.5 million over five years. Eagleson rationalized his cooperation with the WHA, saying, "Orr likely will feel obligated to offer compensation to the Bruins. Bobby has some concern about his new club giving up too much and that is why the WHA teams can't be ruled out."

Then he took a new tack: "It's a million and a half for signing and a million for each year he plays. Hell, all the Bruins would have to do is invest $2.5 million at 10 percent and pay Bobby the interest. We don't care what the combination is; all we want for Bobby is lifetime security!"

But Boston wanted Orr's signed confirmation of what he reportedly said verbally to them: "If I'm not able to play, the contract will be talked over again. I just want some kind of security." The Bruins didn't get it. Chicago, meanwhile, was willing to accept Orr's word that he would resign if unable to play and left it up to Orr to take or leave their offer. In his usual brief response to questions about his finances, Orr says, "That was it ... exactly." Chicago reportedly signed Orr to a $3 million, five-year contract entitling him to the entire amount whether or not he played a single game.

By the end of June, Eagleson had won the last two contracts needed to secure the Canada Cup. The players were granted the right under the new agreement to share in the profits of international games, and the right to be released to participate in any international series. He also obtained doctors' approval to allow Orr to play in the World Cup.

During a tournament committee meeting Eagleson warned CTV's Johnny Esaw, a sports broadcaster and close associate of Hockey Canada board member John Bassett, Jr., that the series should not become the "Carling Cup". Some other considerations pertaining to the press were outlined in a letter sent by Lou Lefaive, president of the National Sport and Recreation Centre, Ottawa, to Doug Fisher on June 14, 1976:

This one is rather delicate and is perhaps of less concern in 1976 than it was in 1972 when we were in the midst of an election campaign, but you should discuss now who controls camera positions and selects close-up shots, i.e., does the camera focus on Joe Clark vs. Pierre Trudeau vs. Bill Davis vs. Harold Ballard (some people might even insist on Ed Broadbent).

In general, our relationships with the TV people in both 1972 and 1974 were reasonably good if distant. I know that Johnny Esaw will quickly read to you the pertinent sections of the broadcasting act which precludes anyone other than the major producer having any right to interfere with programming. It is my view that this section of the act is ignored more often in its breach than its observance. . . .

The final format of the tournament was drawn up. Team Canada was to include NHL and WHA players, who would be paid $5,000 for eight weeks' work. It would be a single round-robin tournament. Two referees would be selected from each of the participating European countries, and four each from Canada and the U.S. Each game of the tourney would be handled by a neutral referee. Officials would be selected by a committee chaired by Eagleson.

One major problem Eagleson encountered was booking Maple Leaf Gardens. The negotiations went on for several weeks before a deal could be made. Eagleson reportedly offered the Gardens' president $25,000; but Ballard wanted a $50,000 rental fee for each of the three games scheduled (originally six games had been planned there). After Eagleson threatened to put the "whole show" in Quebec, Ballard settled. "Ballard took a little less, I settled for a little more and now we have the games set for the big rink," said Eagleson.

Sam Pollock, another friend of Eagleson's, was the strong, silent arm of the Montreal Canadiens executive. A solid, unpretentious stalwart of hockey, Pollock had the responsibility of selecting and directing Team Canada '76.

"When I announced his name at the meeting of international professional, government, and amateur hockey officials, their mouths fell open," Eagleson bragged. "Did you notice when the team was announced there wasn't a whisper of criticism? How are you going to argue with a man who runs an organization that withstands the loss of Frank Mahovlich, J.C. Tremblay, Marc Tardif, and Réjean Houle to the WHA, sustains the retirements of Jean Beliveau, John Ferguson, Jacques Laperrière, and Henri Richard, then skates out on the ice and knocks off Philadelphia four straight?"

Pollock doesn't figure Eagleson has a conflict of interest. "As the union representative and as a negotiator I have always found [Eagleson] very fair and honest to deal with," says Pollock. "He strikes a hard bargain for his members. In my mind it's helpful that he represents a great many hockey players — it gives him a great insight into many of the problems confronting players and hockey in general.''

The next confrontation was with the players themselves. Bobby Orr had suffered several serious bouts of depression throughout the summer of 1976, but when he appeared at Team Canada's training camp, Eagleson boasted that "Orr sacrificed $3 million and his career to play for his country because I asked him to." When Orr was questioned about his disappearance during the Boston–Chicago contract talks in 1976 he simply says: "[Eagleson] got the hell kicked out of him, I know; ... but that's his job. He knows what has to be done." Orr calls Eagleson "a fast-talking wheeler-dealer with a sharp mind". Nonetheless, having Orr's coattails to hang on to was great for morale. "They [the players] don't like the idea of a big series at that time of year", admitted Eagleson. "I agree with them. But it was September or nothing." Then he summed up his feelings: "The first series ['72] was won on heart alone. In the '74 series, the WHA players filling the Team Canada roster were physically in shape but they lost the series because of a lack of talent. This will be the penultimate [*sic*] series to combine talent and physical preparedness with knowledge of what to expect from the Russians."

Some players were still not too keen, but that's where Orr's presence helped.* For example, when Rick Martin of the Buffalo Sabres reported to Team Canada's training camp in August, the first thing he said was, "I'll be honest, I just got married and I don't feel like playing." Canadiens' star defenceman Guy Lapointe said he needed a longer vacation after winning the Stanley Cup four years in a row and didn't want to play for Team Canada. "But I relented when I saw Bobby Orr on television signing in for his physical."

Later Eagleson said, "Orr was the only player who put his whole career on the line ... something he didn't have to do ... it cost him $3 million in the bank.... Orr did it to play for his country. ... He did it while others backed off."

Seventeen games were played in all, in Quebec City, Montreal, Toronto, Winnipeg, and Philadelphia. Eagleson's client Sittler scored the winning overtime goal in Montreal in the best-of-three final

---

* Orr had agreed to play with a bad knee. His playing career was virtually over by the time of the Canada Cup. The last knee operation left him with little strength. He received only a small part of the $3 million contract with Chicago and didn't play a full season.

against Czechoslovakia, and Team Canada was the first team to have its name inscribed on the Canada Cup, a piece of hardware valued at some $60,000.

Orr proved once again that he was the world's finest hockey player, winning several "player of the game" awards throughout the series.

The Eagle had brought it off. The bottom line proved it. Profits for the series were well over $3 million.

THE EMPIRE STRIKES BACK

*My sympathies and admiration are so
strongly with Eagleson in this conflict with
the CAHA . . . that I have to keep pulling
myself back from statements that are
openly libellous.*

Doug Fisher

After his success in staging the first World-Cup hockey tourney, Eagleson was left with a powerful organization. Its power began to spread over into the amateur sector, the grass-roots vanguard of Canada's hockey lifeline. As new Eurodollars entered hockey through international exhibition meets, he honed his reputation for arranging lucrative financial deals for domestic (amateur) and foreign hockey concerns. His corporate business empire was now a far-reaching extravaganza. Eagleson himself sat on the boards of more than twenty organizations and companies, yet his power was elusive and undefined.

His reputation as a benevolent despot, earned by handing over $1 million of "tied aid" to amateur hockey from the profits of the first world cup and then dictating how they should spend it, made him a monolithic power at once too visible and too seemingly untouchable not to challenge.

A series of attacks from the corporate sector and amateur ranks and then a subsequent lifting of the tarpaulin by the media threatened the Eagleson corporate dynasty's continued invincibility.

The first assault to his empire caused a severe weakening in one of the main pillars of support, his ability to guarantee sponsorships for international tournaments from his corporate contacts. After publicly announcing that sponsors for Team Canada's re-entry at the 1977

World Championships in Vienna were committed, one of the two main sponsors appeared to be backing down. General Motors and Carling O'Keefe were apparently committed to splitting ninety minutes of TV advertising time during the series at $10,000 a minute. Just three months before the tournament, however, Arthur Harnett Enterprises Ltd. told Eagleson that there was a problem getting General Motors' cheque. As usual, Eagleson, as head of the tournament committee, applied a little muscle on Harnett's behalf. In his letter to Jack Newby of Foster Advertising, agents for General Motors, he said:

> Apparently some confusion has arisen with respect to General Motors' participation in Team Canada '77. I have had more confusion with my dealings with you and General Motors than I had in the entire Canada Cup of Hockey with all sponsors combined.
>
> In view of the confusion I am prepared at this stage to permit General Motors to withdraw completely from Team Canada sponsorship.

The discount rate Harnett apparently offered GM at the outset was 50 percent. Carling O'Keefe and GM together were expected to split the 90 minutes of prime commercial time for $500,000, a sum which would cover nearly all expenses incurred by Team Canada for the Vienna tourney in April 1977. In the event, Team Canada finished in fourth place at the world championships.*

At the same time, another force was gathering speed to attack the integrity of Eagleson's empire. The amateur constituency (CAHA) of Hockey Canada was coming after him with all guns blazing on two issues: first, how the CAHA's portion of Canada Cup profits — in the form of a $1 million trust agreement — was allocated; and second, how he spent money for Team Canada's involvement in the 1977 World Championships in Vienna.

On January 27, 1977, CAHA president Don Johnson, then Assistant Deputy Minister of Recreation for the Newfoundland government, wrote to each of the four western provincial Major Junior A hockey presidents, defending Eagleson on the matter of the trust agreement.

---

* General Motors and Carling O'Keefe were the major sponsors in April 1977. According to Newby, Carling bought half of the 90 minutes and General Motors took a smaller share (40 percent) at the $10,000-per-minute rate. In addition, says Newby, General Motors bought more time in Vienna for approximately $2,000 per minute because Canada's performance had picked up.

Johnson reminded the provincial presidents that although the CAHA was not involved in any way, shape, or form with the Canada Cup, $150,000 from the 1976 proceeds was paid to junior hockey. "Mr. Ballard simply paid the $50,000 over to the Ontario teams himself rather than go through Hockey Canada. It was only a gentleman's agreement that he had with Alan so no one objected anyway. Sam Pollock had the same agreement, and delivered $50,000 to Major Junior A Hockey teams in Quebec. This, of course, left the Western Canada Junior Hockey League [WCJHL] out in the cold." After raising the issue with Eagleson, Doug Fisher was instructed to deliver $50,000 of Hockey Canada's funds to the Western Canada Junior Hockey League. In addition, Hockey Canada gave the CAHA $111,185 to pay off its hockey development account deficit, plus $40,000 towards sending the Ontario team to the World Championships in Czechoslovakia.

In the letter, Johnson explains why amateur hockey participation was dropped from the Canada Cup: " ... Hockey Canada was presented with a bill by CBC for some $252,000.* Mr. Eagleson was so annoyed that he subsequently called off all the side deals and special arrangements that he had made with me and Amateur Hockey. Quite frankly, I did not blame him one bit." Then, in confidence, Johnson broke the news about the $1 million trust agreement. "This is a million dollars that will be placed on deposit [for five years] and Amateur Hockey is to have the interest without any strings attached. We will also have our say with regard to the million dollars itself; however, it is hoped that it will stay on deposit where it can help us year after year."

Later, at a full meeting of the Hockey Canada board in March 1977, it became clear that the CAHA did not receive the $1 million with "no strings attached". At the meeting, it was decided the accrued interest on the principal would go for CAHA development, but the Hockey Canada board would decide the future use of the principal. Fisher and Johnson were named trustees. When the CAHA questioned how the $1 million would be paid, Eagleson then demanded the CAHA account for all funds received from Hockey Canada over the past years.

Today, the controversy over the $1 million trust agreement rages

---

* In an effort to ensure than every Canadian had a chance to see the Canada Cup, CBC supplied extra line reach and air time, at a cost of $252,000, in pockets of Quebec, New Brunswick, and the Prairies that the two private television networks, CTV and TVA, couldn't reach.

on. On May 26, 1981, a Canadian Press article stated that "The CAHA claims it should have received $200,000 in interest from the fund during the last two years, a sum still sitting in the Montreal Trust Company in Toronto." The problem is that neither Hockey Canada nor Eagleson can agree on the terms originally set out when the trust fund was set up in 1976. Eagleson claims the CAHA was told it would get a total of $1 million from the Canada Cup. The CAHA feels that it has the right to the $1 million trust fund (including interest for two years). To date, the CAHA has received a total of $301,185, and Eagleson says it is now owed only $698,815. However, the CAHA feels it should get the accumulated interest on the $1 million (9 percent a year for 5 years) which comes to $450,000, plus the $301,185 received initially, plus the $1 million in the bank, a total of $1,751,185. Before the problem can be settled three questions must be answered: What was the original deal? Who is entitled to the $1 million? What happens after five years?

Few could outwit Eagleson in the boardroom or on the streets. However, just as he appeared to have the world of hockey won over to his side, the big kid on the block was soon accused of bullying. After the 1977 World Championships in Vienna, with Team Canada finishing in fourth place, it took a search-and-rescue squad from the IIHF home office to clean up the rubble left in its wake. Eagleson had apparently accused IIHF secretary general Walter Wasservogel of "stealing money from [my] pockets". He then admitted to a news conference, "stolen may be a strong word. All I know is somebody screwed me out of $20 Gs."

Eagleson claimed his Canadian delegation purchased $50,000 worth of tickets for the Vienna series, "but $20,000 worth of tickets are useless." He said that in order to purchase 100 seats for the Canada-Czech game, Canada was forced to buy 100 seats for the U.S.-Finland game. "The only money they [the organizing Committee] will make will be what they stole from us," he was quoted as saying.

When the dust finally settled, the real issue surfaced. Apparently what caused the sabre rattling was the IIHF's new president, Dr. Gunther Sabetzki, telling a Canadian newspaper that the Canadian team "was out of shape and perhaps drinking too much and the IIHF would find it difficult to sanction the 1980 Canada Cup because of this poor performance."

Of course Sabetzki denied having made the remarks, but Eagleson was boiling. "He probably said it. I've heard from other guys that he said it." Here was Canada's long-awaited return to the world championships, playing against national teams from Finland, Japan, Germany, and Romania in the presence of heads of state. "I made it clear right from the start we were coming here with a fourth-place team that might jell and wind up third. ... The Canadian public might not like it but I can't ask the NHL to stop doing business," Eagleson explained.

It would be a memorable spring for Eagleson. Vienna was suddenly blossoming with outraged tournament officials. The Canadian public and press were upset, as were a few Canadian politicians. Federal MP Arnold Peters (NDP–Timiskaming) informed Eagleson and Fisher that he was going to ask for an inquiry to explain Team Canada's embarrassing performance throughout the 1977 tournament. Eagleson told a reporter for the *Montreal Gazette*, "Arnold Peters is a jerk NDPer from Timiskaming. ... He's mad at Doug Fisher for leaving the NDP and I guess he's mad at me for being a Tory."

Scotty Bowman, who coached the victorious Team Canada in the 1976 Canada Cup series, said that the poor showing during the Vienna games was a result of lack of preparation and "not being given the same opportunities as we were".

Wilf Paiement, the Colorado Rockies forward who took eleven minutes in penalties during Team Canada's 11-1 loss to the U.S.S.R., told reporters, "I had nothing to lose. The game was over and I figured I could hurt somebody, make them think twice in the next game. I always like to win."

Another incident sent Kent-Erik Andersson, a Swedish player, to hospital with suspected internal injuries. Carol Vadnais, a New York Ranger member of Team Canada, jabbed Andersson during the second period of a game (won by Canada 7-0). It was reported that Vadnais was getting even for a 1972 incident during a Team Canada exhibition tour when Wayne Cashman — then his teammate with Boston Bruins — was cut by the stick of Swedish player Ulf Sterner. "I promised Cash I'd get a Swede for him," Vadnais said.

Eagleson had hoped that these Vienna games would provide "a bit of glue for national unity".* His wish was fulfilled. Not since 1972 and the Moscow incident had the country been so united in its stand — against Eagleson.

Two federal government departments also attacked Hockey

* A phrase coined by former U.S. Vice-President Spiro Agnew.

Canada's international committee. On September 16, 1977, Marc Lalonde, now federal Minister of Health and Welfare, sent a formal reprimand to Derek Holmes, the federal government representative and executive director of Hockey Canada, reminding him of proper decorum, as suggested in 1976 by the President of the Treasury Board in the House of Commons:

> While recognizing that Hockey Canada Inc. is not a Crown corporation, it is still important that any corporation in which there is a significant degree of federal government ownership or control maintain a very high standard of conduct. My colleagues in the Cabinet have, therefore, directed me to write to each of the government-appointed directors and commend to them the policy and guidelines set out in the Minister's statement. It is the government's wish that the policy be brought to the attention of the full Board of Directors at the earliest possible moment, and that the Board implement the spirit of the policy and guidelines through appropriate corporate policies and procedures.

Iona Campagnolo, Minister of State for Fitness and Amateur Sport, set up an *ad hoc* committee of five prominent politicians in September 1978, "to evaluate Canada's participation in international hockey competition". Senator Sidney Buckwold, a Liberal from Saskatchewan, headed the inquiry. He informed Doug Fisher of the minister's plans, which had come "as a result of Canada's return to world hockey competition and the controversy which surrounded our team".

Members of the press who were strong Eagleson supporters violently opposed the cost of the inquiry (estimated at $100,000) as a "scandalous waste of taxpayers' money". The inquiry was finally terminated in November 1979 because of "financial restraints".

At about the same time that Campagnolo announced the federal inquiry, Don Johnson cabled Eagleson from St. John's, Newfoundland: "If you or Doug ever need me, it is simply a matter of giving me a shout." That was in May; by June, Johnson was no longer president of CAHA. One of his last duties was to draw Eagleson's attention to some "confidential minutes" he had received with regard to the Hockey Hall of Fame: " ... the Federal government said the [Canada] Cup belongs to the government. Did you ever officially let them have it as Chairman of the Canada Cup Committee? ... I know we both wanted the Cup to go to the Hall of Fame; however, apparently our wishes are being ignored. Is there anything we can do to get this Cup in its proper resting place?"

Amid the federal government's mucking about, Eagleson proved resilient, only to find there was more to come. For a time, the empire was going to fight back. On July 18, 1977, Hockey Canada reappointed Eagleson as chairman of the International Committee, with a new first lieutenant — his personal comptroller, Marvin Goldblatt, was named the committee's comptroller. Another piece of business (which would provoke abundant controversy by the end of the summer) the summer) was the election of Eagleson as chairman of the new World Junior Tournament scheduled for December 1977 in Quebec.

At this time another member of the Eagleson "mafia", Rick Curran, was brought into Hockey Canada under the title of business manager. Curran was an employee of the Orr–Walton hockey camp and later assisted Eagleson in recruiting junior hockey players and running the day-to-day operations of the NHLPA. Also, Eagleson's accounting firm (Clarkson, Gordon), was appointed auditors for Hockey Canada. Another employee, Bill Watters, head of Eagleson's company, Sports Management Ltd., was introduced to the board by Eagleson as his assistant under the title of "tournament co-ordinator", and his buddy, Professor Robert Mackay, was retained as counsel. CAHA president Gordon Renwick was appointed co-chairman. Eagleson intended that Hockey Canada, through its international committee, would oversee every aspect of the World Junior Tournament Committee. He set up a tournament directorate headed by Jack Devine, Renwick, and himself, as well as a rep from each of the countries participating. Renwick was added to the legal, technical, and banking committee then composed of Chris Lang, Walter Bowen (a lawyer with Blaney, Pasternak — Hockey Canada's legal representatives), Eagleson, and Goldblatt. Eagleson then informed the board: "The CAHA acknowledges that HC owns all international hockey rights for Canada and the rights of membership in the IIHF. The CAHA further acknowledges that HC has one seat for its appointee and one seat for the president of the CAHA on the IIHF."

Criticisms of Team Canada '77 were voiced at the July meeting, and it was rep Georges Larivière's opinion that "Team Canada '77 went to Europe and other than participate ... nothing had been accomplished ... there appeared to be a good deal of money spent but nothing was set aside to assist in studying the Europeans in their approach to the game."

At the meeting in Toronto, Eagleson tabled a draft financial statement showing a net loss of $12,000 for the series.

One of the most common complaints from most senior officers in Canadian amateur hockey was: "The international committee, the most powerful arm of Hockey Canada, should not be operating out of Eagleson's office." Eagleson responded by saying, "I suggested we operate Hockey Canada in my office. They were paying about $4,000 a month in rent before, and I said we could run it on a shoestring here."

When the Major Junior A Hockey officials were asking for details about the organization and financial arrangements for the scheduled junior tourney, the junior group asked the CAHA to hold a meeting of HC's international committee in September. Three items were questioned; they appeared on an allegedly "incomplete" confidential financial paper released to an Ottawa newspaper. An item called "office" (for $39,516) was suggested to be the "shoestring" costs Eagleson meant. Other items referred to "souvenirs, gifts and miscellaneous" ($36,093), and to "accommodation" ($167,000). Eagleson claimed that, as fund raiser for the international tourneys, he shouldn't be criticized. Just how did he spend $36,000 on "gifts"? He argued that the money spent was not Hockey Canada's but that of two major sponsors of the team. "We bought some people some very nice gifts," he said. "There was a list of about fifty people. We gave the players nice commemorative watches, and we gave their wives sterling silver charms, and all the international federations got nice gifts." Arguing that since professional players would "play for nothing" once every four years, "we put them in good hotels to generate goodwill." Eagleson placed the visiting junior tourney teams in the Hotel Toronto and the Montreal Four Seasons. While the CAHA had been willing to pay travel costs of visiting teams, Eagleson had asked them to pay their own costs. "We saved $70,000. I don't want credit for that, but I don't want to be criticized for spending money somewhere else." Then he countered threat with threat: "If I get anything but total approval of what I've done. ... If [the CAHA] can't support the concepts I have in mind, I'll resign from the junior tournament. [CAHA officials] ask me to raise the money: they don't want to share that part of it. All they want to do is share in the spending of it. Well, damn it, if I raise it, I should have some input into how the money is spent."

He continued to defend his actions, suggesting, "I can change hats faster than most of those guys [amateur hockey officials] can think, I have no trouble with that at all. Furthermore, many of my friends and associates are volunteering to work for HC during international tour-

neys, which saves the organization money. I can strongarm my friends.
. . . I can tell them to work eighteen hours a day and they will. I can
get them to cut their fees by 15 to 20 percent; if any friend of mine
gets a contract or job it's because they offer the best deal or because
they are the best men for the job.''

A Canadian Press article ran a counterattack by CAHA hockey official
Ed Chynoweth, Western Canada Junior Hockey League president.
''Why is he so touchy?'' Chynoweth asked. ''I am sure that most
hockey fans in Canada are sick and tired of hearing another of his
sermons from the mount. . . . If he has nothing to hide in how he runs
HC, why is he constantly defending what he does?'' Eagleson had
been annoyed by a letter from Howard Darwin of Ottawa, the major
junior hockey rep on the Hockey Canada international committee. Ed
Chynoweth said that all Darwin wanted was a copy of the proposed
budget for the tournament, copies of sponsorship agreements and TV
contracts, and a list of people to be hired.

In January 1978, Eagleson threatened to quit his post as chairman
of the international committee: ''Unless I make a move now, I'll be
caught in a difficult situation between the NHL and the IIHF.'' He
maintained that he had had time for little else but Hockey Canada
since 1975, and in the past three years had been overseas twenty
times. Now he wanted to turn over the reins to Bill Hay, already
a committee member. Eagleson would remain a member of the committee: ''What I'll do will be the same as everybody else on the
committee — represent my constituents, the NHL players.''

He said he would stay around to oversee the 1978 tournament in
Prague, which was to run from late April to mid-May.

NHL president Campbell said, ''There was a serious split between
HC and CAHA in which some federal intervention was required and
there is no doubt that [Eagleson] looked to Mme Campagnolo, as the
federal minister of sports, for assistance and support and he got it. To
the extent necessary, I think Alan would have been happy to see the
CAHA supplanted by some other Canadian organization even under
federal sponsorship. Such a move could not have been effectively
implemented under the Canadian constitution as the subject matter
was clearly within the ambit of Section 92 of the BNA act (which gives
that area of jurisdiction to the provinces).''

The split Campbell referred to was between the NHL and the junior
pros over the handling of ''development fees'' to the thirty-four clubs
in the junior league. There was a standard player contract issued by

the CMJHL, which Eagleson had advised players not to sign. The contract meant that the NHL would compensate the junior club for players taken. Eagleson called this "a form of blackmail. It's the same as a promissory note." The maximum compensation fee ($20,000 1978) is paid by the NHL club that drafts the junior, and is supposed to protect the supply source. Junior hockey is the NHL's major farm system. More than 75 percent of NHL players graduate from junior clubs. During the 1976-77 season only six of the thirty-four junior clubs made money.

Another major attack on the Eagleson empire came from the players' association. Arthur Kaminsky, a New York attorney and agent for Ken Dryden, became an agent during the expansion years. Kaminsky publicly asked Eagleson to renounce either his stewardship of the players' union or forfeit his "conflicting" role as agent to individual players. He also took offence at Eagleson's suggestion that weak NHL teams should fold. In November 1977, Kaminsky said that Eagleson was lax: "Only recently has he been meeting with the players from each team to explain the new contracts. That's something that should have been done at training camp, not in the middle of the season."

Kaminsky singled out the Ken Linesman issue, saying that Eagleson was flaunting his power. Eagleson had attempted to prevent nineteen-year-old Linesman, of Kingston, Ontario, from signing a pro contract with the Birmingham Bulls of the WHA. Kaminsky, Linesman's lawyer, says, "Eagle threatened to use his power to cancel a tournament the WHA had scheduled with the Czechs and Russians if he didn't get his way. WHA needed the money; it would have hurt them if he called it off. He has too much power. We later tried to negotiate a settlement and he singlehandedly stopped it." On October 28, 1977, a federal judge in Hartford, Connecticut, ruled that what Eagleson desired in effect violated U.S. anti-trust laws. "Eagleson used his monopolistic power to basically boycott anyone under twenty years from making a living — it's against the law," says Kaminsky. Linesman, an outstanding young rookie, was leading his team in scoring. Kaminsky had an agreement from Linesman's junior club saying they would let him turn pro as a special underage junior. "Eagle tried to prevent the move by using his verbal shield of protecting junior hockey, saying that, if Linesman played for the Bulls, he would cancel the WHA's lucrative international series."

Then, Rangers player Phil Esposito and Detroit's general manager

Ted Lindsay criticized Eagleson for throwing the players into too many international games. "It was at the owners' insistence that we amended the agreement to permit eighteen games a year, rather than eight," Eagleson said. Eagleson wrote a letter to John Ziegler, who replaced Campbell as NHL president in June 1977, asking for a clear statement about the league's future intentions concerning international hockey. On behalf of the players' association, he suggested the possibility of scrapping the whole idea if it couldn't be "handled properly". Dr. Sabetzki, who worried about killing the goose that laid the golden egg, said: "We must see not only the money but also the sport. And we must not do a bad job for the spectators."

Eagleson was still hanging tough. At an NHLPA meeting scheduled in Buffalo on January 23, 1978, he presented a letter signed by NHLPA president Bobby Clarke of the Philadelphia Flyers and vice-president Phil Esposito of the New York Rangers. The letter, addressed to Doug Fisher, outlined problems with the Team Canada format for Prague in April. Players who had been in Vienna "came home with a bad taste in their mouths. They felt that Canadian amateur hockey officials and some HC officials made the team a scapegoat. ... I know the players felt they were let down by many of the amateur officials who were very critical of our team members." The letter cited Gordon Juckes' complaint that "'this was one of Canada's worst hockey teams'. ... It certainly was not appreciated by any of our players to hear such an authority as Mr. Juckes describe our team in that fashion." The letter went on to say several players had indicated to Clarke that they were not interested in going to Prague under any circumstances. "All of them have advised me that unless Mr. Eagleson commits himself to the project and is heavily involved in representing the rights of our players, they will not be interested. If you wish to make other arrangements [for the Prague tourney] with the WHA or amateur players, our association will not be offended in the least. I feel that the NHLPA honoured its obligation that arose out of the Canada Cup of Hockey by participating in Vienna and that obligation has ended."

Eagleson wrote a note on the letter, saying it represented the opinion of most of the players. "I'm sure Bobby didn't write that letter," says Doug Fisher.

Eagleson said he figured he alone could make or break the series. "If I'm involved, I'm certain they'll be available for Team Canada. I don't think they'll do it if I'm not in the picture." Again, he said the only thing standing in his way was CAHA criticism. "It makes me reluctant to get back into the meat grinder and devote the time to it that the project demands. I've been squeezed by too many people and see no reason to continue. It's my contention that the CAHA should not be in international hockey. ..."

Gordon Juckes later blamed Hockey Canada for a $100,000 loss in marketing opportunity from the junior tournament in Quebec. At the same time Eagleson wrote to Fisher, saying, "I have misgivings about dealing with the CAHA in future. I made a commitment to the NHL and WHA and made certain that HC honoured it. I made a commitment to the CAHA and made sure that HC would honour it to the extent of $1 million [the trust agreement]. The board members have now improved upon that commitment to the extent of more than $300,000 and I consider this to be totally unfair. ... I was very frustrated by the results of the meeting and I accept the decision of the Board even though I am satisfied that most of the members who voted on the issue were unaware of the commitments made by the committee of the Canada Cup with respect to the NHL, WHA and both Players' Associations and the CAHA."

In April 1978, Eagleson was off to Italy, selling Canadian hockey futures under his new title of chief negotiator for Hockey Canada. On February 16, 1978, the directors of Hockey Canada had done away with the international committee and all other committees giving power back to the board. They had decided that Eagleson alone would represent Hockey Canada and sit in on IIHF tournament committee meetings. Canada would continue to send less than its strongest reps to the world championships in exchange for pledges for NHL–European hockey matches. With respect to working with CAHA president Gordon Renwick, Eagleson had agreed to compromise: "We've agreed to bury the hatchet — and not in each other."

PALACE REVOLT

Any power I have comes directly from the
players. If the players lose confidence in me
then I don't have a hell of a lot of power.
R. Alan Eagleson

At its peak, the Eagleson network was a thriving multi-million dollar business cartel. His corporate empire had cornered most major sectors of the Canadian hockey entertainment field, from endorsements to TV licensing rights to running private pension plans and personal financial consulting companies. As agent for Hockey Canada, a publicly financed oligopoly, Eagleson and his associates conducted hundreds of profitable ventures under IIHF tacit agreement free of the restraints of most combine or anti-trust laws. Eagleson and his network won contracts by setting prices which undercut the competition (such as Harnett's 50 percent rate reduction on TV advertising sales). While club owners reported combined losses in the tens of millions, Eagleson's investments soared, yet he never invested a dime in a franchise. To the corporate world the name Eagleson had become a byword. At the time of the NHL-WHA merger, in March 1979, Eagleson was close to being a millionaire twice over, and could afford to buy out the Canadian business interests of his wealthiest client, millionaire Bobby Orr.

His reason for leaving Blaney, Pasternak had crystallized. His tenth-floor corner suite of offices in the heart of Toronto's business community housed the country's largest sports agency. His switchboard was constantly lit up like a stock exchange in a downturn with giant manufacturing firms and food conglomerates playing "let's make a deal".

Then, suddenly, the lights began to go out. Like the final act of a Shakespeare tragedy, Eagleson's empire slowly crumbled.

In July 1978, the NHL handed down its first suspension of a hockey player for the use of illicit drugs. Don Murdoch, the $120,000-a-season right winger for the New York Rangers, had pleaded guilty to a criminal charge of possession of cocaine. Murdoch was fined $400 and had his U.S. work visa revoked by an Ontario provincial court judge. (Later, the work permit was reinstated after an appeal by his agent's lawyers.) NHL president John Ziegler suspended Murdoch without pay for the 1978–79 season. The twenty-one-year-old native of Cranbrook, B.C., screamed foul, saying he had been used as a "fall guy". Murdoch's lawyers announced plans to appeal the NHL decision to the board of governors.

Ballard called the length and severity of the suspension "ludicrous", saying, "but considering who we have for a president it doesn't surprise me." He said although he didn't condone the use of drugs, "a lot of young guys without the pressures of a Murdoch make a mistake now and again" and added that Ziegler wasn't playing ball. Eagleson and the NHLPA, however, backed Ziegler, not Murdoch. In its official statement, the NHLPA said it had "little sympathy for Don Murdoch". Peter Smith, Canadian spokesman for International Management Group, Murdoch's agents, strongly criticized Eagleson: "I seriously question Alan Eagleson's statement. . . . It is one thing not to take a stance but [Eagleson] is kicking him when he is down . . . he's gone out of his way to jump on Don Murdoch and I personally question if Eagleson would have said those things if one of his clients and not Murdoch was in this unfortunate position." On December 15, 1978, Murdoch's sentence was altered by the NHL to suspension from exhibition and forty regular season games.

Next there was the McCourt case. The Los Angeles Kings demanded rights to Detroit Red Wing centre Dale McCourt as compensation for Kings goalie Rogatien Vachon, who had become a free agent in 1978 and signed a long-term contract with Detroit. An arbitration decision awarded McCourt to Los Angeles. Then, McCourt filed a suit in an attempt to overturn the arbitrator's decision. He accused five parties — the NHL, the NHLPA, the Red Wings, the L.A. Kings, and the Kings' parent organization, California Sports Inc. — of restraint of trade, restraint of employment, two counts of breach of contract, and abuse of an arbitration award. McCourt threatened not to play for the NHL if he did not get his contract assigned to the Red Wings.

McCourt appealed to U.S. District Court Judge Robert de Mascio, who ruled that McCourt did not have to play for the Kings. He said the compensation rule — set out in the collective-bargaining agreement — is not necessary to maintain a balance in calibre of players in the league and that it could not be justified as serving any legitimate purpose.

The NHL issued its statement: "It is our counsel's firm opinion that the court committed reversible error in its conclusion of facts and interpretation of the applicable law. ... " Ziegler said he was calling for the preservation and sanctioning of the collective-bargaining agreement which included equalization as one of its essential provisions.

Meanwhile, Judge de Mascio had issued a temporary restraining order, which allowed McCourt to stay with the Red Wings while the court heard McCourt's case. If the case went as far as the U.S. Supreme Court, it could cost the NHL an estimated $1 million in legal fees. "If the owners drag the McCourt case out, it will cost them a bundle," Eagleson said. "Hell, it has already cost the NHLPA $40,000 and we aren't carrying the ball."

The threat of NHL-WHA merger was strengthened by Ziegler. "Unless we can maintain some form of equalization for free agents and keep collective bargaining intact, several owners will be forced into a position of re-examination, deciding whether it's worth their while to continue."

At the time of McCourt's case, Eagleson said that Harold Ballard's way of opposing McCourt's action was not to release Darryl Sittler or Lanny McDonald as free agents in 1977, but instead sign them to seven-year contracts. However, McCourt's lawyer said he felt there was too much uncertainty in the rule. "Because of the rule, how can any general manager deal in good faith with an athlete? A specific formula must be laid out." He chose the example of the National Football League's codified formula for dealing with free agents — draft picks (someone not actively playing, such as a junior), a player, or money.

McCourt's case was to come to trial in Detroit on October 18, 1978. One week earlier, Eagleson addressed the subject of compensation. In a newspaper article, he proposed compensation — draft choices and money based on the player's salary — for free agents. "We tabled our proposals in July and the owners have sat on their butts since then and done nothing about it." He suggested now that the McCourt case had come up, perhaps the owners wished they had acted. "If the McCourt decision is upheld, it will help the players over the short haul, but it will hurt the game down the road." (The case was settled out of court, and McCourt remained with Detroit.)

At the same time, Eagleson ran into another snare over the compensation issue with Pierre Bouchard, a personal client. Bouchard was left unprotected by Montreal in the intraleague draft on October 9, 1978, and was immediately picked up by the Washington Capitals. Then, within twenty-four hours, Bouchard was traded back to Montreal for Rodney Schutt, American Hockey League Rookie of the Year in 1977, then with the Nova Scotia Voyageurs. John Ziegler declared the trade of Bouchard void because it contravened a league by-law which said a player who was claimed in an intraleague draft could not be transferred unless he first cleared waivers.* But Eagleson wished to ignore the waiver draft, stating simply: "Bouchard is not leaving Montreal and if he can't play hockey in Montreal I am certain that Pierre will retire." On October 16, 1978, Bouchard announced his retirement.† A few days later Eagleson accused other teams of opportunism at the expense of Schutt and Bouchard: "They pounced on this mistake like vultures ... we will be making a formal complaint from the players' association about the waiver draft. We will make a formal request to have it expunged and to have it replaced by some other type of draft at the June talks in Nassau." He called the draft a joke because it resulted in displacement of families just a few days before the regular season began.

The new year brought talks of the NHL's fifth historic expansion (to twenty-one teams) and Eagleson was accused of waffling on the NHLPA's stand opposing merger.

In 1973, the players' association had specifically stated that there would be no merger talks. If the two leagues were amalgamated, there would be less bidding for talent, and therefore skyrocketing inflation of salaries would be curbed. At that time, a deal was proposed with

---

* One example of league waivers is that an NHL player in the major league cannot be sent down to the minors until a list is circulated to each club in the league, giving the rest of the clubs a chance to pick up that player or waive the right to do so.
† Bouchard resumed his playing career with the Washington Capitals of the WHA in 1979.

the NHLPA whereby no member would be able to join the WHA for one year. Then, in 1974, Eagleson threatened anti-trust suits against both leagues and charged the NHL with a breach of trust for holding secret talks and planning exhibition games and playoff games between two leagues.

Merger attempts in 1977 between the NHL and the WHA failed. In the spring of 1978, the NHLPA suggested that it was ready to enlist the aid of the courts to oppose the merger, which now appeared imminent because the National Basketball Association and the American Basketball Association were to merge. The NBA Players' Association had won a court injunction against the merger in 1970.*

It appeared the last hope for the debt-plagued leagues was winning a lucrative TV contract with one of the huge American networks. Ziegler (and, some say, Eagleson) made one last-ditch effort to net a TV commitment. They came up with the 1979 Challenge Cup. It was designed to replace the annual NHL All-Star match, which was termed a ''yawner'' because hockey players were keen to avoid injuries mid-season.

The NHL All-Stars were pitted against the Soviet Nationals in New York for the one-time Challenge Cup in the hope that the American public might become excited about hockey. With a star-studded NHL roster including six Leafs (Palmateer, Sittler, McDonald, Salming, Turnbull, and Burrows), it looked as if once again Eagleson had to tap his source of personal clients for ''debts owing''. The Soviet Nats won the game 6-0 and the Challenge Cup failed to do anything more than attract a tiny nibble from a small U.S. cable network. Bobby Orr, who was becoming well acquainted with the marketing field, commented on the situation: ''The network bought a section of one period of one game . . . very small . . . we have to watch the ratings to see how they do. It all depends on the ratings.'' Still, Ziegler could not sit idly by watching other pro league sports like baseball obtain TV deals for as much as $60 million in one season.

* One architect of the National Football League's eventual absorption of the American Football League was Ed Snider, part owner of the NFL Philadelphia Eagles. In 1972, Snider, chairman of the board of the Philadelphia Flyers and owner of the Spectrum, felt hockey was still operating in the 1940s and had fallen behind both baseball and football. He met with league officials to present his master plan for the NHL's takeover of 11 WHA franchises for a reported $4 million each for the right to play league division games, until the WHA schedule would eventually match the NHL's. His deal was shot down in 1972, a move he claims cost the league a huge TV package deal with CBS.

Ziegler again met bad luck on another count. In May 1979 the Montreal Canadiens eliminated the New York Rangers in the fifth game of the Stanley Cup finals. It cost the NHL the $450,000 that ABC had guaranteed for rights to the seventh game in the best-of-seven series.

Waiting for the elusive TV contract was like waiting for Godot. Without the huge TV network contracts to increase exposure, new investors were scarce. When Team U.S.A. won the gold medal in the 1980 Lake Placid Olympics but still couldn't generate the TV ratings, the NHL's hopes of winning a major TV network contract were dashed.

After the Challenge Cup disaster, merger talks resumed. In March 1979, at an NHL board meeting in Chicago, a 14-3 vote approved what it termed an "expansion" with the WHA. The Maple Leafs, the Boston Bruins, and the L.A. Kings opposed it.

At the time the NHL entered its fifth expansion, results of a *Globe and Mail* poll of NHL governors showed how bleak the economic picture was. Ten out of seventeen clubs anticipated projected losses of $12 million in 1977–78 year, something of an improvement over the 1976–77 period when combined losses were $18 million. The clubs reporting losses in 1977–78 included the Cleveland Barons, with a payroll of $2 million (the average league payroll size), which had losses of $2.7 million; the Colorado Rockies lost $1.8 million, down from losses of approximately $3.7 million for the 1976–77 period; the Chicago Black Hawks saw the Wirtz family owners absorb a $1.3 million debt; the Detroit Red Wings' owner Bruce Norris reported projected losses of $1 million; the Minnesota North Stars lost $1 million; Ralston-Purina had purchased the St. Louis Blues, inheriting a $2.2 million payroll and losses of $800,000; the Atlanta Flames had $800,000 in losses; the Washington Capitals, $750,000; and the Los Angeles Kings reported a deficit of $500,000.

The WHA had been a seven-year itch that cost $100 million to scratch; only four of the original twelve teams survived.*

Walter Bush, vice-president of the Minnesota North Stars, claims the war between the leagues cost his club between four and six million dollars over the years. Each of the four remaining WHA teams

---

* When the league held its first chalk talks in Anaheim, California, in February 1972, its roster reached from Alberta to Miami with teams in major capitals including the Calgary Broncos, Chicago Cougars, Edmonton Oilers, Los Angeles Sharks, Miami Screaming Eagles, Minnesota Fighting Saints, New England Whalers, New York Golden Blades, Ottawa Nationals, Quebec Nordiques, and Winnipeg Jets.

(Winnipeg, Edmonton, Quebec, and New England) was expected to pay $6 million to join the older league. Payments were to be made in two instalments: $4.6 million (Canadian) on joining (June 1, 1979) and $1.4 million, free of interest charges, to be paid at any time.

WHA president Howard Baldwin, who owned a 12 percent share of the New England Whalers, was jubilant about the merger: "I feel we're giving the NHL four sound franchises with good owners who worked hard and paid their bills."

During the first expansion season of 1979-80, the *Globe and Mail* reported that the twenty-one NHL teams shared total gate receipts of close to $100 million during the 1979–80 season. League estimates showed that nine teams experienced losses after meeting operating and salary costs averaging $4.5 million. Losers for the 1979–80 season included Colorado, Pittsburgh, Atlanta, St. Louis, Chicago, Washington, Los Angeles, Hartford, and Quebec.

Before the merger could be finalized, the remaining WHA teams not joining the NHL had to be compensated. One estimate placed payments to the Birmingham Bulls and Cincinnati Stingers at nearly $6.5 million — $3.5 million and $2.85 million respectively.

Another difficulty was Eagleson's claim that the players' association viewed what the NHL called "expansion" as a "merger". NHLPA approval of the amalgamation was necessary according to the 1976 collective-bargaining agreement. Eagleson's settlement plans at the time included payment to the association of half of the expected $24 million WHA entry fees from the four teams, as well as the maintenance of the agreement. Suddenly, on March 27, Eagleson said he had put both Ziegler and Wirtz "on notice" that the NHLPA was prepared to file anti-trust action against the NHL unless the agreement was renegotiated. He said the association wanted to adopt a compensation system familiar to the NFL's — a team losing a free agent would be compensated with draft picks to permit more freedom of movement.* Eagleson also wanted changes in amateur drafting to allow two clubs to compete for a player's services.

A couple of days later, Ziegler announced that the "expansion" meant the players were "legally ... not entitled to anything and we don't believe we have any legal obligation to the players to reopen or

* Of the 310 NFL players who had their contracts expire or became free agents during 1976–79, only one player, Norm Thompson, changed teams. Detroit labour lawyer Brian Smith said of the NFL's new free-agent rule, "An equalization like the one employed in football leads to collusion among owners and price fixing."

renegotiate the collective agreement. Our legal position is based on the premise this is an expansion and not a merger.''

On March 30 (the deadline for the amalgamation), Harold Ballard ran a one-man demonstration against the ''expansion''. As league governors gathered in New York, they were greeted on their arrival by Ballard carrying a placard reading: FIRST THING WE DO IS KILL ALL THE LAWYERS.

Eagleson had always said, ''The only thing that affects salaries is a WHA–NHL merger.'' In May, after the merger seemed to be more than a definite possibility, Eagleson said it wouldn't happen for a couple of years. What about the $12 million share Eagleson wanted in WHA entry fees?''I will have to settle for about $9 million, but so are the owners settling for less,'' he replied.

In a time of private and public restraint, it appeared that Eagleson too would be forced to reduce his demands. ''What I want are some freedoms. . . . not huge million dollar signing bonuses. What I want is for Mike Palmateer to be able to go to Chicago, get a salary, get a job, and not worry about them not signing Mike because they might have to give up [Tony] Esposito.''

But the very next month, at the Nassau annual meetings, the NHLPA members opted for a moderate rather than a hard-line approach in their negotiations with the league governors and owners. When the subject of redrafting the collective-bargaining agreement came up (the 1975 agreement became obsolete with termination of the WHA), the NHLPA rejected the stand they and Eagleson had originally formulated, by choosing more financial benefits in place of more freedom of movement. As it was, the question of whether the players actually chose equalization was a moot point. It was generally believed that had the NHLPA not agreed to the expansion, the NHL might have backed off, the players still would have been subject to equalization, and the WHA probably would have folded, as it was not expected to survive the next season. If the WHA collapsed, there would be four fewer teams and eighty fewer jobs.

One player in particular who didn't take too well to the ''squeeze'' was Mike Milbury. The summer of 1979 brought evidence of a palace revolt in Eagleson's empire. Two devastating things happened simultaneously. One was Bobby Orr's departure from Eagleson's fold; the other came from the all-important power base itself — the players' association. At its annual meeting in June, player reps of seventeen teams voted in a new collective-bargaining agreement with the board of NHL governors by a 30-1 sweep. The one dissenting vote came from the founding team of the NHLPA, the Boston Bruins. Milbury's dissenting vote as the Bruins' rep ended the record of unanimous votes within the NHLPA. The players voted to retain equalization and binding arbitration, and extended the agreement until 1982. The players reportedly received $7.25 million in extra pension, medical, dental, and playoff benefits. Milbury told reporters: ''I just agreed to disagree. . . . I think the association took a total retreat. Under this system there will be no freedom of movement for the players. It is my view that we should have forced the issue with the owners on equalization and earned much greater freedom of movement. They threatened to cancel the expansion of the NHL [with Edmonton, Winnipeg, Quebec, and New England] if we didn't reach an agreement. But I feel they would have bulled ahead with it anyway, no matter what happened to the agreement.'' Milbury said the owners insisted on the right of first refusal on all free agents who desired to change teams. ''I feel we should have pushed harder to get them to change their minds on it.'' He said his vote reflected the views of his teammates, but ''mostly it was my personal view. I'm unhappy we didn't make a stronger stand.'' But other reps disagreed: Chicago Black Hawks goalie Tony Esposito (who was elected NHLPA president in 1981) welcomed the ''merger'', acknowledging the owners' victory: ''I think [the owners] did better on the deal than we did. I had more to lose than anyone because of my position [as a free agent] if we had been able to change the equalization rule. But I'm worried about the game, which is in big trouble with so many teams losing so much money. When we agreed to the new deal, we gave the owners a chance to get things straightened out a little. If they can't there will be a great many less jobs for hockey players before long. The good owners aren't going to lose money forever.''

One agent, however, even went so far as to claim ''Eagleson's waffling was horrible''. Norman Caplan, whose list of 125 top NHL clients (including Canadiens' Larry Robinson and Minnesota North Stars' rookie sensation Bobby Smith) now rivalled Eagleson's roster, said that Eagleson's manoeuvres were ''damaging to the market place. Where's the leverage? Where's the freedom of movement?'' He further questioned the NHLPA's agreeing to extend the collective agreement to 1982 and being governed by the same ''restrictive'' compensation and final arbitration rule as when the WHA was operating. He commented on the $7.5 million the players would receive in extra benefits: "What does $7.5 million mean? It's rather academic, especially when you divide the amount of money by the number of player years." Caplan felt Eagleson had been caught in a conflict. Because of his other involvements he could not apply all his efforts to collective bargaining like other union bosses. Ed Garvey of the National Football League Players' Association and Marvin Miller of the Major League Baseball Players' Association are said to be full-time labour leaders.

When Milbury returned to Boston, the articulate and bright defenceman set about accomplishing two remarkable victories in exceedingly short order: Eagleson's resignation from the union, and control over selection of his successor. In September, the Bruins issued Eagleson an ultimatum: devote your energies solely to running the 500-man union at an annual salary of $200,000 or step down. Eagleson laughed this off in his usual cavalier manner: "The association couldn't afford it and neither could I."

A month later, a unanimous resolution was passed by the NHLPA to find a permanent replacement for Eagleson. He was notified of the decision at the next association meeting. Brad Park (Boston), then vice-president of the NHLPA, also said that he hoped to get support from the rest of the membership to terminate the collective agreement as of June 1, 1980. Ironically, Boston, which had been the first team to organize, and which had hired Eagleson as its only labour leader, was pushing him out.

Eagleson wanted some say in the naming of his eventual replacement, suggesting that his successor should be "a bilingual Canadian lawyer who has labour law experience". Although the camps were never equally divided against Eagleson, apparently the St. Louis club backed Milbury's oust-Eagleson campaign. The Bruins continued to bolster their support within the membership. In January 1980, Boston commissioned the accounting firm of Price Waterhouse to send ballots by registered mail to each of the NHL players and to tabulate the results.

"I'm sure Alan didn't think we would handle it this way," Milbury says. "We were getting very little action from Alan by taking the conventional channels. We thought action had to begin immediately, in preparation for the upcoming contract talks with the owners." Milbury stated his concerns in the letter accompanying the ballot. The resolution on the ballot asked that the membership either support or reject the selection of Eagleson's successor by an independent screening board of labour-management experts no later than the summer of 1980. Eagleson first told Milbury that he would convey the Bruins' feelings to the entire NHLPA membership, but later told Milbury the resolution was out of order. In a later report, Eagleson offered to resign if the majority of the player reps wanted it. Then he appeared to have a change of heart. "I'm always ready for a fight. .... I'm not going to let these guys scare me away. ... Unfortunately the ballot couldn't have been more cut and dried: Eagleson versus Mike Milbury," he said.

In January Eagleson was asked to appeal the suspension of two Boston Bruins who were involved in a brawl with fans after a New York game. "Ol' Uncle Al has to go down to defend the Bruins despite the fact they want to throw me out," he said during a radio interview. He lost the appeal to the NHL board of governors.

Then Eagleson announced that there would be changes made (such as terminating the collective agreement) on June 30, 1980. At that time, the owners proposed a revised formula whereby players earning more than $110,000 a season would be bound by the existing agreement. The players felt the figures should be closer to $150,000. (In 1980, according to Marvin Goldblatt, the average NHL salary was $90,000.)

At a meeting of players' representatives in Detroit in February 1980, a motion was passed to elect a seven-man committee to find a full-time successor to Eagleson. A vote by secret ballot elected Eagleson, Milbury, Sittler, Tony and Phil Esposito, and two outside lawyers, one a Harvard law professor. But Sittler says he was at both that meeting and at an earlier meeting in Toronto, when the reps voted unanimously that Eagleson should continue as executive director. "There were a number of those players who were not clients of Al's and they were in his corner all the way. I know that guys like Tony and Phil Esposito said strongly they were very disappointed in what Milbury was trying to do, the approach he was taking." Later, Eagleson confirmed he was going to retire in 1982. "And that is guaranteed. If I can retire in 1981 I may do it. I resigned in February, I said 'Listen, there are two ways of doing things, the way we've been doing it and Mr. Milbury's way. If you're going to do it Milbury's way, here's my resignation' and they decided they wanted to do it my way," he says. He agrees he had offered to resign before but "this is more serious. I had retired before but not out of complaint or spite, just felt I had done whatever I had to do. I didn't have any obligations. But this is a serious year. It wouldn't be fair to them if I walk away, but to hell with it!'' Then he reflected a bit, and slowly murmured: ''There is no problem now. I got a unanimous vote. Just Mike Milbury.''

Milbury had cooled off by May but still felt strongly about bringing hockey on stream with other player associations. His game plan was first to hook up the NHLPA with the U.S. National Labor Relations Board (NLRB), the body that certifies unions. ''Baseball and football are certified associations, but hockey is not,'' says Milbury, ''and their pension plans and disability insurance benefits are better.'' As an afterthought he adds, ''they also have legitimate elections and certain rules and regulations they have to adhere to.''

He says then he would like to see the NHLPA affiliate with the largest umbrella union in the U.S., the AFL-CIO. ''I've talked to Garvey, the executive director of the NFLPA, and I know a little more about what they are doing. They have affiliated with the AFL-CIO and are doing some interesting things. I think all of the players should be a whole lot more cooperative.'' Milbury says he would pursue the idea of the NHLPA affiliating with NFLPA and other unions. ''That's still a ways off, but I hope someone from the NFLPA will sit in on our meeting (and vice-versa) to talk about insurance, medical, and dental plans.'' He claims that if hockey affiliated with the AFL-CIO, it would be eligible for ''more benefits ... for example it has a strike pool and because of the NFLPA's association with the federation it is available to the NFLPA should they decide at any time to strike. Right now that is something we don't have.''

As the merger and Milbury dramas unfolded, another thorny issue promised to shake up matters even more. It began in the summer of 1979, when George ''Punch'' Imlach was rehired as the Leafs' general manager. By the middle of the season, Imlach and Eagleson altercations were as famed as the Ali-Frazier knock-abouts. Imlach first tossed the gauntlet in December when he accused Eagleson of ''demanding better deals for his clients than for other NHL members''. He was referring to Eagleson's request to delete a ''buy-out clause''* from any new contract issued to his client, Mike Palmateer. The Leaf goalie was playing out his option year of a $70,000-a-year contract with the Leafs. Eagleson was looking for a $200,000-a-year contract.

---

* The buy-out clause, which is contained in the league's standard player's contract, says if a player is put on waivers and not claimed by another club, his employer can buy out his contract for a third of a year's pay.

Just two days after the Palmateer dispute was aired, the *Globe and Mail* ran a front-page story telling of Imlach's move to trade two Eagleson clients, Lanny McDonald and Joel Quenneville. Eagleson quickly turned the event into another "Let's Get Eagleson" scenario, remarking: "But Imlach suggested to a lot of people that he was going to rid himself of all my clients. If Sittler didn't have a no-cut contract he'd be gone as well." Both McDonald and Sittler had signed seven-year contracts through 1984. Fans were outraged over McDonald's trade (in return for two other Eagleson clients, Pat Hickey and Wilf Paiement), and held a public demonstration in front of the Gardens.

Lanny McDonald had hired Eagleson a couple of years earlier to bail him out of a messy entanglement he had with his first agent, New York attorney Richard Sorkin, who was later convicted of misappropriation of funds. McDonald says he got out "before all the trouble happened, so I wasn't hurt that badly". Reports at the time indicated that McDonald was burned for $100,000. He says he chose Eagleson because he was located in Toronto but also "because of the kind of man Al is and because I like everything to be close. ... it's worked out very well for me."

McDonald says he expects to continue using Eagleson's services even though he is no longer in Toronto. "Nobody likes to leave a city such as Toronto. I would like to have finished my career there. It was unfortunate. Whether my trade had anything to do with being an Eagleson client I don't know. A lot of people have said that, but at the same time maybe you're getting rid of one client but you get one right back." Meanwhile Ballard asserted, "I won't have any more Eagleson clients."

When Mike Palmateer became a free agent, Imlach traded him to the Washington Capitals for Robert Picard and Tim Coulis. The twenty-six-year-old goalkeeper and his agent smiled winningly as Palmateer signed a four-year contract with the Capitals for $200,000 a year.

But before the dust settled on the McDonald trade, news surfaced that two more Eagleson clients, the Leafs' Pat Boutette and Dave Williams, had been traded. In a fit of pique, Darryl Sittler ripped the "C" from his sweater and resigned as Leaf captain. Some observers claimed that Imlach had hassled Sittler because the general manager figured Sittler had divided loyalties as vice-president of the NHLPA and Leaf captain. At the beginning of the season about a dozen of the Leafs were Eagleson's clients, and could supposedly swing a partisan vote at team meetings. This fact was reputed to be the reason for the proposal Imlach offered Sittler — a Florida vacation to cool off.

By the end of the 1979–80 season only nine of the original twenty-one Leafs were around. "That's a big turnover," says McDonald. "[Ballard] got some pretty good players back but I think the key to any trade is character.... Not only what you do on the ice is important — it's what kind of team player you are, what kind of personality you are in the dressing room." McDonald feels the kind of players the Leafs traded that season — Palmateer, Quenneville, McKechnie, Williams, Butler — "these are the secret *team* guys. For example, Patty Boutette is an excellent player. He can win a lot of games, a lot of close games, when you have that extra feeling for each other. Maybe that's what they are missing now."

McDonald is one of the many Eagleson clients who talk openly about their satisfaction with past services. Describing Eagleson's business manner, McDonald finds him "bold, abrasive but honest. What more can you ask for? Just being around Al's clout and character, and because he has a lot of personal contacts in business, you're bound to learn something ... and being with Al you definitely get a little bolder yourself and take advantage of situations."

Marcel Dionne is another big Eagleson supporter. The 5'8" centre from Drummondville, Quebec, first met Eagleson in 1969 on a fishing trip with Bobby Orr, shortly after Dionne was released from the Quebec league. "Al came along and we caught a couple of fish; that's the time [Eagleson] said he would 'negotiate' me," says Dionne. "Eagleson hadn't met me yet, but already had a file on me in his office under the spelling 'Dion'. He had been in touch with my manager [also the owner] of the St. Catharines Black Hawks. He was doing some legal work for the team at the time." In August 1980, Eagleson successfully negotiated a record $3.6 million multi-year contract for Dionne with the Los Angeles Kings.

Still the controversy over Sittler's "no-trade contract" raged on. He was also said to have a "play contract", but Ballard was prepared to pay him to stay home. This raised more heated debate.

The Leafs owner, who has never been averse to stoking a fire, announced during a radio interview at the time: "All the Leafs' problems have been caused by one man; his office is around the corner." Ballard said if the embargo had not been placed on Sittler's contract he wouldn't have missed out on many lucrative deals. One earlier trade would have seen Sittler, Palmateer, and Dave Burrows sent to New York. Whether Sittler signed for less money to secure his future and his endorsement commitments in Toronto, it certainly was not standard league procedure. But it did provide an interesting bargaining position. Eagleson says, "Darryl has a no-trade contract to which there is no price attached"; yet in the next breath he adds, "If Leafs management want to come to us and draw up a new contract for Sittler we'd be happy to talk ... the price would be about twice as much as they are paying him now. If they want to remove the no-trade clause ... I think Darryl would be happy to sign a contract for $350,000 for five years with the right to let them trade him." But Sittler denies being a party to any discussion to this end. He says he wouldn't agree to being traded at any price.

In August 1980 Imlach was hospitalized with a second coronary. While the veteran general manager was still recuperating, Sittler decided to work without Eagleson, and smooth things out with Ballard.

Imlach says when he came back to Toronto in 1979 he heard about the hockey club's no-cuts, no-trades policy, and vowed, "That's all over. I was hired as manager, I'm going to manage but I can't do my job if you have people telling me 'you can't trade me'. Why did you hire me?" He says, "When players start giving the orders that's when you start giving the hockey club away."

In Sittler's case, however, Imlach says the situation is more serious. "I personally think he can be traded. There will be a court case over it but I think he can be traded. It was done kind of shabby as far as the contract was made out ... it probably will go to court and I don't think I'll lose, personally."

While the whole Eagleson empire was being assaulted — first Milbury, then the merger, then the Leafs situation — perhaps the strongest blow of all occurred when Bobby Orr walked out. An epoch in both men's careers and lives was ended.

Unable to play hockey because of crippled knees, Orr, the Canadian hockey legend, became something of a recluse, and perhaps a little bitter. He played his last game with the Black Hawks in November 1978, and then took over management duties by assisting general manager and coach Bob Pulford. Then, on January 10, 1979, a blustery cold Boston day warmed up a little when sobbing fans witnessed the official retiring of Orr's legendary Number Four during a $100-a-ticket exhibition game between the Boston Bruins and the Soviet

Wings at the Boston Garden. It was a sellout. Then, after Senator Edward Kennedy shook Orr's hand, the famed defenceman ended his hockey life.

The public Eagleson–Orr falling-out occurred over an apparent conflict of interest when the Black Hawks management team of Orr and Pulford, both Eagleson clients, wanted to buy the services of another client, Dave Hutchison. Hutchison signed with the Leafs; Orr said Eagleson acted for Hutchison because Sittler asked him to, showing client favouritism. Then, in September 1979, Orr issued a curt statement saying, "Few athletes need agents when they are no longer active participants". That same month Bobby Orr was inducted into the Hockey Hall of Fame. Eagleson's absence was noticed. "I went to Europe that night," says Eagleson. "It was the week after the separation and I didn't feel comfortable attending it. Ordinarily if we did not have a difference of opinion, or if he hadn't decided to terminate the relationship I would have backed up my trip a day."

A few weeks before Orr moved back to Boston in May 1980, he said, "I'm finished with hockey and Eagleson in that order: and now I just want to get on with my new life."

On April 1, 1980, Orr officially disassociated his financial interests from Eagleson, and sold his Canadian properties and assets to Eagleson for $2.4 million over the next ten years. Eagleson says he didn't charge Orr a fee for his services on the Black Hawks contract or Orr's agreement with his new employer, Standard Brands of New York. Eagleson also adds he made the deal on the understanding that Orr wouldn't have any business contact with Bill Watters for at least five years. Watters had left Eagleson the month before. Eagleson didn't want Watters getting pulled along by Orr's coattails to instant credibility. Watters had been Eagleson's chief negotiator and head of Sports Management Ltd., and his leaving was quite a blow. Many saw his break as a repetition of history. "What's hapening to Eagleson is precisely what Eagleson did to us," says Bill McMurtry.

Inside the Watters home, amid the collection of Orr-Walton hockey camp photographs and his sons' hockey trophies, Watters recalls his split with his former employer. In a polite but pointed manner, he says that he has not spoken to any of the "older" clients who have been with Eagleson since 1974. "When I left a lot of the younger guys, guys who I've been dealing with since 1976, called me. The bottom line of this whole deal is, I decided it was in my best interest to go on my own. If that means I don't talk to some of Al's clients about business, then that's it, I just don't see any sense in trying to belittle an operation I was an integral part of for ten years.''

Watters maintains that he left because of a "difference in philosophy over fees". "Ten percent is not standard practice. In some cases there are people in our business who try that, but the major competition don't.'' He thinks Kaminsky in New York and Caplan in Montreal are the major agents in the business. "Gerry Patterson ... sold his client list to Gerry Petrie, who is another major competitor. Then there is Gus Badali in Toronto [Wayne Gretzky's agent]. Their prices aren't 10 percent, yet, mind you, Mark McCormack charges 10 percent.'' Watters says he was pressured into charging the high fee because it was company policy. "Alan and Marvin [Goldblatt] knew I didn't agree with it. If a player bought the full management program and had his contract negotiated, then the fee was 10 percent. I knew we were going to lose business because of such high fees to people I thought couldn't do as good a job as Goldblatt and I were doing. I didn't like the idea.'' He says Sports Management had not lost many clients. "There had been a few, though, and that was a contributing factor to my uneasiness.'' Since starting up his own business, Watters says he charges in the area of 6 or 7 percent. The average pro contract in 1980 was $90,000 a year and the minor pros made $30,000. "I think it's the principle involved. Sure, when you look at the financial difference and when you consider the fee is tax deductible* it's minimal ... I could have rationalized it very easily.'' He also admitted the fee issue was just one of the reasons for his resignation; "of course there were personal reasons.''

Two of Eagleson's chief headhunters, Rick Curran and Al Turner, left with Watters. He attracted an armful of clients, costing Eagleson a reported $150,000 in lost business. Eagleson told the *New York Times*,"It [was] a small dent in the $1 million-a-year enterprise.''

Eagleson says he doubts Watters' leaving was a moral issue. "If the guy was going to disagree with the 10 percent fee charges, he wouldn't have stayed a year and a half ... but we changed that for Bill, we changed the fee structure.'' He says Watters wanted to do business which involved negotiations only, whereas Eagleson was more inclined towards contracts which involved full service (Sports Management). "Bill persuaded me to adopt a stance that would be 10

---

* Agents' fees are deductible only under U.S. tax laws.

percent for full service, 6 percent for negotiations only. Then we went to 5 percent for negotiations only. It was foreign to my thinking because Bill was the one out there selling in the market place.''

Eagleson saw himself cutting back to only full-service clients. He says he held the conviction that ''the player who gets full service will retain you, whereas the player who hires you only to negotiate his contract won't. ... You have no control over the other aspects of his life. ... If I only negotiate contracts, I could double our profit for sure: but how can I say to Marcel Dionne, 'here's a big contract. You figure out what to do with your tax headaches, financing problems, your house purchases, and your marital relationships on that kind of dough'? ... that's why we are not going to lose clients like Dionne and Sittler.''

Yet he admits it was partly his preoccupation with ''big guys'' that permitted his first lieutenant an inside track with juniors. ''Watters will get the young guys because the last few years he has done 75 percent of the amateur draft picks. ... I was too busy looking after the big guys. Right now we have between 90-100 NHLers at the start of the 1980–81 season. I want to cut back to 60-75 because my strength has been personal contact relationships, and there are some clients' wives I don't know and that doesn't make sense.'' All in all, Eagleson figures he can only profit from his employees' exodus. ''You don't make any money on young hockey players who make under $100,000 a year because you are cutting out Sports Managment fees which are 6 percent across the board. I would think that with Bill and the number of employees that have gone with him, we will net out *making* money.'' Eagleson says Watters was paid a bonus and salary plus expenses ''that took him well over $100,000 a year. He feels he can make twice that, I suppose, but I didn't teach him all the tricks. He'll find out in the market place he's had life easy in the last three years — easy because his competitors have been everyone but me!''

He also feels he has scored points in keeping the critics at bay. ''Kaminsky and Caplan and the others used it against me to have others doing contracts. That's what I told the players, for the next five years there will be nobody doing your contracts except R. Alan Eagleson.''

Arthur Kaminsky thinks that the cutting back of Eagleson's empire is good for both Eagleson and hockey, and says he figures Bill Watters' pulling out of the Eagleson camp was inevitable ''because Bill worked like a Trojan and eventually was going to figure out he is earning a great deal of money for Mr. Eagleson and not much for himself ... yet he is doing 70 percent of the work." Kaminsky claims that when Watters left, Eagleson had to pick up the telephone and introduce himself to most of the players. "Al was nothing more than a name, a household word they sold. He's become like a Wizard of Oz, a little man behind the machine ... a voice behind a great façade."

Then to erase any doubt about the Watters/Eagleson split being a press gimmick or a friendly agreement to disagree, Eagleson sued Watters.

In November 1980, Watters and his personal company, Branada Sports Management Ltd., were sued by Eagleson for breach of contract and having induced clients to switch from Sports Management Ltd. to Branada.

Branada filed a counterclaim in the Supreme Court of Ontario in January 1981, alleging that Eagleson and Sports Management Ltd. acted "in bad faith and intentionally misled [Watters] by promising to lower fees charged to clients and merely revising their fee structure so that over billing charges to the client could remain the same."

A final blow was levelled at The Eagle's international hockey reputation when his efforts to stage a 1980 Canada Cup backfired in May.

After executing a four-nation agreement in Sweden, giving Canada control over the entire 1980 Canada Cup operations and total net profits in return for $1.8 million payment — a guarantee of $1 million to the IIHF and the balance to be divided between the six participating countries — Eagleson returned to Canada not a victor but a villain.

The groundswell of public opinion against Moscow's incursion in Afghanistan and the subsequent U.S.-initiated boycott of the summer Moscow Olympics made it awkward for U.S. and Canadian hockey teams to play the Russians three weeks later. And if sponsors were losing interest for fear negative public feelings would undermine their advertising efforts, what was the point in going through with it? But Hockey Canada had agreed to stage the tournament, and was left holding a $1.8 million guarantee.

For 72 hours Eagleson was on a tightrope. "My job was to protect Hockey Canada. I got them into the mess and I had to get them out of it," he says. "The only thing that would save my bacon is for either the Americans or Canadians to back down, and then I would be off the hook." He was referring to a clause in the agreement which said that each country has to ice its best players.

But the American Amateur Hockey Association did just the opposite, and sent a telex to the IIHF agreeing to play. Eagleson's last hope was that Prime Minister Pierre Trudeau would cancel the Cup challenge when he announced that Canada was entering the Olympic boycott — but he didn't. "So here I am, pushed into a corner with a herd of goddamn buffalo coming down on me. I'm waiting for all the other guys who have a better position than me to start shooting at them and nobody would even draw their guns," says Eagleson. "I finally had to dig into my back pocket and find some players who would oppose the Cup, and it was the Canadian players who pulled me out — without 'our best' there was no match."

Dr. Gunther Sabetzki, president of the IIHF, obviously angry at hearing that the tournament was cancelled for the second time in two years,* threatened to pull the event out of Hockey Canada and turn it into a World Cup to be run by the IIHF.

Eagleson said he would make a decision by the end of 1980 as to whether or not he would try for September 1981; "We may never see it again," he warned.†

---

* The Canada Cup scheduled for September 1979 was cancelled when a major sponsor withdrew support.
† Another Canada Cup, a single round-robin tournament with six teams, was scheduled for September 1981. The Soviets took the 1981 series, beating Canada 8 to 1 in the final game.

THE RIGHT STUFF

In the end you only have your family.
R. Alan Eagleson

By June, thick shrubbery partially conceals the entrance to the Rosedale subway station on Price Street. Mercedes, Cadillacs, and BMWs line the tiny dead-end road running east off Yonge Street to the Toronto Lawn Tennis Club. Except for a few dried leaves brushing the pavement and a swimming pool shimmering behind a half-mile of perfectly strung and rolled clay tennis courts, there is no sign of life. But by 10:00 A.M. the chaises longues separating a glass-enclosed clubhouse from the courts are occupied by about thirty women, all with rich suntans and dressed in perfect white linens. Sharply at 3:30 P.M. their children begin appearing through the doorway in various grey and navy-blue school uniforms, wearing sneakers and parachute-nylon backpacks. An hour later the fathers appear. They change from business suits into starched tennis whites. Then, in family units, everyone files onto the courts. Suddenly the air is filled with frenzied shouting ascending from between the white lines.

Within this group, Alan Eagleson looks like any of the other trim, middle-aged men. But the life of this loom fixer's son has touched, at least to a small degree, the lives of over a million Canadians. He has revolutionized a sport, introduced a full-scale industry of total sports management for athletes to the country, and partially created our international image. His name is synonymous with hockey.

What new challenges await Eagleson in the eighties? One important development is Revenue Canada's investigation as to whether Bobby Orr owes $500,000 in taxes on salary paid to him between 1971 and 1976. The issue centres on the question: was it legal to include Orr's playing income in Bobby Orr Enterprises Ltd.?

Eagleson's lawsuit against his former negotiator for Sports Management Ltd., Bill Watters, was settled out of court on May 1, 1981. Watters refuses to say how much money he paid Eagleson for taking "quite a few of [Eagleson's] clients" or how much it cost to buy out the three years (and the three-year option) remaining on his employment contract.

The CAHA is currently suing Eagleson and Hockey Canada for the $1 million trust agreement plus interest owing which Eagleson set up between the amateurs and Hockey Canada from the 1976 Canada Cup proceeds.*

Eagleson's former client, Detroit Red Wings' Vaclav Nedomansky,† launched two separate suits against Eagleson and Sports Management Ltd. in the Supreme Court of Ontario on June 25, 1981 for negligence and breach of contract. The suits for combined damages of $40 million plus legal costs allege that Eagleson and Sports Management did not get Nedomansky the best possible financial deal and future security.

Eagleson negotiated Nedomansky's contract with Detroit in November 1977, and won a new five-year contract for $250,000 a year on June 29, 1979, the date Nedomansky became a free agent. Nedomansky is charging Eagleson with neglecting to file a formal contract with the Detroit club, and says Detroit claims the contract doesn't exist. He alleges in his suit that when Eagleson filed a new contract with Detroit on September 9, 1980, Eagleson "[would have earned] a higher fee with a short-term contract than [with] the one that had been negotiated on June 29, 1979." He charges that Eagleson "literally coerced" him to sign with the Detroit club.

Eagleson's proposal to relinquish his duties as NHLPA union boss by 1982 is still a possibility. He has made good his promise to leave the

---

* For details on the trust agreement, see pages 186–88.
† Before defecting to Canada in 1974, Nedomansky, as captain of the Czechoslovakian national team, was voted Most Valuable Player in his team's 7-2 upset over Russia in Helsinki during the 1974 World Championships. He joined the Toronto Toros of the WHA in 1974 and became Eagleson's client in August 1974.

house in order and has been revising the collective-bargaining agreement.*

Another responsibility Eagleson *says* he would gladly shelve after September 1981 is running the Canada Cup. He appears to be reluctant to part with the hallmark of his achievements, however. He told a daily newspaper he wants to run a third Canada Cup in 1984; "then it would be a tradition."

One decision he appears to have changed his mind about is staying out of politics. Eagleson, who backed Brian Mulroney in the 1976 Progressive Conservative leadership race, was on the Conservative short list to run as the federal candidate in the Spadina riding by-election in August 1981. Eagleson was not chosen, however.

Eagleson has always demonstrated an ability to leap-frog from hockey negotiations to politics. When bogged down in extensive labour talks with the NHL over revamping the collective-bargaining agreement, and apart from his regular duties as player agent, he found time to pick up the spear for Metro Toronto in its attempt to win a twenty-five-year-battle to oust Toronto Island residents from their homes.†

In June 1981, Eagleson permitted his long-time friend and associate, Metro Chairman Paul Godfrey, to talk him into lending instant credibility to Metro's plan to free the island for parkland. Eagleson's services were retained, along with those of the Conroy Hallworth Advertising Agency, for $250,000. The ad campaign, however, seemed doomed from the start. Metro's "Oh, no, Mr. Bill" campaign jingle

---

* The 1976 contract came up for renewal when the WHA and the NHL merged in 1979 (see pages 176–79). In May 1981, both the NHLPA and the NHL voted to terminate the agreement as of September 15, 1982. At the time of the baseball strike in the major leagues over the issue of compensation for free agents in June 1981, Eagleson and the NHL were conducting bargaining talks at the Skyline Hotel in Toronto to settle the problem of equalization and compensation for free agents in hockey (see page 177*ff*). During the meetings, league president John Ziegler said wages amounted to 50 percent of club budgets and that two thirds of the owners were losing money.

† Metro Toronto has issued eviction notices for 250 Island homes (approximately 600 people) but the Ontario government overrode this by passing emergency legislation in January 1981, giving the residents a six-month stay of eviction. Ontario also hired lawyer Barry Swadron to carry out a five-month study. Swadron's one-man report proposed that the islanders be allowed to stay another 25 years provided they pay market-value rents to Metro. Ontario subsequently extended the first stay another six months until December 31, 1981.

was about to be shown on TV when an embarrassing inaccuracy was discovered. Someone had not done his homework thoroughly enough. The hard-sell jingle, which said that wealthy island residents were enjoying cheap rents subsidized by municipal taxes, focused in part on Peter Gzowski, a writer and journalist, while it was in fact his son who lived on the island.

Immediately following Eagleson's acceptance of the job, Tom Wells, provincial government house leader, claimed Metro was wasting its money. "We won't talk to Eagleson," he said. Eagleson's mandate is to get the best deal he can for Metro — namely, a "slow death" clause written into the twenty-five-year reprieve the Ontario government plans to grant as a result of the Swadron report. If Eagleson's plan is put into effect, it will mean that when an islander dies, his property will revert to Metro.

Eagleson's job is clear-cut: now that Metro's ad campaign is botched, he has only one route — through the courts. But what can he try to do that several other lawyers haven't already tried? His deadline is the end of December 1981, when Ontario's present stay of eviction expires.

Eagleson earned his reputation and fortune primarily through hockey as a player's agent and later as a labour leader — a job he never intended to take. He was the only person who had the "right stuff" to do it. As the NHLPA's only boss since its inception in 1967, Eagleson has taken advantage of this power to wheel and deal for the players as well as to execute power-plays for his own network.

Eagleson the agent quickly learned the value of publicity, and built an empire on selling the concept of hockey idolatry to thousands of parents who believe their sons will become sports heroes. This phenomenon is captured in Agnes Eagleson's feelings about *her* son's business: "I never liked hockey, but I enjoyed the Bobby Orr thing."

Eventually, by running Canada's largest agency for hockey players while at the same time setting policy for the NHL through collective bargaining as well as acting as Hockey Canada's agent and chief negotiator in international hockey matters, Eagleson came to hold a monopoly on the billion-dollar hockey industry.

At first glance, Eagleson appears to be all surface: if you scratch the surface, you'll find more surface. But on deeper probing, he's a web of complexity. His strong adherence to the hard-work-is-rewarded ethic has narrowed his vision, and his only goal has been a pragmatic one — to get at the meat. He has embraced an elitist system of hockey whereby only the most talented professionals prosper. He demands total honesty and do-or-die support from everyone in each of his undertakings. Yet he doesn't return the faith. The slightest sign of wavering, a difference of opinion, is interpreted as a stab in the back. Whether the backstabbers will outflank the loyalists is not as important as what appears to be his ultimate goal — securing a position of prestige and power in federal politics.

His recent decision to service fewer clients and to cut down on his hockey commitments suggests he has overcome his earlier disenchantment with partisan politics. In 1976, Eagleson told a national magazine: "I still think I could become prime minister within the next 15 or so years. . . . But let me hasten to add I wouldn't want to be. Not now that I've seen what politics have done to some decent and honest men lately. I don't mean the Nixons and Agnews, of course, but those good men who can't pick up a parking ticket without a national inquisition."

Eagleson has sent both his children to private schools in Toronto: Allen, Jr., goes to Upper Canada College, and Jill attended Havergal. When Allen, Jr., brought home his report card bearing a 78 percent average, the young man knew it wouldn't please his father.

"Let me see it," said Eagleson. "Eighty-five in French, that's better. An eighty-four in physics, seventy in math, eh?"

"I keep trying to get the math up, but I can't."

"Listen, take those two, the eighty-five and the eighty-four and get them up to ninety, don't try to get the seventy to seventy-five, screw it, keep it at seventy and get five more marks here and here. You don't have to be an expert in everything, you have to limit yourself to the things you do well."

Do what you do well is the maxim Eagleson has always followed. Whether it is raising money for Ontario Tories or buttonholing TV sponsors for a nation-versus-nation hockey tournament, Eagleson, the "fixer", has cut himself a lofty niche both in politics and in sports as a singularly important team player. His continued success will depend on two things: how badly the team needs him, and the number of loyalists he has left.

Notes

1. A DAY IN THE LIFE

Chapter 1 is based on a day-long personal interview with R. Alan Eagleson on May 6, 1980, and on lengthy interviews in January and March 1978 and May 1979. Other personal interviews include Nancy Eagleson, April 1978 and December 1980 and Darryl Sittler, May 1980. Material has also been drawn from Deidra Clayton's article in the *Financial Times of Canada*, May 15, 1978, and Ron Base's articles in *Quest Magazine*, November 1977 and in the *Toronto Sun*, August 17, 1975.

page 1
The epigraph to Chapter 1 is adapted from J. E. Cirlot, *Dictionary of Symbols*, 2nd ed. (New York: Philosophical Library, 1976), pp. 91–93.

page 6
The reference to a "closed shop" is from a personal interview with R. Alan Eagleson, May 1980.

page 12
The reference to $500,000 is from the *Globe and Mail*, February 22, 1980.

page 13
The Torrey quote is from a personal interview, January 1978.

page 16
The Lang quote is from a personal interview, November 1978; M & M Systems Research Ltd., "The Organizational Development of Hockey Canada, January 1969–December 1973".

2. POTATOES AND POINTING

Chapter 2 is based on personal interviews with Agnes and Allen Eagleson, December 1979; Margaret Hooey, December 1977 and November 1980; Marguerite Weir, May 1980; Eddie Waring, November 1980; and on John Gault's article in *Toronto Life*, September 1972.

page 18
The epigraph to Chapter 2 is from a personal interview with Morley Kells in August 1980.

page 19
The reference to the "longest overtime game" is from Brian McFarlane's *Sixty Years of Hockey* (Toronto: Pagurian Press, 1976).

page 21
The reference to $7,000 is from the *Toronto Sun*, August 17, 1975.

3. THE IVY LEAGUE

Chapter 3 is based on interviews with R. Alan Eagleson, *op. cit.*; Margaret Hooey, *op. cit.*; Agnes and Allen Eagleson, *op. cit.*; Marguerite Weir, *op. cit.*; Nancy Eagleson, *op. cit.*; Robert S. Mackay, November 1980; Ed McManus, January 1978; Jack Batten, November 1980; and on John Gault's article in *Toronto Life*, *op. cit.*

page 30
The epigraph to Chapter 3 is from a personal interview with R. Alan Eagleson in January 1978.

4. GILDING THE LEAF

Chapter 4 is based on personal interviews with R. Alan Eagleson, *op. cit.*; Bob Watson, December 1980; Morley Kells, August 1980; Harold Ballard, March 1978; Carl Brewer, December 1980; George Imlach, December 1980; and on George Imlach and Scott Young, *Hockey is a Battle: Punch Imlach's Own Story* (Toronto: Macmillan of Canada, 1969).

page 40
The epigraph to Chapter 4 is from a personal interview with Harold Ballard in March 1978.

page 41
The Woodrow quotation is from Leland Ryken's article in *Christianity Today*, October 19, 1979.

page 42
The McLuhan quote is from a personal interview in October 1979; the Nancy Eagleson quote is from an interview, *op. cit.*; and the reference to J. J. Robinette as a "giant oak" is from Barry Pepper as cited in David Lancashire's article in the *Globe and Mail*, November 26, 1979.

page 47
The Ballard quote is from a personal interview, *op. cit.*; the Lilley quote is from a personal interview, December 1979.

5. BOBBY WHO AND THE SUMMER OF '66

Chapter 5 is based on interviews with R. Alan Eagleson, *op. cit.*; Doug Orr, January 1981 and June 1981; Bobby Orr, January 1978 and May 1980; Punch Imlach, *op. cit.*; Ray Smela, January 1981; and on Stan Fischler, *Bobby Orr and The Big Bad Bruins* (New York: Dodd, Mead & Co., 1969) and Dick Beddoes, Stan Fischler, and Ira Gitler, *Hockey! The Story of the World's Fastest Sport* (New York: Macmillan, 1971).

page 52
The epigraph to Chapter 5 is from a personal interview with Punch Imlach in December 1980.

page 53
The Mackay quote is from a personal interview, *op. cit.*

page 55
Maclean's, February 20, 1965.

page 56
The Beddoes quote is from *Hockey! The Story of the World's Fastest Sport*, *op. cit.*, p. 264.

page 59
The reference to Heindl's $150-per-week wage is from Peter Gzowski's article in *Saturday Night*, January 1981.

page 60
The reference to Butterfield is from Trent Frayne's article in *Maclean's*, September 1967.

page 61
The Brewer quote is from a personal interview, *op. cit.*; the reference to the Canadian Football League is from Jack Batten's column in *The Canadian*, August 27, 1966.

6. THE EMANCIPATOR

Chapter 6 is based on interviews with Red Fisher, January 1980; R. Alan Eagleson, *op. cit.*; Morley Kells, *op. cit.*; and on Gerald Eskenazi, *A Thinking Man's Guide to Pro Hockey* (New York: Dutton, 1976); Brian Conacher, *Hockey in Canada: The Way It Is!* (Toronto: Gateway Press, 1970); Bruce Kidd and John Macfarlane, *The Death of Hockey* (Toronto: New Press, 1972); and George Gross's article in the *Toronto Telegram*, June 8, 1967.

page 63
The epigraph to Chapter 6 is from a personal interview with Conn Smythe in January 1978.

page 64
The Smela quote is from a personal interview, *op. cit.*

page 69
The Lindsay quote is as cited in Stan and Shirley Fischler, *Fischlers' Ice Hockey Encyclopedia* (Toronto: Fitzhenry & Whiteside, 1979), p. 333.

page 71
Imlach's first quote about Mahovlich is as cited in *A Thinking Man's Guide to Pro Hockey*, *op. cit.*, p. 165; Imlach's second quote is from *Hockey is a Battle*, *op. cit.*, p. 168; and the Beddoes quote is as cited in *Maclean's*, September 1967.

pages 71–72
Excerpts are from *A Thinking Man's Guide to Pro Hockey*, *op. cit.*, pp. 162–66.

page 73
The quoted material is from Hans Pohl's interview with R. Alan Eagleson in *Maclean's*, November 17, 1975.

7. BALANCE OF POWER

Chapter 7 is based on the entire collection of Hockey Canada documentation from 1969 to 1980; on personal interviews with Doug Fisher, January 1981, and Chris Lang, November 1978 and May 1981; and on Doug Fisher's article in *International Perspectives*, November-December 1972, *The Death of Hockey*, *op. cit.*, Scott Young, *War on Ice: Canada in International Hockey, 1918-1976* (Toronto: McClelland and Stewart, 1976), Anatoli Tarasov's article in the *Toronto Star*, February 4, 1979, N. Norman Shneidman, *The Soviet Road to Olympus* (Toronto: Ontario Institute for Studies in Education, 1978), and *Hockey in Canada: The Way It Is!*, *op. cit.*

page 76
The epigraph to Chapter 7 is from a letter to Doug Fisher from Robert F. McNeil, dated June 18, 1973.

pages 77–78
The excerpts are from "The Organizational Development of Hockey Canada", *op. cit.* and Chris Lang's "Preface" and "Historical Background" in the same document.

page 79
The reference to the "national team" is from the draft agreement between the CAHA and Hockey Canada, June 1969.

pages 80–82
The excerpts are from Doug Fisher's article in *Canadian Commentator*, 1969, pp. 5–9.

page 81
The Brundage quote is from *War on Ice, op. cit.*; the Tarasov quote is from the *Toronto Star*, February 4, 1979.

page 84
"The Organizational Development of Hockey Canada", pp. I:9 and II:4.

pages 84–85
M & M Systems Research Ltd. consultant's report, January 1974–March 1975.

page 86
The reference to Haggert and the Lefaive quote are from *War on Ice, op. cit.*

pages 88–89
The reference to Campbell is from R. Alan Eagleson's letter to the Committee on International Hockey, September 26, 1977.

page 90
Jack Ludwig, *Hockey Night in Moscow* (Toronto: McClelland and Stewart, 1972); the Campbell quote is from his letter to the author, dated July 6, 1979; the footnote material is from *Fischlers' Ice Hockey Encyclopedia, op. cit.*, p. 613.

pages 90–91
Hockey Night in Moscow, op. cit., p. 16.

pages 91–92
The excerpt about the federal government is from "The Organizational Development of Hockey Canada", *op. cit.*, p. 5

page 92
The Fisher quote is from his article in *International Perspectives, op. cit.*; the McNeil quote is from his letter to Doug Fisher, dated June 18, 1973.

8. GETTING THE STEAK TO MATCH THE SIZZLE

Chapter 8 is based on personal interviews with R. Alan Eagleson, *op. cit.*;

Bobby Orr, *op. cit.*; Lyman MacInnis, January 1978 and July 1981; William McMurtry, December 1980; Eddie Waring, *op. cit.*; Punch Imlach, *op. cit.*; Ken Dryden, January 1978; and on Christie Blatchford's article in the *Globe and Mail*, June 20, 1973; Deidra Clayton's article in the *Financial Times of Canada*, *op. cit.*; Ron Base's articles in *Quest Magazine*, November 1977, and the *Toronto Sun*, August 17, 1975; Rex MacLeod's article in the *Toronto Star*, March 11, 1979; *Maclean's*, *op. cit.*, November 17, 1975; Ken McKee's article in the *Toronto Star*, August 4, 1973; Trent Frayne's article in *Maclean's*, December 1973; and *Hockey in Canada: The Way It Is!*, *op. cit.*

page 93
The epigraph to Chapter 8 is from a personal interview with Bobby Orr, January 1978.

page 94
The reference to $7 million in contracts is from the *Toronto Star*, August 4, 1973.

page 97
The reference to *Sports Illustrated* is from *Hockey! The Story of the World's Fastest Sport*, *op. cit.*, p. 262; the reference to $2.5 million for Orr is from *Maclean's*, December 1973.

page 98
The Godfrey quote is from a personal interview, March 1978; the Morrison reference is from Jonathan Manthorpe, *The Power and the Tories* (Toronto: Macmillan of Canada, 1974); the reference to McDougal is from personal interviews with him in January 1978 and June 1981.

page 99
The Kirke quote is from a personal interview, July 1981.

page 100
The footnote references to IMG and Arnold Palmer are from an Associated Press article in the *Globe and Mail*, May 26, 1981.

page 101
The references to Howe and his sons' contracts are from the *Toronto Star*, August 4, 1973.

pages 106–07
The references to player contracts, the WHA and NHL settlement, and the New York Raiders are from *Fischlers' Ice Hockey Encyclopedia*, *op. cit.*

pages 107–08
The reference to Bassett is from the *Toronto Star*, May 19, 1973.

page 108
The references to pensions and hockey franchises are from the *Toronto Star*, August 4, 1973.

page 109
The insurance references are from the *Globe and Mail*, August 17, 1972.

9. HIGH NOON IN MOSCOW

Chapter 9 is based on personal interviews with R. Alan Eagleson, *op. cit.*; Red Fisher, *op. cit.*; Chris Lang, *op. cit.*; Hockey Canada documentation; *Hockey Showdown*, *op. cit.*; and *War on Ice*, *op. cit.*

page 110
The epigraph to Chapter 9 is from *War on Ice*, *op. cit.*; the Beddoes quote is from his column in the *Globe and Mail*, September 4, 1972.

page 111
The reference to Joe Lapointe of the *Chicago Sun-Times* is as cited in the *Toronto Star*, March 29, 1977; the footnote reference is based on *Hockey Showdown*, *op. cit.*

page 112
The Ballard quote is as cited in Beddoes' column in the *Globe and Mail*, September 4, 1972.

page 113
The Eagleson quote is from Dick Beddoes' column in the *Globe and Mail*, September 4, 1972.

page 115
The reference to Ballard's offer of $1 million is from the *Toronto Star*, September 4, 1972.

page 116
The Esposito quote is from Don Ramsay's article in the *Globe and Mail*, September 2, 1972; the Kryczka quote is from the *Toronto Star*, September 9, 1972.

page 117
The Eagleson, Esposito, and Dryden quotes are from the *Toronto Star*, September 9, 1972; the reference to Mahovlich is from *Hockey Showdown*, *op. cit.*

pages 119–20
The Whitehead-Eagleson confrontation is from a personal interview with Red Fisher, *op. cit.*

10. NEKULTURNY

Chapter 10 is based on personal interviews with R. Alan Eagleson, *op. cit.*; Morley Kells, *op. cit.*; Christie Blatchford, February 1979; Bobby Orr, *op. cit.*; Harold Ballard, *op. cit.*; Bill Watters, *op. cit.*; Irving Ungerman, January 1978; and on *Hockey Showdown*, *op. cit.*; *War on Ice*, *op. cit.*; *Hockey! The Story of the World's Fastest Sport*, *op. cit.*; and *Toronto Life*, September 1972.

page 123
The epigraph to Chapter 10 is from a personal interview with Morley Kells, *op. cit.*; the reference to homecoming is from *Hockey Showdown*, *op. cit.*, and *War on Ice*, *op. cit.*

page 126
The Eagleson quote "The Russians have only ..." is from *Hockey! The Story of the World's Fastest Sport*, *op. cit.*, p. 343; the Robertson reference to "... diplomatic disaster" is from the same source, p. 344.

page 127
The Frayne quote is from *Maclean's*, December 1973.

page 130
The Kidd quote is from a personal interview, September 1980.

page 131
The Harnett quote is from a personal interview, January 1978; the reference to Team Canada Products is from John Gault's article in *Toronto Life*, September 1972.

11. WHITE MAN'S TRINKETS

Chapter 11 is based on personal interviews with R. Alan Eagleson, *op. cit.*; Bill McMurtry, December 1980; Doug Fisher, *op. cit.*; on Hockey Canada documentation; and on correspondence from Clarence Campbell.

page 134
The epigraph to Chapter 11 is from a letter to Doug Fisher from Robert F. McNeil, dated June 18, 1974.

pages 137–38
Excerpts and quoted material are from "National Hockey League Players' Association brief to the Standing Senate Committee on Banking, Trade and Commerce, Dec. 11, 1974, re: The Advance Study on Proposed Legislation respecting The Combines Investigation Act, Competition in Canada, or any matter relating thereto", pp. 1, 2–3, 12–13.

pages 138–39
Ibid., p. 10 and p. 12 (Campbell quote).

page 139
The Campbell quote is from his letter to the author, dated July 6, 1979; the footnote reference to the Sky Shops affair is from the *Globe and Mail*, March 8 and 14, 1980.

page 140
The reference to $6 million is from the NHLPA brief to the Senate, *op. cit.*, p. 23.

page 141
The reference to development fees is from the NHLPA brief to the Senate, *op. cit.*, p. 26.

page 142
The excerpt is from *The Death of Hockey*, *op. cit.*, p. 163; the quoted material is from the Fisher memo, dated February 12, 1973.

page 143-44
The Scott quote is from his confidential memo to the Hockey Canada committee, dated April 27, 1973.

page 144
The Lefaive quote is from the Scott memo, *op. cit.*

pages 145–46
The excerpt is from Fisher's letter to Walter Stewart, dated March 25, 1979.

page 146
The quoted material is from Fisher's memo to R. Alan Eagleson, dated January 31, 1973; the Lefaive quote is cited in Lang's memo to Fisher, dated June 1973.

pages 146–47
The Wasservogel quote is from his letter to Joe Kryczka, dated August 2, 1973.

page 147
The reference to charitable status is from Lang's memo to the Hockey Canada board, dated October 1978.

page 148
The Fisher excerpts are from his handwritten "record of substantial failures and real successes", undated.

page 149

The reference to $1.4 million is from *Fischlers' Ice Hockey Encyclopedia*, *op. cit.*

page 150

The Fisher excerpts are from his memo to Eagleson, dated May 5, 1974; the reference to Derek Holmes' salary of $24,000 is from a personal interview with Chris Lang, *op. cit.*

pages 151–52

The Fisher excerpts are from his memo to Eagleson, dated August 23, 1974.

page 152

The Eagleson quote is from his memo to Fisher, dated August 28, 1974; the *Globe and Mail*, October 7, 1974; the Lang quote is from a personal interview, *op. cit.*

page 153

"Eagle is given royal welcome" is from the *Toronto Star*, October 3, 1974; the Eagleson quote about Gresko is from the *Globe and Mail*, December 9, 1974; the reference to Marc Lalonde is from his official press release, dated May 23, 1975.

page 154

The Coleman quote is from his column in the *Toronto Sun*, June 3, 1975.

12. THE SINGULARLY WISE AND ENLIGHTENED AUTOCRAT

Chapter 12 is based on personal interviews with R. Alan Eagleson, *op. cit.*; Ed McManus, *op. cit.*; Nancy Eagleson, *op. cit.*; Marvin Goldblatt, January 1978; Marcel Dionne, June 1980; Bob Watson, *op. cit.*; Bill McMurtry, *op. cit.*; and on Deidra Clayton's article in the *Financial Times of Canada*, *op. cit.*

page 155

The epigraph to Chapter 12 is from a personal interview with Conn Smythe, January 1978; the reference to Mulroney is from the *Toronto Star*, January 5, 1976.

page 159

The reference to Ross Johnson is from an article by Ron Base in the *Toronto Sun*, August 17, 1975.

pages 159–60

The Crombe quote is from a personal interview, November 1980.

page 161
The Ballard quote is from a personal interview, *op. cit.*; the Eagleson quote about Mrs. Davis actually appeared in Dick Beddoes' column in the *Globe and Mail*, May 9, 1977, as follows: "We only need to do one more thing to win the next election . . . we've got to make Mrs. Davis stop wearing such tacky clothes."

page 166
The McMurtry excerpts are from his pamphlet *Investigation and Inquiry into Violence in Amateur Hockey* (Toronto: Ontario Ministry of Community and Social Services, August 21, 1974).

page 167
The reference to 1976 criminal charges is from the *Toronto Star*, June 5, 1976; the McMurtry quote is from the *Toronto Star*, October 29, 1975; the Bassett quote and the Ballard quote are from *ibid*.

pages 167–68
The references to the Forbes-Boucha case and Green and Maki are from the *Toronto Star*, October 29, 1975.

page 168
Washington Post, September 12, 1975; the Eagleson quote on wearing helmets is from Jim Proudfoot's column in the *Toronto Star*, November 8, 1975; the Eagleson quote on goon hockey and the newspaper headline are from the *Toronto Star*, May 11, 1976.

13. WHERE EAGLE DARED

Chapter 13 is based on personal interviews with R. Alan Eagleson, *op. cit.*; Chris Lang, *op. cit.*; Doug Fisher, *op. cit.*; Sam Pollock, January 1980; Bobby Orr, *op. cit.*; and on Hockey Canada documents and financial statements.

page 170
The epigraph to Chapter 13 is from a personal interview with Steve Shutt, January 1980; *Ottawa Citizen*, January 14, 1975.

page 172
The excerpt relating to Canada's financial commitment to the '76 Cup is from the report of the International Committee presentation to the Russian Ice Hockey Federation, dated July 14, 1975; the reference to $25,000 paid to the IIHF is from a confidential report of the agreement by six nations to participate in the Canadian Invitational Tournament (1976) at the Stockholm meetings on November 23 and 24, 1975.

page 176
The Eagleson quote about a "$2,400 increase" is as cited in the *Toronto Star*, January 18, 1975; the references to AIB controls on Maple Leaf Gardens' season ticket prices are from the *Globe and Mail*, January 29, 1978.

page 177
Ray Kroc with Robert Anderson, *Grinding It Out: The Making of McDonald's* (Chicago: H. Regnery, 1977); the reference to $22,000 is from the *Globe and Mail*, September 2, 1975; the Campbell quote is from a personal letter to the author, *op. cit.*

pages 177-78
Details about the first five-year collective-bargaining agreement (September 15, 1975–September 14, 1980) are from the *Toronto Star*, April 2, 1976.

page 179
The Campbell quote "It was a great day . . ." is from the *Toronto Star*, October 7, 1975; the Campbell quote "The NHLPA has the best . . ." is from a personal interview, *op. cit.*; the Campbell quote "The league is afraid . . ." is from the *Globe and Mail*, October 22, 1976.

page 180
The Ball quote is from the *Toronto Star*, April 2, 1976; the Eagleson quote "So far ten teams are pitching for [Orr] . . ." is from the *Toronto Star*, June 3, 1976.

page 181
The reference to "It's a million and a half. . ." is from the *Toronto Star*, August 7, 1975; the Orr quote is from a personal interview, *op. cit.*

pages 181-82
The Lefaive excerpts are from his letter to Doug Fisher, dated June 14, 1976.

page 184
The reference to $60,000 is from a letter to Hockey Canada from Mary Pilon of Canada's Sports Hall of Fame, dated July 24, 1978; the reference to $3 million is from Eagleson's report to the Committee on International Hockey, September 26, 1977.

14. THE EMPIRE STRIKES BACK

Chapter 14 is based on personal interviews with R. Alan Eagleson, *op. cit.*; Chris Lang, *op. cit.*; Arthur Kaminsky, November 1977 and May 1980; Mike Milbury, May 1980; Doug Fisher, *op. cit.*; and on Hockey Canada documentation.

page 185
The epigraph to Chapter 14 is from a letter to Hockey Canada from Doug Fisher, dated October 13, 1978.

page 186
The excerpt is from Eagleson's letter to Jack Newby, dated February 15, 1977.

page 188
The reference to "stolen. . .$20 G's. . ." is from the *Toronto Star*, April 28, 1977; the Sabetzki quote and the Peters quote are from the *Montreal Gazette*, April 27, 1977.

page 189
The Paiement quote is from the *Ottawa Journal*, April 26, 1977; the Vadnais quote is from the *Toronto Star*, May 6, 1977.

page 190
The Lalonde excerpt is from his letter to Derek Holmes, dated September 16, 1977; the Johnson quote is from his letter to Eagleson, dated June 28, 1977.

page 191
The Eagleson quote "The CAHA acknowledges . . ." is from his memo to the Hockey Canada board, dated September 22, 1977; the reference to $12,000 is from the same source, p. 5.

page 192
The reference to $4,000 is from the *Globe and Mail*, September 2, 1977; the reference to "confidential financial paper" is from the *Ottawa Citizen*, September 8, 1977; the Eagleson quote is from *ibid*.

page 193
The Eagleson quote is from the *Globe and Mail*, January 27, 1978; the Campbell quote is from a personal letter to the author, *op. cit.*; the Eagleson quote is from the *Globe and Mail*, August 31, 1977.

page 195
The Eagleson quote "It was at the owners' insistence . . .", the reference to Eagleson's letter to John Ziegler, and the Sabetzki quote "We must see . . ." are from the *Toronto Star*, January 4, 1978; the Bobby Clarke letter on behalf of the NHLPA is dated January 24, 1978.

page 196
The reference to the $1 million trust agreement is from Eagleson's letter to Doug Fisher, dated October 31, 1977.

15. PALACE REVOLT

Chapter 15 is based on personal interviews with R. Alan Eagleson, *op. cit.*; Gil Stein, July 1981; Darryl Sittler, *op. cit.*; Bobby Orr, *op. cit.*; Bill Watters, *op. cit.*; Lanny McDonald, *op. cit.*; Punch Imlach, *op. cit.*; Harold Ballard, *op. cit.*; and Marcel Dionne, *op. cit.*

page 197
The epigraph to Chapter 15 is from Clancy Loranger's column in the *Vancouver Province*, September 9, 1977.

page 198
Eagleson's reference to Don Murdoch is from the *Globe and Mail*, July 29 and October 14, 1978, and the *Toronto Star*, October 11, 1978.

page 199
The Ziegler quote about merger is from the *Globe and Mail*, October 10, 1978.

page 201
The reference to Ziegler and the TV contract is from the *Globe and Mail*, October 11, 1978; the Orr quote is from a personal interview, *op. cit.*

page 202
The reference to $450,000 is from the *Globe and Mail*, May 22, 1979; the reference to club losses is from the *Globe and Mail*, May 1, 1980.

page 203
The Eagleson reference to anti-trust action is from the *Globe and Mail*, March 27, 1981; the footnote material is from the *Globe and Mail*, May 26, 1979.

pages 205–06
The Milbury quotes are from a personal interview, *op. cit.*, and the *Globe and Mail*, June 7, 1979.

page 207
The Eagleson quote about resigning is from the *Globe and Mail*, September 21, 1979, and June 9, 1980.

page 209
Globe and Mail, December 29, 1979; the Eagleson quote about "Let's get Eagleson" is from *ibid*.

page 212
The McMurtry quote is from a personal interview, *op. cit.*

page 213
New York Times, August 31, 1980.

16. THE RIGHT STUFF

Chapter 16 is based on personal interviews with R. Alan Eagleson, *op. cit.*; Bill Watters, *op. cit.*; and Gil Stein, *op. cit.*

page 217
The epigraph to Chapter 16 is from a personal interview with Eagleson, May 1980.

page 218
The reference to the Nedomansky suits is based on a writ of summons with the Supreme Court of Ontario, dated June 25, 1981.

page 220
The quote attributed to Agnes Eagleson is from a personal interview with Agnes and Allen Eagleson, December 1979.

page 221
The Eagleson quote "I still think I could become prime minister" is from Ted Blackman's article in *Weekend Magazine*, September 4, 1976.

Index

237